UNDERMINING
the
GOSPEL

UNDERMINING
the
GOSPEL

The Case for Church Discipline

RONNIE W. ROGERS

Foreword by Dr. Paige Patterson

Pleasant W rd

ISBN 1-4141-0152-X
Library of Congress Catalog Card Number: 2004103018

Dedication

I dedicate this book to my wife Gina who is my dearest
of all friends, my most trusted partner in ministry, and the
true love of my life. I owe everything that I am, have, or
know first to my Lord Jesus Christ and second to Gina, who
is my heroine in the faith, and who on more than one occasion has forsaken the securities of this life to walk with me
on this path of holiness.

Contents

Endorsements 9

Foreword 11

Acknowledgements 15

Introduction 17

Chapter 1: Liberated through Discipline: The Five
Kinds of Discipline 21

Chapter 2: The Day the Gospel Died: The Five Reasons
for Discipline 49

Chapter 3: Discipline and the Great Commission: The Essential Relationship Between Church Discipline
and the Great Commission 87

Chapter 4: When the Church Disciplined Church
Discipline: The Theological Reasons for the
Banishment of Church Discipline Answered 105

Chapter 5: They Say Church Discipline Is No Longer
Practical: The Practical Reasons for the Banishment
of Church Discipline Answered 157

Chapter 6: Can the Church Be the Church Without
    Discipline? The Biblical and Practical Reasons for
    Church Discipline 183
Chapter 7: Church Discipline Requires a Tender Heart:
    Love Not Legalism 241
Chapter 8: What Did Jesus Say? 279
Chapter 9: Will the Church Discipline Candidates
    Please Stand? 311
Chapter 10: Navigating the "Mind" Fields of Church
    Discipline: Facing the Factual, Theological, and
    Practical Realities of Church Discipline 351

Appendix 1—Resolution on Church Discipline by LeRoy
    Wagner 369
Appendix 2—Bylaws on Church Discipline 373
Appendix 3—A Story of Temptation, Tragedy, and Tri-
    umph: A True Story of How a Church's Willingness to
    Practice Church Discipline Resulted in Restoration
    and Rejoicing 377
Index 387
Notes 393

Endorsements

It's hypocrisy for a local church to claim to believe the Bible and then willingly ignore the Bible's teaching on church discipline. It's refreshing to see a local church pastor like Ronnie Rogers cry out so clearly against the apathy and disobedience that prevails in most churches on this issue. Perhaps the Lord will be pleased to use this book to increase the growing number of church leaders who are awakening to their responsibility to practice biblical church discipline.

—Donald S. Whitney
Associate Professor of Spiritual Formation
Midwestern Baptist Theological Seminary
Kansas City, Missouri

Here is a true pastoral theology for church discipline, one of the most difficult and most critical pastoral issues of this or any age. Writing as a biblical theologian, Ronnie Rogers explains the significance of discipline in principle, and establishes the foundation for church discipline in practice. He demonstrates that church discipline not only does not contradict love and grace, it is essential to express fully both love and grace. But Ronnie writes also as an experienced pastor who has worked out the biblical teaching on church discipline in real life, over many years, prayerfully and thoughtfully, faithfully and compassionately. And God has blessed it. If pastoral theology is simply biblical teaching, deeply understood and faithfully applied within the body of Christ, then this is as good an example as you could ever hope to find.

Here is biblical truth, wisely applied by someone who knows by experience the power of that truth in real life.

—C. Richard Wells
Distinguished Professor of Pastoral Theology
The Criswell College
Dallas Texas
Senior Pastor of South Canyon Baptist Church
Rapid City, South Dakota

Foreword

Prospects for another great awakening in the United States are the subject of many church discussions and not a few books. My own hope and prayer for the United States is that it would be the scene of the outbreak of revival, and that Southwestern Baptist Theological Seminary could be a contributing part of that effort.

But the truth of the matter is that it is exceedingly doubtful that revival will come or a third great awakening sweep the Nation when the Nation's churches are generally speaking in such carnal state. For example, Baptist churches affiliated with the Southern Baptist Convention love to brag about a total membership of 15–16 million. But a candid assessment shows that five to six million of those are almost never in the church in which they hold membership, if they go anywhere. On top of this, those who do attend church often have lives that are indistinguishable from the lives of the secularists among whom they live and work in terms of basic morality or commitment to kingdom endeavor.

Worse still is the realization that it is far more difficult to join and remain a member of the Rotary Club or the Lions Club than it is to join an evangelical church and to remain a member of it. If you belong to one of the service clubs in your city, you must either attend or be dropped from membership. If you are out of town for an extended period of time, it is common for members of those service clubs to visit other service clubs and bring back proof of their having attended a club meeting elsewhere.

But the sad truth for evangelical churches is that you could sooner get pastors to talk about a surgical procedure that they just had than you could to get them to talk about the possibility of a disciplined church. America and America's churches have become so carnal that thought of a disciplined church membership is the farthest conceivable notion from the mind of most.

And this is all exactly what makes Pastor Ronnie Rogers' superb volume on discipline so critically important. Not only has Pastor Rogers clearly indicated kinds of discipline called for in the New Testament but also he has indicated the reasons for such discipline and the attitudes with which the church should proceed. He has given ordered and rational assessment of why, if revival comes, we must have a disciplined church. Furthermore, he has tied the matter carefully to its scriptural roots and has provided the most detailed study that to my knowledge has been written in recent years. The concluding chapter of the book entitled, "Navigating the 'Mind' Fields of Church Discipline" is alone worth the price of the book. Here the author acknowledges the misuse and abuse of church discipline across the years, but he also gives clear demonstration of why church discipline cannot be dismissed simply because it has sometimes been abused. That kind of thinking, of course, is the kind of thinking that would cause a person to say that he would not seek medical help because mistakes were often made by physicians and hospitals. Rogers shows why that thinking only contributes to an anemic church.

Undermining the Gospel will not be comfortable reading for anyone. When a pastor thinks of preaching such material and implementing those things that are necessary for a genuinely committed church and for a revival, many will quail before the assignment. But any pastor who wants to have a genuinely New Testament congregation and who wishes to see the outbreak of meaningful church membership and, hence, of genuine revival cannot afford to avoid the subject. And if one cannot afford to avoid the subject, then there is no better place to start than with this superb volume by a pastor who has made it work and seen it blessed of God in his own ministry. I thank God for someone willing to tackle this delicate subject who approaches it in sensitive yet New Testament fashion.

—Paige Patterson, President
Southwestern Baptist Theological Seminary
Pecan Manor
Fort Worth, Texas

Acknowledgements

So many people have been a part of my spiritual life and the preparation of this book that I am truly a debtor to all. There is nothing original in me, but only what my Lord Jesus Christ has taught me through His Word and the lives of others.

I would like to thank Sam and Marian Whitlow for being committed to our Lord Jesus enough to come to my home on a cold January night nearly 25 years ago with the glorious gospel of Jesus Christ and unending sacrificial love for my family and me.

I would also like to thank all who had a part in the preparation of this book: Lance Witt for his invaluable insights that helped to clarify my points and improve my style without compromising my conviction, Anita Charlson for her superb and untiring work on the manuscript, Trinity Baptist Church for being willing to follow Christ in the demanding areas of discipleship, and the elders of Trinity for their encouragement and support of this book.

With profoundest emotion and undying admiration, I lovingly thank Bill and Pat Bledsoe, Mark and Donna Park, Mace and Christie Robinson, and Harris and Martha Shuffield. Without these dear saints who love our Lord Jesus Christ and His church more than their own personal peace and comfort, much of what is in this book could not have been written. I will always be indebted to all of you for your love, trust, and support. Harris went to be with the Lord a few years ago, but the impact he had upon my life is more obvious now than ever.

Introduction

One thing is certain. Every pastor and local church will
face challenges that threaten the spiritual life of the church.
To seek to meet those challenges without a thorough understanding of church discipline affords Satan a permanent foot-
hold in the church. In addition, a proper understanding of
church discipline reveals that it is interconnected with every
aspect of church life. Maybe this is why Christ's first mention
of the local church was regarding church discipline (Matthew
18:15–20).

I have studied and practiced church discipline for over
two decades. It is my desire in writing this book to help pastors and churches realize the biblically compelling need to
restore church discipline in the local church, and to provide
practical insights that will help pastors lead their churches
into the spiritual liberty that comes through church discipline.

Most churches have dismissed the importance of church
discipline by disassociating it from the Great Commission and
spreading the gospel. The consequence of this tragic misjudg-
ment may result in some short-term benefits, like numerical

growth and being relieved of having to deal with some difficult demands of Scripture. However, long-term detrimental effects will ultimately erode the short-term benefits by ravaging the church's biblical fidelity, credibility, unity, spiritual growth, humility, meaningful membership, and undying devotion to follow Christ at all cost.

Difficult church discipline situations will arise from the actions of immature Christians, carnal Christians, or lost people who slip into the church, gain respect and influence, and then bring the desires of their unregenerate heart to influence the life of the local church. How the pastor leads the church to regard the scriptural teaching on church discipline concerning these incidents will determine the fate of the church's spiritual fellowship and whether or not the church becomes complicitous with the world in undermining the gospel.

The lack of church discipline contributes to subverting the gospel in three crucial ways: First, it allows those who are carnal, immoral, divisive, doctrinally deviate, and/or unregenerate to remain in our churches, and thereby, corrupt the purpose, fellowship and credibility of the church. In addition, the energy our Lord commands to be directed toward making disciples is spent on appeasing troublemakers, which results in modifying our message, redefining our mission, and giving place for the flesh.

Second, the lack of church discipline undermines the gospel by implicitly supporting our culture's growing contempt for discipline. Much of the social and medical sciences are seeking to reclassify moral problems as medical problems. This results in man being viewed as sick rather than evil, immoral, or sinful. Therefore, he does not need to be punished, shamed, or held responsible for his actions, but rather he needs treated for his disease. This paradigmatic shift from discipline to treatment arises from a fundamental redefining of man. In the past, our culture viewed man as created by God as a free moral agent, and therefore responsible for his actions. Now, increasingly, he is viewed as merely an evolved, biologically determined being that is not responsible for his actions. Sin is out and sickness is in. Depravity is passé and dysfunction is popular.

Third, when the pastor leads the church to follow our Lord in the easy or popular areas, and overlooks or minimizes the more difficult, members receive an unintentional message of selective obedience with each sermon that undermines any call to follow Christ at all cost. In addition, the church sacrifices the full measure of the presence of Christ. Surely, no one believes that Christ could follow His heavenly Father in the easy matters while neglecting the demanding and still experience His power. If Christ could not, then we should not believe that the modern church could.

When the church relegates church discipline to being unnecessary or an anachronism of the pre-modern era, she necessarily, though not always consciously, aids and abets those who seek to redefine sin as a disease. This destroys the perceived need of the gospel because the gospel is only good news in light of the bad news that man is sinful and a holy God will one day judge him for his sin. This definitional shift degrades the good news of the gospel into merely more news.

The dismissal of discipline by the church reinforces a deterministic view of man, which declares that man is really sick and not sinful, and he needs a physician not a Savior. Tragically, the church, in large measure, has failed to realize that when she adopts the practices and terms of the world she implicitly bolsters their diagnosis and remedy of man's problem thereby contributing to modern man seeing no need for repentance; if there is no repentance, there is no freedom. Therefore, the lack of emphasis on discipline consigns man to animality.

Church discipline is essential for the church to be the church. When the church practices discipline, it vividly portrays to the world that sin is a choice that brings bondage and degradation, that man is to be held accountable, and that God's beautiful and wonderful grace and forgiveness are available to all who repent. Conversely, when the church fails to discipline herself, she sits as a mute herald and darkened light of the truth that man is created in the image of God, fallen and in need of a Savior from the impending wrath of a holy God; thereby becoming complicitous in the devaluing of man as man and undermining the spread of the glorious gospel.

CHAPTER 1

Liberated through Discipline: The Five Kinds of Discipline

I remember well going to my first church after graduating from Criswell Bible College. I was there for about a year when a situation arose requiring church discipline. The situation involved a young lady, and as you might well have guessed, she had several family members in the church, and they had been members for years. Thus, the perfect formula for making a pastor think of sending out a couple of resumes. Her behavior had been out of control for years, and as you can guess again, many wanted me to fix everything—which in pastoral lingo is synonymous with the words, "The honeymoon is over."

I counseled her for several months, but she was unresponsive to the counsel. Consequently, the deacons and I began the process of church discipline, which was the first time for the church to ever consider exercising formal church discipline. The short version of the story is—however, it was anything but short in real life—that she refused every level of discipline.

Her grandfather had been very vocal about his disapproval of the disciplinary action. He also had a significant and vocal following. On one occasion, he entered my study and began to threaten me in no uncertain terms. He vowed that he was going to destroy me, and that he would do whatever it took to get me. At a pause in his brief but fierce diatribe, I tried to explain the gravity of what he was doing by explaining that it could hurt his granddaughter even more, the testimony of the church, and the eternal life of lost people in the area. To which he responded, "I don't care about any of that. I am going to get you no matter what." He told me that he was going to take over the church meeting on Wednesday night in order to stop me. My reply as he was leaving was, "I will be here." Not a very profound response, but I guess I did not know what to do much less what to say at that moment.

In my statement I reminded both of us that regardless what he did, I, by the grace of God, would be here to follow the teachings of Christ. It was lucidly apparent to me at that time that we were headed for an event that I might not be able to survive. We seemed to be moving toward a full-blown split. When he left my study, I vividly remember, with a hollowed out soul and broken heart, bowing my head and praying for the Lord's help. By this time, I was so drained and bewildered that all I could pray was a short and simple prayer, "Lord, You heard what he said. I don't know what else to do but to stand on your Word. Please help me. Amen."

Within a few days of that meeting, this man went to the doctor for a regular checkup and was told everything was great. That same day, he died in his front yard. The second he died, the controversy was over because the conflict within the church died with him. As pastor, I now had to face the issue of how was I to respond to the hurt of this family that I knew hated me and probably blamed me for his death. I felt like I only had one choice. I went to the family's home and sought to minister to them.

The tension was storm thick. It was now clear to me, although at this time it had not been stated, the family and others blamed me for his death. It was etched upon each fleeting glance I received as people passed by me moving about the house or spoke to me in guarded speech. I surely understood their hurt and anger toward me even though I did not kill him.

At the funeral, I assisted. One of the family members came by and said, "I hope you're satisfied." Now, what had been felt and suspected was forcefully stated. To have someone, whom you believe is the assassin, assist at a loved one's funeral must be unimaginably difficult. I know for me it was almost unbearable. I have always wondered why they asked me to assist. Maybe it was simply protocol. Finally, the girl and her family left the church, although not without significant fanfare and damage.

From time to time, we would hear about the young lady. I would see her or a family member around town on occasion, and our dialogue if any, was at best, cordial. Later, maybe three or four years had passed since the implementation of church discipline, we heard that she had received Christ as her Savior. We were so thankful to God. This is what we had prayed for.

But that was not to be the end of the story. Sometime later, I received a call from the young lady. She said she needed to come to the church and apologize. She came and shared her story. She told how she had been saved subsequent to leaving our church, and that it was the discipline of the church that God used to bring her to that point. She said she had always gotten away with everything that she wanted—a pattern developed because of a lack of parental discipline—but the church had made her really examine her life and through that, she came to realize that she was not a true Christian. Therefore, she bowed her heart before our wonderful Lord, and He gloriously saved her.

What prompted her to feel compelled to come to the church and apologize was, no less, the hand of God. She had gone on a mission trip the year before, and while there, God had really burdened her heart for the mission field. Just before she called our church, she was preparing to return to the mission field, but God would not let her. She relayed how God kept convicting her that she had to get things right with the church that disciplined her before He would provide for her and use her. Consequently, out of her new desire to follow God, she came back, apologized and asked for forgiveness, which was joyously granted. She shared how hard the discipline was to go through, but she knew now that we had done the right thing. This was a wonderful ending to the difficult task of church discipline. God granted redemption that was directly related to the church discipline. Discipline is extraordinarily difficult, but can be eternally liberating. May God use her mightily for His kingdom.

The church had spent more than six months on the disciplinary action and then another year coming to grips with the truth that "to obey is better than sacrifice" (1 Samuel 15:22). However, even during the time immediately following the funeral, God began to bless. In the following years, all growth records in the church were broken. During that decade, the church nearly quadrupled in attendance. We saw many people come to Christ, and we were one of the top churches in the state in baptisms for four of those years. That was not because of our size. Our church was still a small to medium size church. We chose to follow God's command and practiced discipline on several more occasions. I believe that the presence of God upon that young lady's life and the life of that church was because both embraced the importance of church discipline and both came to embrace the truth that "to obey is better than sacrifice."

The term *discipline*, both in the Bible and in everyday usage, displays various nuances depending on the particular biblical or life context. The ideas communicated by discipline are that of chastening, instruction, nurturing, training, correction, reproof, and punishment. In the negative sense, the idea of punishment is most prominent. In the positive sense, things like nurturing, training, and instruction come to mind. However, since all discipline is based on the perfect character of God, all discipline is actually positive even though it is not always immediately apparent. Just as the Scripture says, "All discipline for the moment seems not to be joyful, but sorrowful; yet to those who have been trained by it, afterwards it yields the peaceful fruit of righteousness" (Hebrews 12:11).

When discipline is considered with its full range of meaning and application, one must certainly conclude that discipline is essential to life and society,[1] and that discipline is indeed good. The reality is that discipline and discipleship are so closely connected that to minimize discipline is to minimize discipleship. "To separate discipling from discipline is not only to tear words from their etymologically common roots, but also from their organic relationship."[2]

Church discipline is often understood to refer only to the formal action of the church that removes an unrepentant brother. Actually, church discipline encompasses everything that enables the church to be and remain the church. It refers to everything from praying or counseling with a brother or sister who is struggling with a temptation to disfellowshipping someone who refuses to repent and work on his sin. I refer to this final act of discipline, the act of disfellowshipping, as formal church discipline. This is to distinguish the final, more serious and public phase of discipline from the various other forms of discipline such as: exhortation, encouragement, bearing each other's burdens, praying, counseling, and teaching—to name a few.

Most often, discipline is done one-on-one. It does the biblical teaching on church discipline a great disservice to fail to understand and emphasize the full scope of the meaning of church discipline. It is not just expelling people from the church. It is not necessarily the sin that escalates church discipline from one-on-one to formal discipline, most often, it is the response of the wayward that determines whether it must be elevated to the next level.

Having said that, the faithful practice of church discipline must include the willingness to implement formal church discipline. Further, "Church discipline is a means of securing and maintaining the spiritual priority of the Christian church. This exercise arises from the fact that the church is a human institution, and the members of which are subject to the limitations and weaknesses of humanity. The Christian congregation, like every other community, needs a means of self-protection in order to suppress or eliminate whatever might impair or destroy its life."[3] Before looking at church discipline in particular, it is essential to look at the different kinds of discipline, including church discipline, and the reasons for discipline. In this chapter, we will examine the five *kinds* of discipline, and explore the five *reasons* for these disciplines in chapter 2.

The five kinds of discipline mentioned in Scripture are parental, self, governmental, church and divine. These are related in that they are given by God and have the same basic purposes. Also, if disciplines like parental or self-discipline are carried out properly and received by the one disciplined, then the more severe forms of discipline—governmental, church and divine—will usually be avoided. God has designed several levels of discipline to allow a person ample opportunity to mend his ways before more serious disciplinary options become necessary.

The first kind of discipline is parental discipline. "Children, obey your parents in the Lord, for this is right. Honor your father and mother (which is the first commandment with a promise,) so that it may be well with you, and that you may live long on the earth. Fathers, do not provoke your children to anger, but bring them up in the discipline and instruction of the Lord" (Ephesians 6:1–4). *Obey* is the Greek word *hupakouo.* It means to hearken or to hear with the intention of understanding and obeying. Verse 4 translates discipline from the word *paideia,* which carries the idea of "training to provide instruction, with the intent of forming proper habits of behavior."[4]

This relates back to the word *obey* in verse 1. Children are commanded to obey the instruction and discipline they receive, and parents are commanded to bring up their children in the discipline and instruction of the Lord. This is to be done without provoking them to anger. The word *obey* and the two phrases *do not provoke* and *bring them up* are in the imperative mood, signifying each is a command. Consequently, the parents are commanded to discipline, and the children are commanded to obey.

God takes discipline very seriously because of the benefit that comes from it and the harm that is birthed in its absence. Note the benefit given to the child who obeys, "that it may be well with you, and that you may live long on the earth" (Ephesians 6:3). Generally, discipline results in a person living a longer and more enjoyable life. It reduces the likelihood of the child's life being jeopardized while still under the watchful eye of his parents. It also increases the probability of the child growing up to be a responsible adult who will not engage in unnecessarily dangerous pursuits. Parental discipline also increases the likelihood that the child will avoid more serious forms of discipline as he grows up, such as governmental or divine.

Today, it has become rather popular to view corporal discipline as either unloving or in a manner that blurs the distinction between it and child abuse. Opponents of corporal discipline even go so far as attributing a causal relationship between corporal discipline and physical aggression that generates future criminals. Deborah Ausburn, who served as a probation officer with a Georgia juvenile court said, "There is a strong trend among caseworkers to classify any sort of corporal punishment as abuse, at least with older children. Not all agencies and caseworkers subscribe to this theory, but the trend, nevertheless, is to carefully scrutinize corporal punishment. Any discipline, for example, that leaves bruises will likely be considered abuse."[5]

The National Committee for the Prevention of Child Abuse defines corporal punishment as "inflicting of pain on the human body as a penalty for doing something, which has been disapproved of by the punisher."[6] In addition, "they support the adoption of state and local legislation to prohibit corporal punishment in schools and all other institutions, *public or private,* where children are cared for . . . *they advocate an end to the use of all physical punishment in America*"[7] (italics added). Presently, "corporal punishment on the part of school—paddling students who misbehave—is illegal in 27 states. In the 23 states that do allow spankings, the practice is so hedged around by rules, procedures, and paperwork that it is almost never carried out."[8]

The argument against corporal discipline goes like this: when you try to teach someone not to misbehave by hitting him, you actually teach him to hit and become an aggressive criminal and child abuser. Thus, physical discipline is abusive, and everyone agrees that all child abuse is wrong. Therefore, they reason, corporal punishment is wrong. However, it is a fallacy to conclude that punishment, corporal or otherwise, is child abuse.[9] The dissimilarities between discipline and abuse are clearly demonstrated by the undeniable differences in their severity, motives, and goals. Parental discipline seeks to obey God and help the child to have the best life they can. Our children belong to God, and He says discipline them—including spanking (Proverbs 13:24). It is astonishing that modern man in his quest to undermine any value in the role of physical discipline fails to ask why teenage rebellion has increased simultaneously with the decrease in discipline, but especially corporal discipline.[10]

There are three good reasons for practicing corporal discipline. First, small children operate off the pleasure pain principle. They are in fact hedonistic; if it feels good, they do it; and if it feels bad, they refrain. Thus, wrong actions must be associated with discomfort. Modern parents who opt for the democratic approach to parenting with a two year old will be pushed to despair by the undemocratic nature of their child. However, they will soon realize that their two year old is ready for a dictatorship and will assume the throne the moment mom and dad abdicate.

Secondly, children need to be able to associate wrong actions with pain. They do not understand what pain really is or how severe it can be. Before experiencing pain with wrong behavior, they do not understand what it means when a mother says, "Don't run in front of the car because if it hits you, it will hurt or kill you." Thus, by associating pain with a wrong ac-

29

tion, when they are told that running in front of a car brings pain, they will be more likely to obey. Later, much later, you can teach them about the physics of a collision between an automobile and a human body.

Third, wrong actions, especially for small children, need immediate consequences. Their attention span is short, and their inferential thinking abilities are minimal. Therefore, if the consequence does not follow in close proximity to the action, they will not know what to associate the discipline with. This will cause them to fail to learn the intended lesson, and that is the point of parental discipline.

While modernists associate discipline, especially corporal discipline, with child abuse, hate, etc., the Bible does the very opposite. For example, Proverbs 13:24 says, "He who withholds his rod hates his son, but he who loves him disciplines him diligently." As always, biblical discipline is an evidence of love not hate, and the lack of discipline is the evidence of hate not love.

The need for discipline is directly related to our view of human nature. If man is as the humanist says, either a blank slate or inherently good, then one needs only to show him what to do, and he will respond appropriately. But if the biblical view of man is correct, and it is; then discipline is essential for, "Foolishness is bound up in the heart of a child; the rod of discipline will remove it far from him." (Proverbs 22:15)

Children that do not respond to parental discipline, or are undisciplined by their parents, can potentiate such a threat to society that they need to be removed from society. For example, Exodus 21:15 says, "He who strikes his father or his mother shall surely be put to death." Leviticus 20:9 is even stronger. God says, "If *there is* anyone who curses his father or his mother, he shall surely be put to death; he has cursed his father or his mother, his blood guiltiness is upon him." To the modern and undisciplined life that sounds exceedingly harsh.

However, it lucidly demonstrates two truths. First, God is very serious about parental discipline being given and accepted, and the importance of respecting and submitting to His established authority. It is clear that God is far more serious about this truth than the modern church, which at times seems more content flirting with antinomianism. Second, when a child rebels uncontrollably against his parents, he not only disgraces them and God, but he becomes a threat to society. Every person becomes a role model to someone, and the life of an undisciplined child can negatively impact the behavior of other children and as an adult, impact adults through displaying disrespect toward authority.

If this sort of behavior goes on for an extended period of time, it can have an unraveling effect upon a stable society. In addition, at this level of disrespect, he is a threat to other people's physical well being. Many of the shootings and killings today, like in the postal service, schools, and now churches, are directly related to this. The lack of biblical discipline, coupled with secular psychology's obsessions with self-actualization, self-expression, and individualism, and the secularist devaluing of the uniqueness and value of man as created in the image of God, is a prescription for a culture of death.

It ought to be evident to all that guns are not the problem since guns have been around long before our culture became a culture of death. Further, guns are not the exclusive weapon for the wanton destruction of human life as criminals have demonstrated by using hammers, bombs, etc. What have changed in our culture are not the presence or accessibility of guns but the morals, meaning, and dignity of human life, and discipline.

God knows that it is better, in the long run, to eliminate the threat to the moral fabric and security of society, rather than foster some pseudo compassion, which actually allows dishonor and death to reign. Our sense of correctly placed compassion toward those who obey authorities is lost to the degree that we accept the normalization of disrespect for God and His established authority, whether this comes about through overt rejection of or ignoring biblical discipline.

There is a direct relationship between a person's spiritual life and parental discipline. If a child in Israel was allowed to disregard the discipline of his parents, as commanded by God, it was really a disregard for Scripture. If that disregard went unchallenged, it called into question how serious other commands of God should be taken. Thus, one renegade would jeopardize the spiritual lives of countless people. This eternal perspective is clearly the heart of God and should be the heart and understanding of every Christian toward discipline.

The Bible affords wonderful promises with the exercise of discipline. For example, Proverbs 29:15 and 17 says, "The rod and reproof give wisdom, but a child who gets his own way brings shame to his mother. . . . Correct your son, and he will give you comfort; He will also delight your soul." That is precisely what parents want for their child, and it is what God wants for all of us. He tells us exactly how to obtain it. It only takes faith in God, the discipline to discipline and a strong unwavering love for the child.

Youth of today usually do not fare well when compared with the youth of days gone by. This is often portrayed as though there is something inherently flawed in the youth of today that was not flawed in the youth of the past. In reality, ontologically, children and youth are no different today than at any other period in history. They have always sought to do what they could get by with, and what they are allowed to get by with today is significantly more than in the past. Consequently, their behavior is often worse than that of their predecessors. Therefore, in reality, what has changed is not children and youth but rather parenting. This change is chillingly evident in the area of discipline. Our culture of death should prompt society to reevaluate the effectiveness of the modern disdain for discipline. Those who loathe discipline, especially corporal, as barbaric and unnaturally cruel, have produced the most barbaric and cruel culture in American history. I believe that God will hold parents responsible for abdicating their responsibility to discipline; further, the churches will be held responsible for their role in failing to teach the biblical view of discipline in the face of an increasingly libertarian cultural drift.

Humanly speaking, discipline is directly related to the communication and reception of the gospel. Discipline teaches right and wrong, benefits and consequences, respect and choice, obedience and authority. These are all essential parts of evangelism. Thus, we must conclude that the lack of parental discipline has an adverse impact upon the individual and society, but the most horrible legacy is the damage to a person's spiritual life.

It is no accident that our society has become increasingly more hostile to the gospel or any form of discipline and submission to authority. Christian parents, who have been lured into adopting parenting practices that either anathematize or marginalize biblical discipline, have done undue harm to their children and untold damage to the believability of the Bible to the modern mind. For if the Bible is anachronistic in the area of child rearing, then who is to say that its teachings on judgment, sin, the need for forgiveness, and the entirety of the gospel is not also obsolete.

It seems impossible to plausibly argue that a God, who is supposed to know everything, and yet is found to be wrong or out of step in one area, is still undeniably right in everything else. He may be, but it is improbable that it can be demonstrated. The result is that modern undisciplined man is increasingly willing to live the way he wants and take his chances that the God who is antiquated in one area may also be modernizing His view on judgment, or maybe God himself is outdated. Thus, the loss of parental discipline hinders the spreading of the gospel.

The second kind of discipline is self-discipline. Self-discipline includes both natural self-discipline and spiritual self-discipline. Natural (human) self-discipline is to be exercised by all humans because we are created in God's image. Spiritual discipline is that aspect of self-discipline available to individuals who have been born again by faith in Christ. Self-discipline is afforded to all, as created in the image of God, and will be surveyed first.

Learning self-discipline is integral to the maturation process. We call this becoming a responsible adult. Much of a person's ability to do that is dependent on whether his parents molded him into a spoiled brat or a responsible disciplined person. The quality of parental discipline a child receives influences him, but it does not irrevocably mold him. He still has the freedom to continue to embrace what he learned or reject it. If the discipline was not there, or it was of a low quality, he can still become a disciplined person. This is true of everyone, even the nonbeliever.

There are countless examples of people who grow up in unloving and broken homes, but choose not to have their future controlled by that; many of these are not Christians. They simply value and pursue the things that God esteems. Scores of people have had neighbors who were not Christians, but they were great neighbors. Their ability to choose in this area in no way diminishes their lostness or inability to relate to God. They cannot please God or have totally pure motives, but they can mow their lawn and keep it looking nice and watch your house while you're on vacation. They can exercise the power of choice not to be like what they were taught. It is much harder when they do not know God personally, but it can be done and is done every day. The ability to choose is part of the grandeur of man as created in the image of God. In like manner, the lost or saved man can choose to turn from good and loving childrearing discipline also.

The importance of self-discipline cannot be overemphasized because it is at the heart of every other form of discipline. Self-discipline not only helps to prevent the person from coming under a more serious form of discipline, like government, church, or divine, but it also determines how he will respond to any form of discipline that he is subjected to. His willingness to turn other discipline into self-discipline is the key. The lack of self-discipline is at the core of the recalcitrant who rejects authority and anyone seeking to exercise discipline upon him. Further, if a person accepts the discipline being exercised toward him and repents, he will still need self-discipline from that day forward to learn how to conduct himself to avoid that same fall again. If he does not, his future fall is inevitable. Thus, every area of discipline must emphasize self-discipline.

What is true for a non-Christian is even more true for someone who becomes a believer. Colossians 3:5 says, "Therefore consider the members of your earthly body as dead to immorality, impurity, passion, evil desire, and greed, which amounts to idolatry." Further, 1 Corinthians 6:12, says, "All things are lawful for me, but not all things are profitable. All things are lawful for me, but I will not be mastered by anything." While the lost man can choose the good, he does not have the ability to fully realize the fruit of that choice, but Christians do by the grace of God. A person who may not have learned self-discipline, or at least has not put it into practice, can begin disciplining himself after he is born again.

Spiritual discipline is this second aspect of self-discipline. When a person becomes a Christian, he needs to learn to practice spiritual discipline. Spiritual discipline is Holy Spirit enabled self-discipline to practice certain habits, which result in more godliness and usefulness to God. Don Whitney describes spiritual disciplines as "those personal and corporate disciplines that promote spiritual growth. They are the habits of devotion and experiential Christianity that have been practiced by the people of God since biblical times. . . . The Spiritual Disciplines are the God-given means we are to use in the Spirit-filled pursuit of Godliness."[11] Some of the spiritual disciplines are prayer, Bible study, fasting, and serving.

Some view the emphasis on spiritual disciplines as legalistic and not trusting God. However, nothing could be further from the truth. The Christian life is neither "Let go and let God," nor "Pull yourself up by your own boot straps." Neither idea is biblical. It is by the grace of God that anyone would want to practice spiritual disciplines, and by grace that they can, with the right motives. Without grace, no one can practice spiritual disciplines in a biblical manner, even if they want to. Anyone who suggests that Bible study, prayer, fasting, and other spiritual disciplines do not take personal discipline may not have tried them in a while, or lives on a higher plane than the rest of us common Christians. There is a personal responsibility in embracing discipline. Proverbs 15:32, "He who neglects discipline despises himself, but he who listens to reproof acquires understanding." In addition, Proverbs 8:33 says, "Heed instruction and be wise, and do not neglect it."

The purpose of spiritual discipline is godliness. Paul told the young pastor Timothy, "Discipline yourself for the purpose of godliness" (1 Timothy 4:7). Discipline is the Greek word *gumnazo,* from which we get gymnasium and gymnastics. It means, "to exercise vigorously, in any way, either the body or the mind."[12] The Scripture bespeaks of training, sacrifice, choice, and all the other characteristics associated with athleticism. Paul told Timothy to be a spiritual athlete. While it is undeniable that man cannot do spiritual exercises to the glory of God apart from grace, the same can be said of physical exercises. Although the former is due to special grace and the latter is due to common grace experienced by all of God's creation.

The point of the Scripture's emphasis on spiritual discipline is that it is both a choice and work to grow spiritually. Spiritual growth does not come about by osmosis. Further, *discipline* is in the active voice, which signifies that the subject (the Christian) does the action, which further emphasizes the part the Christian plays. The major difference in physical discipline and spiritual discipline is the goal. Physical discipline seeks a more healthy body while spiritual discipline seeks godliness. The Greek word translated godliness is *eusebeia* and means reverence, piety, or godliness. Spiritual exercises are for the purpose of becoming more godly and reverent.

The analogy of physical exercise, or the lack thereof, gives a graphic picture of the effect exercise has on us. Without physical exercise men tend to experience the "chest of drawers syndrome"—where their chest moves to their waist; and women experience "thunder thighs"—this is self-explanatory. Less exercise results in less overall health. This is easy to see in the physical realm, however deprivation of spiritual exercise is not as easy to see since it is spiritually discerned. So many are in far worse spiritual shape than they are physically that the spiritually unfit seems normal, but in reality, the consequences of being spiritually unfit are exceedingly more lethal. A person who comes to church occasionally, but does not practice spiritual discipline, is in no better spiritual shape than the physical shape of someone who goes to the football game and watches the teams hustle.

Later in that same paragraph Paul told Timothy, "Pay close attention to yourself and to your teaching; persevere in these things; for as you do this you will *insure salvation both for yourself and for those who hear you*" (1 Timothy 4:16, italics added). This verse makes it clear that discipline (spiritual exercise) is essential to the spread of the gospel. The theme of spiritual discipline runs through the Scripture in all the commands and various images of boxers, runners, and soldiers—to name a few (1 Corinthians 9:24–27; Philippians 2:12–16; 2 Timothy 2:3–5).

Self-discipline can be readily seen in the apostle Paul. He says of himself, "but I discipline my body and make it my slave, so that, after I have preached to others, I myself will not be disqualified" (1 Corinthians 9:27). Here is a man greatly used of God, but very aware of his responsibility in the endeavor. Paul would not let his body be in control, but he made it a slave for the Lord Jesus Christ. Paul knew well that "to live is Christ" (Philippians 1:21), and that choosing not to discipline himself would eventuate in being put on the shelf. He had no problem allowing the divine and the human responsibility to operate in concert.

The reality set forth in Scripture of the divine and the human, interacting in a synergistic[13] way, must not be obliterated by excluding one in order to preserve the other or minimizing one by overemphasizing the other. This dynamic is seen in every aspect of human and divine encounter. For example, the

Scripture "is inspired by God" (2 Timothy 3:16), and yet the personality, vocabulary, and background of the different writers is reflected in the portion of Scripture they wrote.

Thus, it is true to say God wrote Romans, and it is also true to say Paul wrote Romans. God superintended the process in order to assure that the product was perfect without obliterating the personality or responsibility of the writer. The divine and the human acted synergistically. That we do not fully understand how God sovereignly superintends in order to accomplish His perfect will, and yet man remains man and does not become a machine, is indeed a mystery. Nevertheless, both truths are taught in Scripture and must be maintained in the balance and relationship they enjoy in Scripture. This synergism is seen in the virgin birth where the conception was divine, but the pregnancy from that time on and the birth were very natural. This synergistic relationship is also unashamedly set forth throughout the biblical revelation regarding salvation, by conjoining the ideas of election and faith. For example, Paul said, "work out your own salvation . . . God who is at work in you . . ." (Philippians 2:12–13). Thus, it is clear that without self-discipline, there will be temporal as well as eternal consequences.

The third kind of discipline is governmental. Throughout the history of man, there has been government. In the garden it was God directly, then human governments like the patriarchs who were the head over all their family and workers, and later the Mosaic government; in the New Testament, Romans 13:1–7 is the definitive passage on government and the Christian's responsibility to respect it. The passage says in part, "Every person is to be in subjection to the governing authorities. For there is no authority except from God, and those that exist are established by God. Therefore, whoever resists authority has opposed the ordinance of God; and they who have opposed will receive condemnation upon themselves. For rulers are not a cause of fear for good behavior, but for evil. Do you want to have no fear of authority? Do what is good and you will have praise from the same; for it is a minister of God to you for good. But if you do what is evil, be afraid; for it does not bear the sword for nothing; for it is a minister of God, an avenger who brings wrath on the one who practices evil" (Romans 13:1–4).

It is the God ordained purpose of human government to protect its citizenry from external and internal aggressors. God has sanctioned human government because without some form of government, man's sinfulness and selfishness eventually produce anarchy, which is the most brutal of all forms of existence and opens the door to totalitarianism. God designed government to punish evil and to reward good. This is its purpose, but one must remember that the government is fallen also, and that there are varying degrees of evil displayed in different forms of government. Every form of government fails to live up to God's design since man is fallen; nevertheless, some government is better than no government, and generally they punish evil.

The evil ones are those who operate outside of the law. They pose a threat to the very fabric of society because of their irresponsibility. I remember talking to a chaplain at Cummins State Prison in Arkansas on one of my visits there— just to be sure no rumors get started, my visits were as a pastor and not a resident. I explained to the chaplain the difficulty that I was having with a particular inmate, and he responded that the number one problem when dealing with inmates is to get them to take responsibility for their crimes. He said, "Eighty percent of them do not take responsibility for their behavior."

Those who have not been taught, or did not accept parental discipline or practice self-discipline, end up suffering the discipline of the state, which is always more severe and costly. The formula for producing a sociopath, or a serious criminal, is a lack of parental and self-discipline. Parents often think they are being cool, modern, or more compassionate when they withhold biblical discipline from their child, only to learn later that their compassion was misdirected and that untold harm has resulted. The reality is, if persons are to live together in a community, there must be discipline. It is essential and inevitable. It can come from either loving parents, self, or it will be implemented by a nonpersonal government; but it must be done. The citizenry has to be protected from the nondisciplined, or else any society, including the church, will become a community of chaos never realizing its full purpose and potential.

The fourth type of discipline is church discipline. Church discipline is an intentional undertaking of the church to discipline herself in order to maintain a conducive atmosphere to meet the priority of fulfilling her mission as mandated by our Lord Jesus Christ to the glory of God. This includes everything from discipline by modeling, teaching, and mentoring, all the way to disfellowshipping someone. The first issue addressed in the Gospels to the local church, was the issue of church discipline (Matthew 18:15–20). Every community of believers must have a means of maintaining order, because the church will inevitably receive people who are unsaved, undisciplined, unwilling to practice spiritual discipline, or revert back to living like a lost person. Therefore, the church must have a means of effectively dealing with those situations, and that is precisely why Jesus gave us church discipline.

Since church discipline is the major theme of this book and will be dealt with extensively in the coming chapters, I will simply call your attention to two things in relation to church discipline. First, church discipline is one of the five biblical disciplines and it interrelates with the other four, and like the other four, it is based upon the nature of God. Second, church discipline, like all the previous disciplines, correlates with evangelism. The church cannot fulfill the Great Commission without obeying the biblical teachings on church discipline. The idea that she can omit discipline and compensate for that loss by emphasizing more palatable ideas like numbers, growth, pseudo-compassion, and love ultimately proves to be nothing more than a molestation of the gospel, whether this is fully realized or not. For without discipline in all of its varied facets, there is no point in having a gospel.

This inextricable relationship between the Great Commission and church discipline will be thoroughly explained in chapters 2 and 3. The following quote should remind us of the importance of church discipline. "The Christian concept of discipline has the same breadth as the Latin word *disciplina*, which signifies the whole range of nurturing, instructional, and training procedures that disciple-making requires. When Reformed theology highlights the importance of church discipline, insisting that there is no spiritual health without it and that it is a vital mark of a true church, more is in view than the judicial processes against immoral persons and heretics. Only where the personal disciplines of learning and devotion, worship and fellowship, righteousness and service are being steadily taught in a context of care and accountability (Matthew 28:20; John 21:15–17; 2 Timothy 2:14–26; Titus 2; Hebrews 13:17) is there a meaningful place for judicial correctives. The New Testament clearly shows, however, that in that context judicial correctives have a significant place in the maturing of churches and individuals (1 Corinthians 5:1–

13; 2 Corinthians 2:5–11; 2 Thessalonians 3:6, 14–15; Titus 1:10–14; 3:9–11)."[14]

The Westminster Confession declares: "Church censures are necessary, for the reclaiming and gaining of offending brethren, for deterring of others from like offenses, for purging out of that leaven which might infect the whole lump, for vindicating the honor of Christ, and the holy profession of the gospel, and for preventing the wrath of God, which might justly fall upon the church, if they should suffer his covenant, and the seals thereof [the sacraments] to be profaned by notorious and obstinate offenders."[15]

The final form of biblical discipline is divine discipline. Although all forms of discipline are divine since they all come from God, this discipline is distinguished from the other forms by use of this term because this discipline does not necessitate an intermediary. There are actually two dimensions or levels of divine discipline. These and their differences can be gleaned from passages such as Hebrews 12:5–8 and Revelation 20:14–15. Hebrews bespeaks of the discipline between a father and His child, which says, "and you have forgotten the exhortation which is addressed to you as sons, 'My son, do not regard lightly the discipline of the Lord, nor faint when you are reproved by Him; for those whom the Lord loves He disciplines, and He scourges every son whom He receives.' It is for discipline that you endure; God deals with you as with sons; for what son is there whom *his* father does not discipline? But if you are without discipline, of which all have become partakers, then you are illegitimate children and not sons."

There are three things to be noted in this passage. First, God's discipline is based on His love. He is the perfectly loving heavenly Father. When He disciplines His children, it is all born out of love. This is also true with parental and church discipline. God's discipline is the evidence of love, not hate.

When a Christian is wayward in his walk with God, the most loving thing God can do is to discipline him, so that the child will see the error of his way and return to an intimate walk with God.

Second, the discipline of God is one of the greatest testimonies to a believer that he is truly saved and thus a child of God. He says in that passage, "He scourges every son whom He receives. . . . But if you are without discipline, of which all have become partakers, then you are illegitimate children and not sons." A person who claims to be a Christian and can live out of the will of God without experiencing divine discipline is clearly not a true Christian. Conversely, when a Christian strays, God's discipline assures him that he is still a child of God.

Third, as with all the previously mentioned forms of discipline, the recipient has an inherent responsibility to respond appropriately to the discipline. This can be seen in the words, "My son, do not regard lightly the discipline of the Lord, nor faint when you are reproved by Him." Regarding discipline lightly is the cause of a person becoming undisciplined and possibly having to undergo the more serious forms of discipline like government or divine.

This dimension of divine discipline can be anything from a loving wooing of the Holy Spirit to rebuke from the Scripture, or death. The Holy Spirit says, "Furthermore, we had earthly fathers to discipline us, and we respected them; shall we not much rather be subject to the Father of spirits, and *live?*" (Hebrews 12:9, italics added). If a true believer continues to resist the discipline of the Lord, He will simply take him to heaven prematurely (1 Corinthians 11:30 and 1 John 5:16).

While all believers experience God's discipline in the sense of God discipling and educating His children, the more serious forms are the result of ineffective parental discipline, scorning discipline, or a lack of self-discipline. If the church practiced church discipline, fewer believers would have to undergo more serious expressions of divine discipline. We often pray for God to do something miraculous about troublemakers in the church, and wonder why He does not do something. Actually, He already has; He gave us church discipline. We often pray for divine intervention in a situation that has arisen in the church, and yet the Father is waiting on us to act upon what He has already given us for such situations.

The second level of divine discipline is somewhat different from all other disciplines. It is often known by the term *judgment*. It is the final act of divine discipline applied to mankind. It is exercised only after man has spurned the grace and discipline of the Lord for the last time. It is when God casts them into hell, the lake of fire (Revelation 20:14–15). This is the end result of a life that spurns the convicting of the Holy Spirit and discipline of God (John 16:8–11). It is the result of man's choice to love his own sin supremely (John 3:19–20). Justice demands this final form of discipline.

Since all the other disciplines have a redemptive aspect, it may seem like this last one is not discipline. But remember the discipline of the Old Testament, which in severe cases meant taking the child's life, was not redemptive (Exodus 21:15; Leviticus 20:9). The same could be said about governmental discipline in the New Testament, which involves capital punishment (Romans 13:1–7). It is often forgotten, or at least not emphasized, that discipline is not *only* for the purpose of redemption. It is also for protecting and purifying.

This final discipline is God's eternal discipline exercised in order to protect heaven from contamination of impurity and antinomianism. This aspect of divine discipline is intimately related to evangelism and the gospel in two ways. First, man will one day give an ultimate account to God, which provides a compelling motivator for pursuing evangelism with urgency, vigor, and passion. Paul put it this way, "Therefore, knowing the fear of the Lord, we persuade men . . ." (2 Corinthians 5:11). Second, if a believer is living in sin, he will not be about witnessing, and if he does, he will lack both the power of God upon him and a credible witness. He will most often do more harm than good. Humanly speaking, he contributes to a person dying without Christ and suffering the eternal discipline of God. Once the impending eternal discipline of God is apprehended, it makes it quite easy to understand that parental, self, government, and church discipline are actually very compassionate; although practicing them at the time may seem quite difficult.

Our Epicurean society overstresses what is perceived as the negativeness of discipline, and overlooks the liberation that discipline produces. Discipline, by design, is liberating. It can liberate a person to live a more fulfilled life now, and avoid God's inevitable and eternal divine discipline. Liberty is the true end of all biblical discipline. Hell is reserved for those who refused discipline. This is not to imply that a person can discipline himself enough to merit God's gift of eternal life. It does mean that man's choice, to accept by faith God's offer of salvation, results in eternal liberation and this choice is often precipitated or aided by one of the forms of discipline. For example, a person could be a part of a local church, but not really be or act like a Christian. Church discipline can awaken him to his self-imposed deception and cause him to have to face his lostness. If he accepts the discipline, it can lead to salvation. Conversely, the lack of church discipline can make the church by default a co-conspirator with Satan in fostering a belief in the fairy tale of hell.

I have enjoyed through the years listening to my daughters play the piano—that is after they got beyond the basic scales. When I hear them play, I think how wonderful it would be to play the piano. To listen is so soothing to the soul, and they make it appear to be so easy. However, I know the liberty they experience on the piano is the result of years of discipline.

I also remember watching my daughters compete in gymnastics, and my never ending amazement when they would turn back flips on a four inch beam or swing continuously on the high bar. They did it with such grace. I often wondered what it would be like to do such acrobatics, but as of this writing, I still can't tell you because I have never played the piano nor am I able to even get up the nerve to walk on a four inch beam, much less turn flips on one. The difference in my daughters and me is, I never disciplined myself in those areas; consequently, I never enjoyed the freedom to play a piano or perform acrobatics like they have. I might add, at this point, the prospect for me being liberated in gymnastics appears to be rather bleak; while the piano is possible but not very probable.

I know what it took for my daughters to play the piano and be gymnasts. I listened to them for years as they disciplined themselves to learn the piano—while I did not discipline myself to learn to play, I did discipline myself to learn how to listen those first few years—and watched them spend countless hours in the gym every week. Because of their willingness to discipline themselves, they experienced much more freedom playing the piano and on the gym floor than I did.

We must never fail to emphasize the liberty that discipline produces. When we have the courage and tenacity to discipline, we are actually liberating the person. The cruelest thing we can do is to let them remain in their sin when there is liberty to be lived.

CHAPTER 2

The Day the Gospel Died: The Five Reasons for Discipline

Thinking about church discipline, or any kind of discipline, in an age of narcissism, naturalism, and relativism is difficult; actually implementing the scriptural truths about discipline in that milieu becomes daunting. However, our present wandering culture actually makes it all the more necessary and urgent. Which worldview, creationism or evolutionism with all their respective corollaries, will direct Western culture in the future is still undecided, although evolutionism presently dominates. However, the worldview that will govern the choices and actions of Christians must be decided now.

The church must live out its faith in every area prescribed by the Scripture; she must live it out in the most difficult and unpopular areas if she expects to be taken seriously in the battle for the American mind and soul. Dr. Francis Schaeffer says it succinctly; "In an age of relativity, the practice of truth when it is costly is the only way to cause the world to take seriously our protestations concerning truth. Cooperation and unity that do not lead to purity of life and purity of doctrine are just as faulty and incomplete as an orthodoxy, which does not lead to a concern for and a reaching out towards those who are lost."[16]

As described in chapter 1, there are five types of discipline set forth in the Scripture. These are all related to the same purpose, which ultimately is that God desires that His creation live according to righteousness. Even though man is sinful, God still desires man to live right. First, God does not operate on a curve. When man sinned, God did not change His standards. Secondly, what is best for man did not change when man fell. Therefore, the need to follow God's Word did not change.

There are also five reasons for the exercise of discipline, regardless which of the five kinds of discipline is being exercised. They are all based on the nature of God and His ownership of His creation. Both creation and the church belong to God, and He has given commands for how they should operate based on who He is. God designed the world and the church to reflect His glory (person). For even natural creation tells of "the glory of God" (Psalm 19:1); He gave the church the designation "the body of Christ" (Ephesians 4:12). Thus, when considering the reasons for discipline, they must always be considered in light of the Scripture, and that they are based upon the very nature of God.

This chapter will focus on discipline in general. The following chapters will focus particular attention on the biblical mandate for church discipline. It is important to keep in mind that the term discipline incorporates actions as mild as a loving reminder, to an eternal hell, and everything in between.

The first reason for discipline is redemption. Redemption means being either instrumental in bringing someone to Christ, restoring a person to the fellowship of the church, or rehabilitating a person in some way. Redemption is the reason most

often cited for exercising any form of discipline. However, too
often this is the *only* reason given to justify the use of discipline. When redemption becomes *the* reason for discipline,
rather than *a* reason, the whole concept of discipline is obscured. This narrow view of discipline inevitably results in
the future rejection of discipline for something more "loving."
Although making redemption so prominent in defending discipline does tend to soften the idea and make it more palatable, the backlash occurs when discipline does not result in
repentance and redemption. Then, an attack against discipline is marshaled based on that one-dimensional view of discipline. People develop a disdain for discipline since it seldom
accomplishes its stated purpose of redemption. However, if
redemption is seen as *one* of the reasons for discipline and
redemption does not occur, discipline can still be appreciated
for what it is beyond its redemptive aspect. When redemption
is promoted as the only purpose of discipline, it will have a
short-lived popularity since some will surely refuse its invitation to be restored. Discontinuing discipline because it did
not obtain certain desired and immediate results relegates discipline to being merely Christian pragmatism.

We should do our part in fulfilling God's commands in discipline, not just because He has commanded it, although that
is enough, but because God desires for everything to display
His glory, as should we. The breakdown of standards and discipline in any of the five areas, self, parent, government,
church, or divine, not only fosters havoc in that particular
area, but it also crosses over into the other areas. In other
words, the lack of discipline in one area will not be long con-
fined to that area. This is particularly true in the age of communication, which desolates communities through the rapid
dissemination of information; consequently, a breakdown in

one of the disciplines, in any place, soon spreads to other places and causes the erosion of other disciplines.

This is undeniably what has happened today. Man cannot compartmentalize sin or its consequences. More importantly, the lack of discipline eventually distorts creation, the purpose of creation, and the perceptible image of the one who is the creator. This inevitably results in a more chaotic society and humanly speaking, fewer people coming to Christ. When God's ordained discipline is minimized or distorted, it must necessarily distort man's perception of God, and that is the eternal tragedy of not understanding and following God's commands in the area of discipline.

Redemption is a wonderful and biblical reason for God's discipline, and it is based on the fact that "God is love" (1 John 4:8). Because of the love of God, He desires that man not be lost—primarily lost in the spiritual sense, but also in the sense of any form of destruction. Even we desire men and women to be saved and grieve when they choose a life of wanton destruction of themselves and others. God will punish every sin, but that does not bring Him pleasure; for He says in Ezekiel 33:11, "'As I live!' declares the Lord GOD, 'I take no pleasure in the death of the wicked, but rather that the wicked turn from his way and live. Turn back, turn back from your evil ways! Why then will you die?'"

The most graphic and profound picture of this love was displayed when our Lord Jesus Christ hanged on the cross bearing the holy wrath of God's justice for humans who are willful, wicked sinners and willful enemies of God (Romans 5:10). That demonstrated the unfathomable truth that God is love, and God loves. Therefore, the redemptive aspect of discipline is always prominent regardless how grievous the sin may be. The love of God is inexhaustible; He always desires the best for His creation.

Understanding the nature of God can help us to grasp the depth and breadth of each of the reasons for discipline. Often we talk about the love of God or that God is love, but simultaneously we are in some sense equating it with the love that we as humans show or have been shown. Our inability to fully comprehend the love of God is due to the fact that He is infinite and we are finite—not to mention our sinfulness. Let me try to explain the infinitude of God and how that relates to the discipline of God. However, I must admit at the outset that any illustration, metaphor, simile, or analogy will unavoidably prove to be inadequate since all of them are finite. I hope that it will help us more fully appreciate the greatness of God, His love, and discipline.

Finite means limited. It means that it has a beginning, end, capacity, and/or a limit. Man is finite in his duration and ability; he had a beginning, and he will never know everything. Infinite is the very opposite of finite. When the word *infinity* is used in our culture, we often think of the sleek car called Infiniti, or else we think of something really big—too large to count. A man with a lot of wisdom, whom people respect, is sometimes spoken of as having infinite wisdom, or someone will speak of the government's power as infinite. I realize that many use the term infinite hyperbolically, realizing that it does not really apply. However, the result is the same. Common usage eventually becomes common definitional understanding. Therein is the problem when we refer to God's discipline.

What does infinity actually mean? It means unlimited, no end or beginning, inexhaustible, not increasing nor decreasing. Let me give an example: A googol is an inconceivably large number. It is a one followed by one hundred zeros, and a googolplex is a googol raised to the googoleth power. "If this number were written out, there would not be space on earth to contain the pages required. In fact, they would more than fill our galaxy."[17]

Now apply that to time. Infinite means that if we lived a googol-plex of time, that we would not have exhausted any of infinitude, for to do so would mean that infinity is a limited amount. Even using time, as I just did, to seek to demonstrate how long infinity is, is inherently flawed since infinity is not in any sense time because time by definition is finite.

In relation to God's infinite knowledge, God has never had a new thought or a new idea. God knows, has always known, and will always know everything. This includes every actuality (thing that is), potentiality (thing that could possibly be), and everything that has ever been. There never was a time when God did not know everything that would or could happen. Before we ever existed, we existed in the mind of God. Anything that has come into being or will ever come into being existed eternally in the mind of God. God has never had a new thought about anything. He is not learning. He knows everything infinitely. If He ever learned one thing, His knowledge would not be infinite since there was a limit; thus, He would not be God. The very definition of God is that He is infinite.

As previously mentioned, God not only knows eternally every actuality, everything that is, He knows eternally every potentiality, everything that could or would be. That means that God has not only always known everything that you or I would do, but He also knew everything that you or I could do. Further, He knew the potential outcome of every one of those actual or potential decisions. He also knew that same thing of every person and creature of His creation. As though that is not enough, He knew every possible scenario, which would or could be produced by those trillions and trillions of choices and potential choices made by His creation and how each choice affected others and their choices. Remember that He knew them all at the same time and forever. That is infinite

54

knowledge. If you are presently experiencing a little mind meltdown and fatigue, just worship the Lord who is infinite in every respect, and chose to love us with infinite love.

The point of seeking to better understand God's character is to help us grasp the whole concept of discipline from God's perspective. God's discipline is based upon His infinite knowledge of the violation, violator, violated, every potential ramification and possible scenario resulting from implementing or withholding discipline—not to mention all of the excuses and reasons man gives for not practicing discipline. No matter how heinous the sin, God's love is not exhausted nor His desire for redemption eliminated. Humanly, it is easy at times to forget the depth and breadth of God's love and allow our desire to redeem man to fade.

It is unfathomable to me that God loved Adolf Hitler enough to pay for all of his sin. That God knew what Hitler would do and still died for him and included him in His love is quite beyond me (John 3:16; 1 John 2:2). I admit that I do not fully understand that kind of love, and I will never fully grasp it since even in eternity I will be learning forever about God and His creation. Even in eternity, we will not become God. We will become *like* Him, but we will not become Him—sorry to be the one to break the news to all the would-be gods.

God's discipline always begins with a desire to redeem and show man his evil way so that man will turn to God and be redeemed. This is what the law is designed for (Galatians 3:24). When we, for whatever reason, undermine God's laws, standards, or discipline to the degree He has allowed us to have a part, we concomitantly undermine the redemptive work of God. Thus, it is inestimably serious and unloving when we, for the sake of some finite distorted mercy, seek to mitigate God's discipline as though He could learn a few things from us about discipline and love.

When we are involved in one of God's prescribed disciplines, we must never lose the desire to see a redemptive conclusion. It is true, that in eternity there will be some who suffer the judgment of God forever without the possibility of redemption, but that is only after they have willfully and finally resisted God's offer of redemption. The reason that they must suffer, without any chance of redemption, is because God is holy and they were created in the image of God. One attribute of God will never violate another attribute of God. We will look at this dimension of discipline more closely later. Suffice it to say; because we do not know the end from the beginning, there must always remain in us a desire to see a redemptive resolution come about in the disciplining process.

Keeping the redemptive focus in view is easy to do when we are exercising parental discipline. There never comes a time when parents do not want to see their child redeemed from evil. However, when it is someone else, and the hurt they have caused creates enormous anger and resentment, we can find ourselves praying, "Lord, do You want us to command fire to come down from heaven and consume them" (Luke 9:54), rather than for redemption.

Sadly, I must admit that I have had those feelings before. Watching someone cause immeasurable harm to our Lord's church and her testimony will at times create an internal battle between praying for their redemption and their destruction. It is good that I am not God, for surely I would have prematurely removed some from the redemptive potential of discipline. Living in the light of the cross every day is the only thing that can keep us from the prayer for premature wrath. We must not allow their wanton lying and carnality to cause us to forget that "God so loved the world that He gave His only begotten Son" (John 3:16).

The second reason for discipline is correction. God's holiness and righteousness is the basis for corrective discipline. Corrective discipline is designed to correct wrong thinking or actions and is related to redemptive discipline in that it seeks to correct our thinking and behavior, which will result in a closer relationship with God. However, unlike the redemptive aspect, the person is not necessarily in willful rebellion against the will of God, although he could be. "The goal of chastening is not mere outward conformity to established standards, but an inner commitment of the heart and will to obey biblical mandates because it is right to obey."[18]

In corrective discipline, the person is most likely willing to change his behavior if he learns he is doing wrong. Consequently, corrective discipline is to a large degree educational. For example, suppose you are driving to Phoenix, Arizona for vacation, and along the way, you stop to buy gas—at least that is what the man tells his wife he is doing. While buying gas, the attendant tells you that you are actually headed toward Santa Fe, New Mexico—men need not tell their wives all of these minor details. Learning this you immediately and willingly change directions. This is how corrective discipline is supposed to operate. Thus, there is a training or educational dimension to this aspect of discipline.

Parental discipline demonstrates this point well. Parents are constantly correcting their children for behavior that often the child does not know is wrong. If the parent did not correct certain behaviors or actions, the child would continue repeating the unsuitable behavior. Thus, the parent disciplines in order to teach the child the right conduct. The parental aspect of corrective discipline lucidly demonstrates the love that is involved in discipline, and it clearly models the love that motivates all biblical discipline. Further, corrective mea-

sures often precede redemptive measures; if they are successful, redemptive measures become unnecessary.

In the church, corrective discipline can be exercised in a
diversity of ways such as counseling a young Christian that is
engaged in activities that are contrary to their new life in
Christ, biblical preaching, one-on-one discipleship, and the
different levels of church discipline. One of the greatest means
of corrective discipline in the church is biblical preaching.
When we exchange biblical preaching and equipping the saints
for orations on the most faddish psychological postulate of
the day, an essential means of church discipline is lost to the
church. Each time that the Word of God is delivered, it affords us the opportunity and mandate to bring "every thought
captive to the obedience of Christ" (2 Corinthians 10:5).

Like every other aspect of discipline, corrective discipline
can be embraced or shunned by the individual. Corrective
discipline may be no more serious than a mother disciplining
a toddler for spilling milk, to taking more serious measures to
correct the behavior of a child who is intentionally doing wrong.
The prison system is one of the more serious forms of corrective discipline. Prisons are often referred to as "correctional
institutions," which emphasizes the contemporary philosophy behind imprisonment. The goal is, in part, to correct the
prisoner's thinking and behavior so that he can one day be
released back into society and be a contributing member rather
than a troublesome member of society.

The third reason for discipline is to protect. Whether in
society or the church, God seeks to protect people from those
who constitute a threat to them. This is in contrast to the
redemptive and corrective aspects, which maintain primary
emphasis on aiding the person carrying out the wrong. The
protective aspect shifts the emphasis to the people that might
be harmed. There still exists a desire and maybe even an ef-

fort to redeem and correct the perpetrator, but that is no longer primary since they have demonstrated a recalcitrant attitude; and their aberrant behavior is now a menace to society.

For a society to remain safe and orderly for the sake of its members, there must be a means of dealing with those who resist correction or redemption, and thereby pose a threat to others and the society itself. By society I do not refer only to society in the sense of a city, state, or country, but rather to any group of individuals living as members of, or associated together as, a religious, cultural, political, or other purposed community. This can be groups as varied as a nation such as Israel, a church body, or family.

For example, in Israel, a child who continually refused to obey his parents' discipline, thus creating a threat to the well-being and safety of a society, was killed. Deuteronomy 21:18–21 says, "If any man has a stubborn and rebellious son who will not obey his father or his mother, and when they chastise him, he will not even listen to them, then his father and mother shall seize him, and bring him out to the elders of his city at the gateway of his home town. They shall say to the elders of his city, 'This son of ours is stubborn and rebellious, he will not obey us, he is a glutton and a drunkard.' Then all the men of his city shall stone him to death; so you shall remove the evil from your midst, and all Israel will hear *of it* and fear."

This seems rather severe to the American mind. However, there are three things to remember when assimilating this into our thinking. First, the person undergoing this kind of punishment has already sufficiently demonstrated that he will not change through corrective or redemptive measures.

Second, there is always the need to protect a society from those who wantonly abuse other people or pose a threat to the viability of the society. The severity of discipline escalates proportionately to the seriousness of the offense and the recalcitrance of the offender. If the offender's unruly conduct continues unabated, and he becomes incorrigible, steps that are even more serious must be taken in order to protect those respectful of the norms of the society. This is not society rejecting him, nor casting him away, but rather he has rejected society by choosing to contemptuously disregard necessary societal norms. Consequently, his choice not to participate in the society, as demonstrated by his behavior, is simply being honored.

Third, this kind of action is not uncompassionate. Whenever stern disciplinary action is taken, someone will inevitably ask, "Where is the compassion?" We must remember these commands were given by God, and because He is infinite compassion, there is compassion present in even the more serious acts of discipline. To be otherwise would violate the nature of God.

When a person questions the compassion of such commands or actions required to carry out the commands, they are actually questioning the infinite compassion and wisdom of God. Implicit in the question is the belief that God might learn something from us about compassion. Regardless of polls or feelings, we can be sure these are compassionate acts based on the nature of God. The child has already received compassionate correction, love, care, time, forgiveness, etc., but all to no avail. Now the compassion is directed toward the society who is either in eminent or potential danger. To allow someone to continue living in the society, with callous disregard for what holds the society together, is the embodiment of being uncompassionate.

Today, we have emphasized individual rights to the point of virtually obliterating the idea of sacrificing personal rights for the good of the community. Personal rights have eclipsed the long held idea of personal responsibility. Because humans are created in the image of God, they have certain inalienable rights, and the dignity and freedom due that creative act should not be abrogated. For example, a person should not be treated as a non-person, animal, or in some way that is degrading to a human being created in the image of God. This includes both enjoyment of certain inalienable rights and acceptance of certain responsibilities. However, the present status of personal rights is at a tyrannical and contradictory level.

How is it that an individual, because of his personal rights, can *trump* the rights of a community, which is merely the expression of multiple individual rights? For example, a community of one hundred does not want the presence of pornography in its community, but because one person does, the community must accept the pornography. The argument for accepting the will of the individual is based on the fact that to disallow it would be to suppress the individual rights of the person who wanted pornography. However, one must now ask, if an individual's right is important, then how can a hundred individuals' rights, in community, not be more important?

In addition, if one hundred individuals' rights are not important, then how much less the lone individual. Moreover, if the value of individual rights is diminished because the individual joins a community, or agrees with the majority, to the point where a hundred individual rights are no match for the lone individual, then we have destroyed the value of community and deified extreme individualism and pop tyranny. This is the end of community, discipline, and reason.

In our modern culture, compassion is often ill defined and misdirected, and misdirected compassion eventually becomes abuse. God has compassion on the sinner, but He can only allow that to go so far without becoming uncompassionate toward society itself. When an individual irrevocably chooses to live narcissistically, God will let him go his way, but his compassion for the community will not be compromised. We often hear an interminable plea for compassion toward the criminals, that we should have compassion for them. However, markedly absent from those *kindhearted* voices, who vociferously call for compassion for the criminal, is any sense of compassion owed society— since in today's secular-minded society, the criminal is a victim, and society is the ultimate culprit.

This presuppositional shift in the way we view discipline for the criminal, the victim, and who should receive compassion, is based on a significant change in Western jurisprudence, which has come about since the eighteenth century. This is the battle between the classical school of justice and the positive school of justice. The classical and the neo-classical believe in the free will[19] of man. "The leader of the classical school was Cesare Beccaria. . . . The underlying philosophy of Beccaria's position was that of free will."[20] Because of the belief in free will, meaning that man is responsible for his choices and should be held accountable, the classical system believed that "punishment should fit the crime."[21] The neo-classical view did allow mental disease to be seen as a sufficient cause to impair responsibility, which gave birth to the insanity plea, but it still upholds the free will of man in every other circumstance and believes that punishment should fit the crime.

Contrary to the classical and neo-classical is the positivist view. The positive school of thought developed in the late eighteenth century. The positive school "substituted the doctrine of determinism for that of free will."[22] "They believed that punishment should fit the criminal, not the crime."[23] The emphasis on the punishment fitting the criminal instead of the crime is based squarely upon the rejection of the free will of man. Positivists maintain that man does not have free choice, but is determined by other forces. What determines the behavior of a person could be any psychic, social, economic, biological, or environmental determinant. An integral part of this system is the pervasive practice of indeterminate sentences. No longer is a responsible criminal being punished because he chose to do wrong, but rather the sentence is tailored to meet the needs of the individual criminal because he is a victim of other determinants. In other words, he is sick, and the only purpose for incarceration is to help him get better, and no one can know how long that will take; hence, the indeterminate sentence. Furthermore, the nature of the crime is relevant only for what it tells us about what is needed to rehabilitate the offender. This whole shift from man being viewed as responsible for his actions to being a determined victim can be seen in the continual changing of the name of penal institutions to penitentiaries, then reformatories, to correctional centers and now rehabilitation facilities.

The insanity plea is designed to absolve a person whose mental ability makes him incapable of acting responsibly. While virtually no one would deny some rare instances where the criminal may actually be insane, there are two basic essentials in maintaining the viability of the plea. First, the committing of insane acts does not constitute insanity. If it did, then the committal of every insane act would be automatic proof that the aggressor is insane and therefore not criminally culpable. Therefore, the intelligent person would always commit insane acts, and thus always be protected from being found culpable. The view that equates committing an insane act with being insane is expressed in phrases like "A person would have to be insane to do such a thing." However, that is actually fallacious reasoning and is at the heart of abusing the insanity plea. Second, the plea must be used cautiously and rarely. Although it is not used as often as people believe, it is still used too often. The abuse usually takes place when someone is caught in the act, and there is no rational defense that can be marshaled, which potentiates exonerating the criminal. One of the most notorious cases is that of John W. Hinckley, Jr. Even though the defense presented substantial evidence that Hinckley was sane, he was acquitted of the attempted assassination of President Ronald Reagan. Hinckley said, "I was not responsible for my actions."[24]

Now what could be true in rare cases is now seen as a legitimate and normal defense posture. The words of Clarence Darrow, the attorney who defended Darwinism in the 1925 Scopes trial, have become normal in American law and society. He said in a published speech to the prisoners in Chicago's Cook County Jail, "I do not believe that people are in jail because they deserve to be. They are in jail simply because they cannot avoid it on account of circumstances, which are entirely beyond their control and for which they are in no way responsible."[25]

The acceptance of man as determined has led to absurd legal defenses like, "The Twinkie Defense named for a 1978 case, in which a man pleaded temporary insanity after shooting the mayor and the city supervisor in San Francisco's City Hall. He insisted that a steady diet of junk food had raised his blood sugar and addled his brain. Twinkies made him do it."[26] Not to mention the plethora of lawsuits like: the woman who sued McDonald's because she spilt her coffee, and it was hot; the man suing the Las Vegas casinos because they made him gamble; or the class action lawsuit against McDonald's, Burger King, Wendy's and Taco Bell because the restaurants made the plaintiffs fat. How you might ask? They did it by making good food. Now people are suing gun manufacturers for guns used in crimes. This trend is based on the degrading, naturalistic view of man as being determined rather than being responsible for his actions. The determined person must blame someone or something.

The positive school of jurisprudence sees two victims: the criminal who is a victim of a ruthless society that made him the way he is, and the victim of the criminal's actions. Make no mistake about it, under this philosophy, the real criminal that should be punished is society. The change in the view of man from being created in the image of God and responsible for his actions to being determined through biological evolution is foundational for the death penalty falling into disfavor. In contemporary thought, it should never be invoked since there is no real standard of justice, and the criminal is actually a victim of internal and external determinants, which ruthless society did not do anything about. Therefore, society should have to pay for its crime toward the criminal by continually having to order itself in a different way to deal with the criminal who is repeatedly being released back into society, or at the very least, pay for his room and board for the rest of his life. We call this the "society of victims."

The acceptance of the "society of victims" claim, that man is determined, adversely influences how someone views any form of discipline. The victim society is clearly based on a naturalistic view of man. Man's very existence even bolsters the victim status mentality; according to naturalism, he is merely a product of the random chance of nature. Man is, if you will, a post chimpanzee accident of random chance. The degradation of man as something less than created in the image of God can be more poignantly portrayed by emphasizing that the flip side of the vogue victim status is simply materialistic determinism. The foundational belief of victimhood is determinism, which believes that man was not created in the image of God as a free moral agent, but an accident who is caused by purely natural causes. By rejecting determinism, I do not mean to imply that other factors do not *influence* our choices and actions, but only that they do not *control* our choices and actions.

Dr. Norman Geisler explains that man's decision-making ability is determined in one of three ways. "Logically there are only three basic views: self-determinism (self-caused actions), other determinism (acts caused by another), and indeterminism (acts with no cause whatsoever.) Indeterminism is a violation of the law of causality that every event has a cause, and other determinism is a violation of free will, since the moral agent is not causing his own actions."[27]

It is clear that the biblical view of man is that he is self-determined.[28] Russell Chandler says, "Our society of rewards and punishments is predicated upon the belief of biblical religion that human beings are able to choose between good and evil, right and wrong."[29] This does not mean that man controls everything, or that man can do anything he wants, especially in a salvific sense. It does mean that man was created in the image of God, which means that he is a rational, moral, spiritual, and social being, and although the fall corrupted the image of God, it did not destroy it.

He was created as a free moral agent—self determined. When Adam and Eve were told not to eat of the "tree of the knowledge of good and evil" (Genesis 2:17), they actually had the ability to make the choice to eat or not to eat. God knew they would eat, but He did not predetermine that they would eat—in the sense of taking away their choice. God knows everything because God, as God, necessarily knows everything, but that in no way implies God caused man to choose to sin. For if that were true, we are forced to conclude that God caused sin, which is impossible, for then God would no longer be God (James 1:13).

The very nature of true responsibility necessitates the ability to make real choices. Judaism expert Robert Gordis says, "The idea of freedom [of choice] is fundamental to the very nature of man and the universe. Freedom means the right to be wrong."[30] Thus, when God created man, He predetermined to create him with real choice. However, He also knew that man would use his choice for wrong. Hence, sin arose from man's free choice to disobey God. The serpent tempted Adam and Eve, but the serpent did not force or control them. They freely chose to sin. Thus, God held them responsible for their choice as free moral agents, and they incurred the just reward of their choice. This does not fully exonerate Satan; for in Genesis 3:14–15, his sentence was declared because of his part as the tempter. Satan was only culpable for affording the temptation, but Adam and Eve were culpable for their choice.

If you go back to the origin of sin, when Lucifer fell as described in Isaiah 14:12–15 and Ezekiel 28:11–19, the evidence of self-determinism is even clearer. When Lucifer sinned by choosing to rebel against God, there was nothing outside of himself that would have caused him to sin or even have tempted him. For everything was created perfect, and at that time sin did not exist. Even Lucifer was perfect, meaning that there were no internal flaws like a sin nature or sin principle. Since there were no internal flaws or external forces to blame for Satan's choice, it is clear that the first sin arose out of the nature of free will. Therefore, the free moral agent is the efficient cause of an act, and free choice is the power by which he acts.

In other words, since sin did not exist before that choice, the potential for evil is necessarily inherent in the nature of free will, via the exercise of the free will to do wrong. For, if either external sin or a sin nature existed prior to that first wrong choice of a free moral agent, that would mean that God is responsible for *creating* sin, which is impossible. Hebrews 6:18 says, "it is impossible for God to lie." In addition, James 1:13–16 says "Let no one say when he is tempted, 'I am being tempted by God'; for God cannot be tempted by evil, and He Himself does not tempt anyone. But each one is tempted when he is carried away and enticed by his own lust. Then when lust has conceived, it gives birth to sin; and when sin is accomplished, it brings forth death. Do not be deceived, my beloved brethren." Consequently, sin arose from the wrong choice made by a free moral agent.

In addition, God cannot be impugned with creating sin because He created free moral agents who could and did choose wrong. "In the beginning man was innocent of sin and was endowed by his Creator with freedom of choice. By his free choice man sinned against God and brought sin into the human race."[31] For example, an actor is the efficient cause for his performance, without going back and blaming everyone who gave him the job. Further, free choice by definition means that the person is capable of choosing good or bad, and therefore is ultimately responsible. The question asked is, "Why did God give us free will and allow us to misuse it? The question is misleading. One gives a polish to a table, or a pony to a schoolboy, but one does not give three sides to a triangle or free will to a human being. Free will is part of our essence. There can be no human being without it. The alternative to free will is not being a human but an animal or a machine."[32]

It is true now, that man is fallen and no longer has true free will. He does not have the full freedom of choice as Lucifer, Adam, or Eve exercised; however, while the fall damaged, marred, and effaced the *Imago Dei*, it did not erase it or utterly destroy it. When man sinned, he did not become an animal, machine, or a nothing. He still is man created in the image of God, albeit now with sin. Man is spiritually dead. This does not mean he, as man, is annihilated.

Death in the Bible means separation, along with all that entails. Spiritual death is separation from God, physical death is separation of the spirit from the body, and eternal death is eternal separation from God. When the Bible speaks of man being spiritually dead, it means that he can no longer relate to God. His being was so altered by the fall that in order to relate to God he must be born again (John 3:3; 1 Peter 1:3). It means not only that man cannot come to God on his own, but also that man will not even *will* to come to God (Psalm 14:1–3; Romans 3:10–11).

Any spiritual relationship with God must be initiated by God. Man, because of the inherited consequences of original sin, is no longer able to choose God on his own as Lucifer, Adam and Eve were able to do. However, the Scripture teaches that man is capable of receiving God's offer of salvation by faith or rejecting it after God's initiation through the sharing of the gospel, and illumination and conviction of the Holy Spirit of "sin, righteousness, and judgment" (John 16:8); and he is eternally responsible for that choice. It may be that the work of the Holy Spirit in illuminating and convicting of "sin, righteousness, and judgment" places man in somewhat of a pre-fall position with the ability to make a real choice. Regardless of exactly how the process works, to suppose that man is able to come on his own depreciates the damage done by sin. To postulate that man does not make a real choice after God's initiation depreciates man as created in the image of God and undermines the clear teaching of Scripture.

It is a dreadful mistake to equate man being fallen with totally eradicating man's ability to choose in any area. For that is to press the point further than the Bible, reason, or experience would corroborate. The Bible is full of commands for man to do and consequences for not doing them. Each of which, by the grace of God, implies the ability to respond. The Bible says, "Thou shall not bear false witness . . ." (Exodus 20:16). Even lost people can read that and choose not to lie in a certain circumstance. They, as all of us, will at some-time inevitably lie because they are sinners, but they can and do choose to tell the truth even in the face of great personal cost. The stories of soldiers, many of whom are not Christians, who undergo some of the most inhumane treatment as prisoners of war are stirring examples of this ability.

The Scripture is replete with laying choices before the believer. Christians are told in Philippians 2:12 to "work out your salvation." There again is the choice. When Jesus laments over Jerusalem in Matthew 23:37–39, He says in part, "Jerusalem, Jerusalem, who kills the prophets and stones those who are sent to her! How often I wanted to gather your children together, the way a hen gathers her chicks under her wings, and *you were unwilling*" (italics added).

Regardless of how one balances the sovereignty of God and man being responsible for his actions, he must not conclude that man is now a robot; or that because he has some incapacities, he has no capabilities. In other words, because he cannot choose certain things (to come to God on his own or perform spiritually righteous deeds) he cannot choose anything. In our quest to protect the sovereignty of God, we must not make his crowning creation nothing more than a mindless robot. That would indeed be a tragedy, and it leads to the belief that man is not self-determined and therefore not culpable. Conversely, man's freedom is limited by his nature and the sovereign plan of God.

We must not minimize man's depravity and his capacity to cause enormous tragedies, but concomitantly we must remember that he was created in the image of God. He bears that

70

image today albeit a marred and disfigured image (Genesis 9:6); thus, man is valuable and responsible for his actions. The erosion of discipline results in the erosion of viewing man as created in the image of God. If discipline dies, man as man dies with it; thus, the loss of a day of reckoning, without which, the gospel means nothing.

The late Francis Schaeffer said it well. "The fact that man has fallen does not mean that he has ceased to bear God's image. He has not ceased to be man because he is fallen. He can love, though he is fallen. It would be a mistake to say that only a Christian can love. Moreover, a non-Christian painter can still paint beauty. And it is because they can still do these things that they manifest that they are God's image-bearers or, to put it another way, they assert their unique 'mannish-ness' as men. Therefore, it is a truly wonderful thing that although man is twisted, corrupted, and lost as a result of the fall, yet he is still man. He has become neither a machine, nor an animal, nor a plant. The marks of 'mannishness' are still upon him—love, rationality, longing for significance, fear of nonbeing, and so on."[33]

Reason also tells us that man has enough freedom to make choices. No Christian would dare equate man with an animal who acts merely out of instincts. Nor are man's actions determined by biology and environment alone. Peter Kreeft says of this, "Heredity plus environment plus free will equals the human act. Heredity and environment condition our acts, but they do not determine them, as the paints and the frame condition a painting but do not determine it. They are necessary causes but not sufficient causes of freely chosen acts."[34] The whole area of ethics, right and wrong, moral and immoral, culpability and responsibility, punishing and blaming are all premised on man being responsible for his actions.

This comes from a biblical view of man, whereas the positive perspective is a non-biblical view. The biblical view is that man is self-determined as opposed to other-determined. Man is influenced, cajoled, and tempted, but he is not controlled or forced. In those times where man is coerced through torture or other manipulative techniques beyond his control, we do not hold the man to be culpable; even those extreme cases do not eradicate his ability to choose.

Everyday experience reminds us of man's freedom to make choices, for each person makes hundreds of choices each and every day. These can be as small as what socks to wear—most wives wish that their husbands would not make that choice alone—to the choice of the man who was drowning in the icy Potomac, as a result of a plane crash, who freely chose twice to hand off the lifeline that had been dropped to save him, to allow others to be rescued first. These choices ultimately cost him his life. When the rescue line came back the third time, he had sunk into an icy, watery grave.

Now, either we are really making these choices, or we must believe that we are all totally self-deceived by our senses and are merely puppets being manipulated on the cruel stage of life, as some extreme predestinarians and fatalists seem to believe. It is true that our natural senses can deceive us; like when a straight stick is halfway into the water and looks crooked. However, it cannot be demonstrated that our senses deceive us every time. For that would cast us into the absurd world of Jean Paul Sartre, rather than the meaningful world of God. Our senses deceive us when they contradict the perfect will of God or some other more valid and objective criteria; at other times they are life savers.

When man is not held accountable and punished for his wrong choices, we diminish the grandeur of man as created uniquely in the image of a thrice-holy, infinite God. What a tragedy for man to believe such a lie, and the tragedy of trag-edies is that a Christian would believe and perpetrate such a demeaning idea about man. The determinist's compassion, which seeks to punish others for another person's choice is degrading to man and man's creator. Man can only assume his rightful place in God's creation, as God's image bearer, if he is held responsible for his choices. At times, there are strong determinate influences brought to bear upon a person, like being held at gunpoint. In such instances, the person bearing the gun should be held accountable for his actions. We al-ready make legal allowances for such choices that are made under duress. However, even in those dire circumstances, man still makes a choice; albeit maybe not the choice he would have made otherwise. In addition, history is replete with men and women who have chosen to do what is right even in the face of inevitable loss of freedom or life.

John Bunyan, the author of *Pilgrim's Progress*, is a classic example. "In 1660 old acts against Nonconformists were re-vived. Meeting houses were closed; all persons were required under severe penalties to attend their parish church; it be-came illegal to conduct worship services except in accordance with Anglican ritual. Bunyan continued to preach in barns, in private homes, under trees, or in a church if an invitation came. He was arrested in November 1660 on his way to con-duct a religious service about twelve miles from Bedford."[35] He spent the next twelve years in jail because he chose not to compromise his faith in God, even while living in great peril. So is the grandeur of man created in the image of God.

Thus, all disciplines have the inherent idea of choice in them, and that man is self-determined. Therefore, any soci-ety is justified in exercising protective discipline. Society is not only justified, but responsible for the protection of the community (Deuteronomy 13:5, 17:7,12, 21:21; 1 Corinthians

5:13). We remove the recalcitrant not because God does not love him, we do not love him, or because we do not have compassion, but rather because he has willfully chosen to reject correction, and is now jeopardizing, by his choice to do wrong, the well being of the whole community who chooses to do what is right. Man cannot permit personal freedom to corrupt the community's well being any more than God can allow His redemptive love to undermine His holiness and justice.

The fourth reason for discipline is purification. Discipline for purification is similar to protective discipline in that it protects, but it is dissimilar in that it seeks not only protection from aggressors but promotes growth in purity and perfection. It is true that if a community is not protected, it will experience a purity meltdown, but merely protecting it does not guarantee the community's advancement in purity. Purity has to do with becoming more God like. Purity is moving toward the glory of the image of God and away from the sinfulness of man. The choice to move toward purity produces a more godly atmosphere. When sin is tolerated, it has an inevitably degrading impact on the purity of the community. Minimizing the seriousness of sin results in more sin being tolerated, which eventuates in a loss of desire for purity and ultimately even a knowledge of what purity is.

The acceptance of wrong, or sin, is normally cloaked in the verbal garment of *compassion*. They say "To discipline is harsh and to tolerate is compassionate." In reality, winking at sin does not ultimately result in more compassion, righteousness, or love, as is often purported or thought at first; but it will always result in more sin. This is what happened in Israel and the Corinthian church. Paul warns the Corinthians of the danger of winking at sin in 1 Corinthians 5:6–7, "Your boasting is not good. Do you not know that a little leaven leavens the whole lump *of dough*? Clean out the old leaven so that you may be a new lump, just as you are *in fact* unleavened. For Christ, our Passover, also has been sacrificed."

Irresponsibility breeds irresponsibility; however, I would quickly add that in a sinful world there will always be a certain level of irresponsibility, so I'm not promoting perfectionism. I am not saying that we do not forgive and forget. For without that none of us would remain. Nor should we become obsessed with eradicating all of fallen man's frailty from him, which only God can do. What I am talking about is the need for discipline at all levels. Further, I am saying that the biblical view of man, as a responsible free moral agent, must be upheld if the dignity of man and the perceived dignity of God are to be upheld. The extreme of what we are discussing is legalism. However, that is not a part of the view under consideration, but a perversion of it; equal in its ugliness as the victimhood mentality.

Any community that emphasizes undue acceptance, tolerance, victimhood, and love without accountability, will never grow in purity as they should because they unduly prize acceptance over holiness. Once this happens, the die is cast; impurity will increase because the ones who are accepted without having to be held accountable will rarely endorse an all out effort to pursue purity. For that would be self incriminating. Thus, the atmosphere of the entire community will be increasingly infected by the naturalistic view of man and his choices. The rhetoric surrounding man's quest for tolerance is so heavily beclouded by demagoguery, it often obscures the inevitable consequences of embracing sin; so that, by the time it becomes evident, it often becomes bitterly and irrevocably evident.

American culture affords irrefutable evidence of this downgrading. It is hard for younger people to believe that thousands of people walked out of the theaters in outrage over

Clark Gable's expletive at the end of the movie *Gone With The Wind* in 1939. That was over 60 years ago, and few can grasp why people would walk out over one word. Their disbelief is because they have yet to fully grasp the desensitizing that takes place when sin is tolerated; along with that desensitizing comes a lower view of discipline, and the redefining of and desire for purity. Lurking just beneath the surface of the modern humanistic man and woman's declaration "Man is inherently good" is the fact that man, although gloriously created in the image of God, has a dark side whose quest for sin cannot be satiated. Whichever dimension of man is encouraged, whether the glorious image of God, which is faith, love, respect, pursuit of purity, nobleness; or the dark side of man which is his sinfulness, self love, immorality, irresponsibility, corruption, lying, stealing, etc., will most often be the one which predominates the culture.

The church's lack of will to exercise biblical church discipline has diminished her ability and desire to pursue purity. Some would say that the lack of desire for purity in the church diminishes her will to exercise church discipline. In either case, the demoralizing result is the same. In churches without discipline, purity becomes at best a heavenly abstraction and at worst a worn-out cliché, which disfigures and cripples the society of believers since God intended for purity to be an experiential reality of the church community.

Since the fall of man, the reality is that neither personal nor corporate purity is without cost. This is the consequence of the fall. To a large degree, the church seems unwilling to pay the price. The cross demonstrates the ultimate price, which God paid in order to be able to offer purity to man. The church that pursues purity will inevitably pay a price; even though the members are supposed to be saved, each still possesses his fallen humanity. Thus, purity will not come without

76

pursuit. The resounding message of our time appears to be that the god of size, respect, and unity has snuffed out the passion of the church's soul for purity.

Local churches must admit that their failure to be zealous for purity among their own flock, as demonstrated by the absence of church discipline, has facilitated the devaluing of man as a free moral agent created in the image of God, the advancement of the victim society, and the overall decline of American culture. Liberal churches embrace modernity and postmodernity openly, by rejecting the full biblical view of man. Conservative churches embrace them by default because of failure to follow the hard sayings of Christ concerning discipline. Whether these ideas are embraced openly or by default, the tragic consequences are the same; man is devalued and the gospel is undermined.

The reality is that most of the people in politics, the justice system, public education, and the American work force claim to be Christians. Therefore, it is undeniable that the failure of the church to be the church has contributed greatly to the rising tide of our secular society. While the church should not bear all of the responsibility, she must reckon with what she has taught and practiced as a community that would allow so many "Christians" to be contributors to the decline of the biblical view of man and God's discipline in the public square. The church's unwillingness to discipline ungodly behavior within each local church has become so pervasive that it makes discipline seem antiquated—even though we still preach about it. Until the contemporary church is willing to admit that she has either explicitly or implicitly adopted some of the philosophical implications of evolutionism's determinism, she will not really begin the ascension back to the place of holding man accountable because he is created in the image of God and extolling discipline as loving and honorable. It is one thing to preach on discipline and purity. It is quite another to follow what our Lord said about them.

It is a grave failure of contemporary Christianity to see no correlation between the loss of church discipline, the devaluing of man created in the image of God, the loss of the pursuit of purity within the local church, and how all these undermine the very heart of the gospel and evangelism. But this does not automatically absolve the church to dismiss America as simply gospel hardened. The question must be asked, why is America hardened? It seems undeniable that part of the blame must be attributed to the church's lack of discipline within its community, which continually underscores the secular view that man is determined and not accountable to anyone, not even God. If all sin, crime, and evil are a product of determinates acting upon man then he has nothing to account for. Ultimately, discipline is as essential to the gospel as conviction is to salvation.

The presuppositional shift concerning man, from a free moral agent to an other-determined victim, moves the essential questions of morality from the moral model to the medical model. Under the medical model, a person is neither right nor wrong, nor guilty or innocent, but merely sick or healthy. Under the biblical model, man is a sinner and needs a Savior. Under the medical model, man is sick and needs a physician. The result is man is no longer self determined but blames all his problems on genetics or environment. He is a victim. Furthermore, everyone knows that a God who holds man accountable for contracting a sickness, over which he had no control, is no better than any of the myriad of other capricious gods in the pantheon. Surely, this is not a God worthy of obedience and reverence from modern man. It must necessarily be, that undermining the discipline of God results in a loss of desire for purity, leading to minimizing the importance of purity, which ultimately results in a corrupted view of the gospel and God. Thus, as stated in chapter 1, church discipline is inextricably bound to the Great Commission.

With a loss of discipline in our various societies, but especially the church, the truth and desirability of the gospel have been severely discredited. Many people in America really have no problem believing that God loves them; especially when self-esteem mantras continually tell them how wonderful they are, the deification of rights over the past four decades, plus the ever expanding victim society, which means whatever wrong a person did or appears to have done can easily be blamed on someone else. This has culminated in a dulled sense of man's own sinfulness, lostness, and ultimate accountability for his actions.

If that is not enough to perceptibly devalue the gospel, add to that the church's new love affair with merely preaching a positive message based on felt needs. With all of that working in concert, one must ask why would they not believe God loves them; or go even further and conclude that they are themselves gods. The milieu of a deterministic, evolutionary worldview coupled with the church's exchanging exposition of Scripture for a message based on man's felt needs, which actually arises out of that deterministic environment, obfuscates man's high honor of being created in the image of God and his ultimate accountability to Him.

If anything is in disfavor today, it is the idea of hell, which is a place of eternal discipline. Without boldly proclaiming this day of reckoning, there is little need for the gospel, which calls a person to take up his cross and follow Jesus Christ. This is the part of the gospel that must be declared through word and the practice of the disciplines of God. If this is not restored to a place of visible prominence, we will continue to see a decline in America's receptivity to the gospel.

I have predicted for years that evangelicalism will one day awaken to the reality that she has welcomed a Trojan horse. That Trojan horse is psychology. Selected techniques connected with psychology, like listening skills and observing body language, are helpful in any setting where someone is seeking to assist another person with a problem. However, certain methods and terms associated with psychotherapy or psychology only have limited value in particular circumstances like counseling in a state hospital where people have complex and profound disorders. When those same methods and terms are normalized in society at large, the perceived relevance of the gospel is marginalized.

The failure to maintain this domanial distinction is a major contributor to the church's love affair with this spiritual harlot. What moving sexual relations from the marriage bed to prime time did to morality vividly pictures what moving psychology from the rehabilitation ward to society does for the gospel. What was called heresy thirty years ago has now been adopted by many of the most conservative churches. Psychological terms and ideas have become ever present within the body of Christ, which necessarily displaces biblical terms, along with their definitions and corollaries.

Some examples of this displacement are: codependency undermining the beauty of biblical compassion, dysfunctional replacing sinful, and the ever-present emphasis on self love, which has no biblical support and must depend on a misinterpretation of Matthew 22:39, and parallel passages Matthew 19:19, Mark 12:31, 33 and Luke 10:27, for its biblical defense. The paucity of biblical support for modern psychology has not seemed to be a hindrance to the church's burgeoning love affair with it.

The seriousness of this can be seen by realizing that if the problem is sin, then a person needs forgiveness and a Savior;

but if the problem is merely dysfunctional behavior then they simply need understanding, time, and a psychologist. The term dysfunctional and sin are definitional worlds apart, and so are their cures. The cure for sin is God and the cure for dysfunction is man. Before the Christianizing of psychology, evangelicals referred to a troubled family as sinful and saw Christ as the answer. Now, often the same situation is referred to as dysfunctional although maintaining that the answer is Christ. This comes from the church's flawed understanding of what dysfunctional means, and the secular world knows this. The adopting of psychological terms to describe biblical problems means also adopting their cures by either choice or default. If you accept their diagnosis, you either will openly or naively accept their remedies. Nothing less than the gospel of Christ is at stake.

We must never forget that Freud, the father of modern psychology, was an atheist and viewed man as being "other determined."[36] He believed that "personality is a closed energy system fueled by instinctive biological urges. Human action is never free in the sense of being random or spontaneous."[37] The premise of psychoanalysis is that the unconscious is the repository of repressed material and "change occurs in psychoanalysis when the unconscious becomes conscious."[38] Therefore, Freud took the evolutionary theory of Darwin, which presented a plausible naturalistic explanation for man, and created a completely naturalistic and deterministic explanation for man's behavior. This is why a Freudian psychologist has to reach into the patient's subconscious, which really controls the patient, in order to help the patient.

Behaviorism, the system of psychology founded by John B. Watson, and widely associated with B.F. Skinner, is equally deterministic. It sees, "human action as being determined. Humans are stimulus-response mechanisms who behave in response to some input or stimulus. Human beings do not have the power to make actual choices, since they just respond to stimuli present in the environment."[39]

Both psychoanalysis and behaviorism are deterministic. The former is based primarily on internal determinants and the latter external. Albert Ellis' Rational Emotive therapy postulates that there is "very little free will."[40] He espouses a *soft determinism*. Reality therapy teaches that "punishment should be abandoned completely as a parenting modality"[41] and really goes as far as promoting "no punishment" at any level.[42] Along with these are New Age meditation, hypnosis, and other mind-altering theories that all embrace a deterministic view of man.

For example, hypnosis implies that the hypnotist can facilitate bringing about an altered state of consciousness, and then he can reach into your subconscious, unleash the power and will to quit smoking, be pain free, or a host of other extraordinary feats. While some of the most popular and dominate humanistic psychological theories of our day, like Carl Rogers' Client Centered counseling, are not deterministic, their view of humans as innately good and able to pull themselves up by their own boot straps undermines the gospel as much as determinism does.

All secular psychological theories are based on naturalism. They may vary in their views of man, but they are united in rejecting the biblical view of man, his problem, and the cure. When the church seeks to adopt their terms, she becomes complicitous in the devaluing of man and the gospel.

My first experience in understanding how pervasive the acceptance of secular psychology is in evangelicalism was when I was in graduate school. I studied psychology and counseling from a purely secular perspective at Henderson State University. The alarm came not when I began to understand more

about secular psychology, nor even when I began to understand its immense influence upon our culture, although I found
both of these immeasurably disheartening. The distress came
as I began to pay particular attention to the theories being
presented as *Christian* and *Bible-centered* and hearing sermons that were merely secular psychology shoddily clothed
in Christian terminology.

The fact is, secular psychology is a comprehensive system
that includes a view of man, the world, behavior, morals,
thoughts, will, illnesses, and cures to name a few. These conflict with the Scripture in their most salient points. I remember asking one of my professors if he knew of any recognized
counseling theory that was theistic. His answer was an unequivocal, "No!" Even a rudimentary understanding of modern psychology makes it clear that they have not been able to
divest their theories of their atheism, not that they have tried,
and to date Christianity has been equally unsuccessful. Christians need biblical counseling and not some Christianized athe-
istic postulate.

The final reason for discipline is for the sake of justice.
This is the reason for hell. It is the eternal judgment or discipline of God exercised upon all who willfully reject His grace.
This discipline does not incorporate the idea of correction
or redemption, for by this time that has been sufficiently
rejected. This discipline does incorporate the last two reasons, protective and purity. The final judgment of God must
happen in order to afford eternal protection for the new community of heaven and an environment conducive to perfect
security and purity.

Furthermore, there must be a final discipline for those who
have spurned the grace of God and have chosen to live in
their sin. Since God is holy, He must judge sin. While he judged
the sin of mankind in Christ when He hanged on the cross,

the benefit is not applied until man chooses to accept the gracious offer of God to be forgiven. This is based upon man being created in the image of God as a free moral agent. While, as stated before, man cannot initiate this new relationship, it does seem that he can respond to God's initiation of it by accepting the offer by faith or rejecting it. As man freely chose to leave God's presence and lordship in the garden, he must now choose to come back. Man is not a god but neither is man a pre-programmed machine.

Some propose that it is unusually cruel of God to punish man for eternity, regardless of what man did. This is erroneous for three reasons. First, it is based on an inadequate view of the heinousness of sin. Because man is sinful, he is utterly incapable of apprehending or appreciating the sinfulness of sin. Only a thrice-holy God is in a position to evaluate the nefariousness of sin. Secondly, man fails to fully grasp that while sin is committed in time and space against a finite man—like when a man kills another man—it is first and foremost a sin against an infinite God (Psalm 54:1). Hence, the penalty must be infinite. Third, it is based on an inadequate view of the grandeur of man being created in the image of God and thus being a free moral agent fully endowed and fully responsible. These must not be lost in the spoken and life message of the church. Man must constantly be reminded by the church (the voice of Christ) that he has the privilege of being a free moral agent and must use his freedom wisely, so as not to choose an undesirable and irreversible end.

Communities avoid discipline because of the inherent difficulty and its sometimes lack of immediate benefits; however, it is precisely that inherent difficulty that man must experience in order to keep indelibly imprinted upon his consciousness his grandeur as God's image bearer and his sinfulness as fallen man. Without this temporal reminder that man,

God's image bearer, must live with the consequences of his decisions, he loses the knowledge that he may very well have to live with those consequences forever. When temporal accountability is lost, the believability of eternal accountability is lost with it; then the gospel is consigned to merely being more news, but not the Good News.

The erosion of the value of discipline within American culture, and to an alarming degree in the church, continues unabated. The magnitude of this erosion can scarcely be overstated. Tragically, the loss of discipline is viewed as merely a single issue, and not really related to anything but more freedom. American culture celebrates and perpetuates this singular loss as a coming of age of modern man where rights and wrongs are replaced by health and sickness, evil is replaced with dysfunction and community with selfism. The church, heavily influenced by culture, begins to view discipline as overly harsh, and subsequently refers to it pejoratively as legalism. Thus, she acquiesces and revamps the gospel to reflect this coming of age of man and the discarding of discipline.

However, this is an extraordinary and dangerously simplistic view; for what is at stake is nothing less than man himself. Discipline is a necessary corollary to man being created in the image of God as a free moral agent and thus accountable for his actions. Being created in the very image of God is the grandeur of man. It is what separates him from the rest of creation. When we speak of discipline and accountability for one's actions, we are speaking in terms derived from the grandeur of man as God's image bearer. It is not merely coincidental that this increasing disregard for discipline has paralleled the escalating prominence of evolutionism, scientism, and humanistic psychology in America; but rather it is essential since there is a causal relationship that exists between these views and the decline of discipline.

When discipline is marginalized or discarded, it is based on the devaluing of man, created in the image of God, and each degree of depreciation of discipline that is accepted carries with it the concomitant degree of the devaluation of man. Be warned that the evolutionary anti-disciplinarians, inside and outside of the church, will not be satisfied with anything less than the total death of biblical discipline. This loss of discipline results not just in the loss of discipline, responsibility, accountability, civility, and order, but the death of discipline necessarily involves the death of man as man. Man becomes a determined product compelled by internal or external determinants and chance; thus, man as man dies. When man as created in the image of God dies, the gospel dies with him; for if man is not morally accountable for his actions, the offer of forgiveness is meaningless. Therefore, it is imperative that the church once again honor the five kinds of discipline, as well as the five reasons for discipline.

CHAPTER 3

Discipline and the Great Commission: The Essential Relationship Between Church Discipline and the Great Commission

On one occasion, the chief priests and elders approached Jesus while He was teaching and asked Him, "By what authority are You doing these things, and who gave You this authority?" (Matthew 21:23). While it is obvious that the priests and elders were disputing rather than making careful inquiry, the question they ask is a good question and deserves being asked and answered.

By what authority do we practice church discipline? The Scripture makes it clear that it is the authority of the Lord Jesus Christ. Matthew 18:15–20 makes this lucidly clear, particularly in Matthew 18:18–20, which says, "Truly I say to you, whatever you bind on earth shall have been bound in heaven; and whatever you loose on earth shall have been loosed in heaven. Again I say to you, that if two of you agree on earth about anything that they may ask, it shall be done for them by My Father who is in heaven. For where two or three have gathered together in My name, I am there in their midst." Christ is church discipline's *raison d'etre.*

Since Christ purchased the church with His own blood (Acts 20:28) and is the head of the body (Colossians 1:18; Ephesians 5:23), He is the supreme authority. Since He is God, no one can trump His authority. This being undeniably true, one must ask by what authority do churches excuse themselves from carrying out church discipline. Since Christ made it undeniably clear that the church is to practice church discipline, therefore, it is no less than willful disobedience to our Commander and Chief; it is cafeteria Christianity to fail to practice church discipline.

Many perpetually seek to depose Christ as the sovereign over the church. Some of these *would-be* potentates are: comfortable Christianity that focuses on the seemingly more loving aspects of Christianity, the striving for unity built around something other than the Scripture, desire for a long pastorate, desire to be liked, tradition, the will of the lost or carnal, and the list goes on ad infinitum. Regardless of which demigod has seized control of a local church and precluded following Christ in the difficult things, it is no less than an insurrection.

Christ not only commanded church discipline, but He explained the process. It is important to note, that the word for *church, ekkasia,* is found in the Gospels in only two places. The first time is Matthew 16:18, where Christ says, "I will build My church." In this first mention of the church, Christ establishes that it is His church—and that never changes. He never abdicates His headship or ownership of the church to any self-enthroned monarchy or oligarchy. Also, this passage speaks of the universal church.

The only other time that the word *church* is mentioned in the Gospels is in Matthew 18:15–20. It should startle us that the first and only time that Christ mentioned the word *church* in regard to the local church, He did so in order to explain church discipline—that is, before the Great Commission and the empowering or gifting of the church. This makes discipline indubitably essential to being an authentic New Testament church.

Church discipline can be defined as the personal or corporate actions of the local church concerning one of her members that preserve her holiness, testimony, and doctrinal purity, with the purpose of maintaining a conducive atmosphere for following Christ and experiencing His presence and power. It is redemptive, corrective, protective, purifying and just.

Today, people even wonder if a church has the right to practice church discipline. Not only does the church have the right, but also she has the moral and spiritual obligation to practice church discipline according to the Scripture. To fail to carry out the command to practice church discipline is no less than insubordination. Pastors teach, and rightly so, that if a person has an area of his life he is not subjecting to the lordship of Christ—obeying what He says in His Word—he cannot walk with God, have the blessings of God upon his life, and if he persists, he will undergo the discipline of the Lord.

How can it be any different for the church? Think of it this way. What if tomorrow the church decided to simply not pray, and not even make an attempt at prayer? Not only does she quit praying but also begins to ridicule those who do. Pastors around the coffee table—where no church members can hear—say, "You know it's just too hard to pray, so we do other things." They say, "I believe in it, but we don't practice it. People get offended when you emphasize prayer so we focus on other things to keep the unity." Or what if the subject were the Great Commission. A church says they love Christ. They sing about Him, and they even have Bible studies, but they simply decide that our culture is too secular, and that trying to reach people in America causes too many problems and costs too much in personal sacrifice. Consequently, they emphasize fellowship, preaching, and worship. This would be nothing less than willful disobedience. The same is true of relegating the commands concerning church discipline to some obscure theological closet talk.

Do we think biblical fidelity can be attained if someone says that our church may not evangelize, but we do many other *good things*? There is a prima facie hollowness to these words, and we all know it. They would immediately be branded a heretic and traitor, for they willfully decided not to follow the commands of Christ because they were either too hard or unpopular. It is no less serious to consign church discipline to the Jurassic Park of church history.

Just because there are many who have chosen to exclude the commands of our Lord Jesus Christ concerning church discipline, does not make it any more right than if they chose to exclude the commands to pray. Greater numbers practicing disobedience makes disobedience easier, but never makes it right. If the contemporary church ignores the first command of our Lord given to the local church, one has to ask, can we still call ourselves the church? If something so vital to the gospel can be turned into the leprosy of the church by some hermeneutical gymnastics; it is not hard to see how many other things like prayer, evangelism, and missions can become empty clichés or spiritual painkillers for hearts that have turned from our Lord's commands. Once we consign church discipline to the nonimportant, then others will surely dismiss things that are difficult for them. Pastors set the standard. Even if we preach powerfully and vociferously, if we usurp the authority of Christ in an area, there is a disingenuousness to our message, and people will soon realize it. Herein is the seedbed of church mediocrity.

My point is not to make someone feel unduly guilty if he is not practicing church discipline in his church, but rather to cause us to assign the same importance to it as Christ does. This book is intended to help those who desire to follow Christ in this area, but it is also to expose the hypocrisy of simply choosing to ignore the issue. It is by its very nature inextricably bound to the rest of the commands to the church. To choose to practice one absolute given by Christ and ignore another absolute given by Christ is nothing but pure old relativism outfitted in Christian clothing. Although the direct command of Jesus in Matthew 18:15–20 is amply sufficient, the mandate for practicing church discipline is also found in the Great Commission. It, as well as all the other spiritual disciplines and commands, are necessarily included in the phrase, "teaching them to observe all that I commanded you" (Matthew 28:20).

The Great Commission is talked about, promoted, and extolled as much as anything in Christendom. The Great Commission is the mandate given by Jesus in Matthew 28:18–20, "And Jesus came up and spoke to them, saying, 'All authority has been given to Me in heaven and on earth. Go therefore and make disciples of all the nations, baptizing them in the name of the Father and the Son and the Holy Spirit, teaching them to observe all that I commanded you; and lo, I am with you always, even to the end of the age.'" If someone preaches about reaching people with the gospel, everyone is rightly excited and supportive—even though they may not actually contribute more than an expected amen. When someone is baptized, there are numerous amens, hallelujahs, or applause because the Great Commission is being carried out. While people and churches may fail to live up to the challenge to take the gospel to our neighbors and the uttermost part of the earth, at least there is a serious attempt by most and an esteeming of its importance by almost all. To do less would be heresy and willful disobedience to our Lord who redeemed us.

However, there is a profound misunderstanding of the Great Commission by some, and a serious lack of clear communication of what the Great Commission is by others. We know this because church discipline is often viewed as irrelevant to the Great Commission, and is even seen as a deterrent. For if it were relevant, then church discipline would receive appropriate attention when discussing the Great Commission.

The vividness of this misunderstanding about the Great Commission's relationship to church discipline was graphically demonstrated once at a Baptist state convention. A friend of mine, LeRoy Wagner, submitted a resolution to the Resolutions Committee, which articulated the vital relationship between church discipline and the Great Commission. LeRoy told me that later in the day the committee "had rejected the resolution on the grounds that the language was divisive and inflammatory, and that they wanted to keep their resolutions on a 'high plane.'" After the committee had rejected the resolution, LeRoy submitted the same resolution in an open business session. He explains what took place. "After an opportunity to speak for my resolution, the committee chair attacked the resolution with fervor, scoffing at the idea of church discipline having any connection with the Great Commission. The fervor of the chairman was unlike anything I have ever heard in twenty-two years of attending conventions. The resolution was soundly defeated."[43]

I have no doubt that the committee members have a great desire to carry out the Great Commission. However, it is indeed tragic when the Great Commission is so misunderstood by the leaders of churches and conventions. Further, it is equally tragic to see church discipline relegated to such a disparaging rank.

The very passage known as the "Great Commission" (Matthew 28:18–20), demonstrates the inextricable relationship between church discipline and the Great Commission. Jesus said, "All authority has been given to me in heaven and on earth" (verse 18). This does not make His post-resurrection authority greater than His pre-resurrection authority, but rather the sphere in which He exercises authority is now all encompassing. This is both an encouragement and a call to submission. Although the assignment to follow is humanly impossible, it is encouraging because the one commissioning has absolute power and authority to empower the commissioned. There is also the idea of encouragement in the words, ". . . lo I am with you always even to the end of the age" (verse 20). The absolute power is always available because He not only sends His people but He goes with them. It is a call to unwavering and unreserved surrender to Him as God. His followers are called to be completely and humbly submitted to Him.

Having established His all-encompassing, absolute authority, He now sends His disciples into all of the world to reproduce. Three components of the assigned task are: *go, baptizing*, and *teaching*. These three verbs are participles in the Greek. *Matheteuo* is translated *make disciples*. It is the main verb, and it is in the imperative, which makes it the central command in the passage. It means to make learners and followers of Christ. Jesus command can be summed up in the following way, "I command you to make learners who follow Me and who continue the commission to make disciples who follow Me." The participles—*go, baptizing*, and *teaching*—are dependent on the main verb, and appear that "at least some imperatival force tinges the participle."[44] *Go* is an aorist passive participle, which is best translated as *having gone*. Since they were His disciples, they were to continue His work

93

"to seek and to save that which was lost" (Luke 19:10), which involves going. In other words, He assumed as followers, they would go.

The two other participles, *baptizing* and *teaching*, are in the present tense, which signifies continuous action. Baptizing and teaching are not the means of making disciples, but they do characterize it. In other words, to become a disciple, a person becomes a disciple by faith in Christ, then as a disciple, he is to be baptized and taught. The response of a true disciple will be to be baptized as a sign of Christ's death, burial, and resurrection and his allegiance to Christ, and to submit his life to Christ's instructions.

The verb *observe*, is translated from the Greek word *tareo*, which means, "to attend to carefully, take care of;"[45] "to cause to continue, to keep."[46] The clear meaning is to obey. A disciple is to train other disciples to live in continued obedience to the commands of Christ. Notice that disciples are to observe *all*. There are no exceptions. The meaning of the Great Commission is to make disciples through the preaching of the gospel, then to baptize the new disciples, and train and teach them to follow Christ in *everything* He commanded. To do any less is to disobey the Great Commission; to tell others to do any less than *all* He taught is to misrepresent and molest the Great Commission.

This is not to say that we can teach everything in the first day or year, nor is it to say that some things should not take priority over others in discipling. It is to say that when we fail to teach and follow certain commands or ignore them because of their difficulty, we necessarily fail to "teach others to observe all" and we fail to "observe all." Thus, we irrefutably fail to fulfill the Great Commission. A person's failure to fulfill the Great Commission because he does not know or because he continues to fail, even though his heart's desire is to obey, is categorically different than someone who intentionally disassociates what Christ intentionally bound together.

Jesus always called people to follow Him. He used believing and following interchangeably. The call to follow was a call to obey (Matthew 4:19, 8:22, 9:9). Both philosophers and Pharisees had disciples, but Jesus' call to be a disciple was different. The primary difference between Jesus' disciples and the disciples of philosophers and Pharisees was that they were committed to the person of Jesus—not just His teachings. "A unique aspect of NT discipleship is that it is commitment to the person of Jesus. His teaching has force only when there is first this commitment to His person. This personal commitment explains the deep depression of the disciples after the crucifixion (Luke 24:19ff.). It is not enough that they have the legacy of His Word. They have lost Jesus himself. The crucial importance of the resurrection reinforces this."[47]

The New Testament disciple is committed to the person of Jesus, not merely some of His teachings. Following the clear commands of Jesus is what one desires when he is committed to Christ above everything—pleasure, popularity, acceptance, comfort, and security. It is true that the Scripture clearly teaches that some commands are weightier than others. For example, Jesus excoriates the Pharisees for neglecting the weightier provisions of the law while majoring on minors. However, it is important to note that He then commanded them to keep the weightier commands "without neglecting the others" (Matthew 23:23). Even if church discipline was not a weightier command, it is still Pharisaism to choose not to emphasize and keep it.

Moreover, it is obviously not a lighter command when considered in light of chapters 1 and 2 of this book, the command of Christ in Matthew 18, the wording of the Great Commission, and the things Christ referred to as "weightier" in Matthew 23:23, which are, "justice and mercy and faithfulness." Clearly, church discipline is one of the weightier since discipline, contrary to popular caricatures, is an act of mercy, justice, and faithfulness, and is essential to evangelism and the Great Commission.

Considering everything, this passage brings us face to face with the stark reality that the Great Commission cannot be carried out, in the fullest sense, without teaching and practicing church discipline. The Great Commission cannot be carried out without teaching and following the whole counsel of God because the command is to make disciples who are committed to all that Jesus teaches. Jesus summed it up by saying in John 14:15, "If you love Me, you will keep My commandments" (see also John 8:31). In Jesus' final discourse to the disciples, He said, "If anyone loves Me, he will keep My word; and My Father will love him, and We will come to him, and make Our abode with him. He who does not love Me does not keep My words; and the word which you hear is not Mine, but the Father's who sent me. These things I have spoken to you, while abiding with you. But the Helper, the Holy Spirit, whom the Father will send in My name, He will teach you all things, and bring to your remembrance all that I said to you" (John 14:23–26).

Selective obedience only demonstrates that a person does not love Christ as much as he says. As a matter of fact, church discipline has a great deal to do with whether we love Christ and His church more than we love ourselves. There are many things in the Christian life which bespeak of how much we love Christ, but perhaps none so much as our willingness to follow the teachings of Christ in areas like church discipline, where the potential for personal loss, difficulty, and misunderstanding is so great. To only follow Christ where it is easy is what Dietrich Bonhoeffer called "cheap grace." He wrote,

"Cheap grace is the preaching of forgiveness without requiring repentance, baptism without *church discipline*, communion without confession, absolution without personal confession. Cheap grace is grace without discipleship, grace without the cross, grace without Jesus Christ, living and incarnate"[48] (italics added).

One of the undeniable features of godly love is biblical discipline. This can be seen in parental love (Ephesians 6:1–4), or divine love (Hebrews 12:6). Throughout the Scripture, biblical discipline is seen as an expression of real love. Conversely, the unwillingness to discipline is seen us unloving and poor stewardship. We even acknowledge today that a person who does not discipline his child does not really love his child. We recognize that discipline is love and non-discipline is non-love; and the church is to walk in love, which it cannot do if it forsakes disciplining a sinning brother. Bonhoeffer said, "Nothing could be more cruel than the tenderness that consigns another to his sin. Nothing could be more compassionate than the severe rebuke that calls a brother back from the path of sin."[49]

Our love for Christ is shown by our willingness to follow. This is not the same as perfectionism. We will never follow perfectly in this life, but to use that as an excuse for not following is playing loose with the Word of God. My understanding of the Scripture and my experience as well indicate clearly that discipline is something that is not done for earthly praise. If praise is what someone seeks, he will surely shy away from church discipline. Often the unwillingness to follow Christ in the arduous things like discipline, is cloaked in euphemisms like let's just love them, we will just pray for them, or some other non-threatening statement. Thus, whether intentional or unintentional, the implication is that when you practice church discipline, you don't love them or you are not praying for them. Again, only an abandoned and devotional love for

God, His church, and Word will be sufficient to motivate a church to practice church discipline. This is not to demean love and prayer since they are vital to the Christian life and to carrying out biblical church discipline, but they are inadequate to accomplish the task in and of themselves. If they were adequate, Jesus would never have commanded the process of church discipline. When the temple needs cleansing, nothing else will do.

It is important to note that the phrase *The Great Commission* is not in the biblical text, but rather it is added as the topic of Matthew 28:16–20. It is the Great Commission in the sense that everything culminates in that commissioning. However it is, according to the biblical text, a command. Thus the added term "Great" makes it no more significant than the command to practice church discipline since it is also a command, and an undeniable and inseparable part of the commission. The mandate of the church is to glorify God, and we do that by obeying Him.

The time in which we live serves as another stimulus for church discipline. The time and country in which a Christian lives is not to be determinative of whether he will follow Christ's teaching in the area of church discipline; however, it does influence how often it will need to be practiced. When the church is under severe persecution, there is very little need for formal church discipline. Persecution serves as a natural purifier of the church. In countries where it is illegal to be a Christian, and a Christian can be executed for meeting in house churches, few attend for the novelty of Christianity. In contrast, when Christianity is culturally acceptable, or even somewhat fashionable, many will belong to a church that may not be Christians or at least do not live like they are. In this case, church discipline must become more prevalent for the church to be the church. Without it, there will be undue worldly influence in the church, and authentic Christianity will be jeopardized. The contemporary American church serves as a perdurable and unsettling reminder of this truth.

The cry from church leaders across America reverberates with a deafening voice bemoaning the worldliness and credulity of the church. The church is many times far too anxious to court the newest ideas and redefinitions of biblical Christianity. This problem is titanic in size and catastrophic in its impact. The loss of many mainline denominations to a Kierkegaardian "blind leap of faith," which resulted in accepting higher criticism and other destructive approaches to the Scripture, is one of the most glaring examples in modern times, but it is certainly not the only one.

The church often embraces ideas that have been designed by the world for the world to operate without God. Some of these ideas are an unbridled acceptance of modern psychology, Wall Street management models, the church as a mere democracy, numerical growth as the peerless badge of a New Testament church, and love means never having to say you're sorry, to name a few. None of which lends itself to church discipline.

Maybe, when history is complete and engraved upon eternity, the most ruinous belief ever embraced by the church will turn out to be that believing rightly about the Bible, that it is inerrant, infallible, and authoritative, sufficiently pleases God apart from faithfulness to the Bible. I call this "nonfunctional inerrancy" because there is an unnatural disjuncture between belief and action. Rarely is this belief heard in verbal affirmations, but it is easily detected by the choices that are made. It is far more subtle and less detectable than other destructive beliefs because of its strong faith affirmations and appropriate use of religious jargon. It is also more insidious because it is actually the open door to every non-biblical idea that captures the attention and heart of the church. For without this belief, liberalism, abortion, church discipline falling into disfavor, ad infinitum could never find a pew of the church on which to sit. Further, it arbitrarily categorizes various biblical teachings as unnecessary, unimportant, irrelevant, or too difficult, which results in the same disastrous outcome as any other heresy, only without having to be exposed as the real culprit. The lack of discipline is an outflow of nonfunctional inerrancy, and the lack of discipline results in a church that is undisciplined doctrinally and organizationally. Nonfunctional inerrancy is the church's stealth entrance opened to the host of hell. James says it best, "But are you willing to recognize, you foolish fellow, that faith without works is useless?" (James 2:20).

Maybe Christ mentioned the local church in connection with church discipline first because He not only knew that it would be a very difficult and unpopular thing to do, but also, and I think more importantly, Christ knew that the church could not have the power of God upon her without purity. It is evident to all that when Christ was upon the earth as a man, He experienced the power of God upon Him. However, what is not noted as often is that if sin had come into His life, the power of God would have been diminished if not removed. We are not perfect like Him, but we are the body of Christ; and without purity, we can no more expect God's power upon the church than our Lord Jesus Christ, the head of the body, could. Thus, everything we seek and hold dear, power, peace, unity, credibility, believability and being imitators of Christ, is inextricably bound with church discipline. Holiness cannot be relegated to a secondary or tertiary place of importance without forfeiting the unique presence of God. The lack of discipline does not cause the church to lose her salvation, but because of impurity, it does cause her to sacrifice everything that salvation brings in this life. The church prays for power, and yet power is capsized in a sea of accepted impurity.

As noted earlier, persecution purifies the church, but without it, the church must exercise church discipline to maintain a pure body. Today, to remove someone's name from a church roll is seen as one of the cardinal sins of the church, even if they have not darkened the door of the church in years or live in another state. Some argue that names of these stealth members should not be removed from the church roll under the guise that it is either judgmental, or irrevocably eliminates the possibility of ministering to them. This is merely Christian pragmatism since the Bible makes it clear; the church is a body not a lodge. The way that some respond to removing names from a church roll makes it seem tantamount to erasing their name out of the Lamb's book of life—yes even Baptists often equate salvation in some mystical way with an extant church letter.

One of the most practical mandates for church discipline is its inevitable need. Every pastor will one day face the issue of church discipline. Actually, that is a naively optimistic statement because every pastor and every church will face the issue of church discipline many times. This is particularly true in the day in which we live, where normal moral restraints are marginalized or diminished, and Christians are more knowledgeable about Microsoft Word than God's Word.

The pastor must take this very seriously since he serves as the undershepherd of one of the Great Shepherd's flocks. If anyone is going to follow the teachings of Christ, it has to be His undershepherds. While I believe that a church split can usually be avoided when exercising discipline, it still always remains a possibility, and I will share some things later that can help prevent a split. Shepherds must come to grips with two things in this regard. First, the problems with church discipline are not because of church discipline, but because of the lack of it. Second, the worst thing that can happen in a church is not a split, but a failure to obey Christ. The one who seeks to care for himself, and not provide what the sheep really need is called a hired hand—hireling in the KJV (John 10:12–13). This term signifies someone who does not love the flock like the real shepherd, but who is merely doing his job. Jesus asked Peter three times if he loved Him, and after each time Peter answered yes; Jesus' response to Peter was, "tend" or "shepherd" my sheep (John 21:15–17). Thus, the undershepherd's love for the Great Shepherd is seen in whether he loves the sheep like Christ.

Tolerance of sin eventuates in an increased pervasiveness of sin, which then feeds the desire to overlook more and more sin, since by this time everyone is involved in some kind of sin. Someone will eventually say, "It is not as bad as some sins you know." I have pastored small to medium-size churches over the past twenty-two years, and there has been an unremitting flow of challenges to the purity of the church. People have simply become comfortable with their sin by compartmentalizing it and seeking to make up for that weakness by overcompensating in another area. But the fact remains, that sin is being allowed to thrive inside the camp.

Consequently, every pastor decides, almost daily, whether he will succumb to societal redefinition of what the church should be or follow the pattern laid out in Scripture. I have never talked with a fellow pastor in private conversation who did not express his belief in the commands for church discipline. All see the urgent and critical need for church discipline in the church at large and for theirs in particular. To the man, they each shared whether in the past or in the present, their struggle with what to do about a certain person sowing discord, teaching heresy, or living a life that besmirched the testimony of their church. My heart truly goes out to each of these pastors. I understand their struggle in light of the Scripture and the potential price these pastors may pay. Yet, for all of us, it always comes down to whether we follow Jesus at all costs.

Jesus never said what size our church is to be, or whether it is to be traditional or contemporary in decorum—all traditional music, worship styles, etc., were contemporary styles when they began—but He did command us to practice church discipline and systematically explained how to do it.

This brings us back to the question: By what authority do we dare to practice church discipline? To put it another way, by what authority does a church decide what she will emphasize, do, and pursue? Is it the authority of Scripture or is there a rival authority that the church follows when convenient? When faced with the inevitable and repeated challenges of whether or not to practice church discipline, the simple question will always be, will we remain faithful or compromise?

I remember one time we were in the wonderful Christmas season, and the choir was preparing for a Christmas cantata. It seemed as though the Lord had sent us someone who could help make it a wonderful presentation. She played the piano wonderfully and sang beautifully. Needless to say, she had a major part in the play.

Just weeks before the cantata, a youth came to us who had baby-sat for the pianist. The young girl, I'll call her Jan, came to our music minister and told him that the lady had liquor in her refrigerator and had gone out night clubbing the Saturday night that she baby-sat for her. The youth was confused at how we could teach against drinking, based on our understanding of Scripture, and yet allow this lady to help lead in worship and help portray the wonderful birth of our Lord. The fact is, we did not know anything about it until Jan told us.

The worship leader came to me with the information, and we both agreed that the lady had to be approached. To do any less would surely appear to be hypocrisy, and rightly so, because that is exactly what it would have been. Our teaching and our actions would have been contrary one to the other.

The worship leader went to her home and told her what Jan had told us. The young lady made no qualms about it. She said she did "drink and go to the nightclubs on Saturday nights," but she saw no reason why that should affect what she did on Sunday morning. That she did what she did was indeed a problem, but the greater problem was that she did not see a relationship between what she did during the week and what she did in church on Sunday. The music minister told her that she would have to apologize to the baby-sitter and to cease drinking and clubbing in order to continue to play the piano and be in the play. She flatly refused.

That was the last time we ever saw her. Yes, it did hurt our piano playing for a while, and there was a noticeable void in the cantata, but that was eclipsed by knowing there was a youth who knew for sure that we took seriously the teaching of the Scripture. As a matter a fact, we found out that Jan had talked with other youth about the situation—as she showed her concern and sought their counsel about whether to tell the staff—which resulted in many who were watching to see if we valued the quality of production above fidelity to the Scripture. Our music minister stands as an example of many music ministers who love truth more than they love their presentations. They present to portray truth by both song and vehicle. Most of all, whatever may have happened, we had sought to be faithful to Jesus. And that was our Christmas song.

CHAPTER 4

When the Church Disciplined Church Discipline: The Theological Reasons for the Banishment of Church Discipline Answered

Since church discipline is vital to the church, the gospel, the Great Commission, and the commands of Christ, you would expect it to be a common occurrence in the church today. Its marked absence is all the more noticeable in light of church history because church discipline has been practiced throughout the history of the church, albeit in various forms. In the New Testament and the early church, it was carried out by the entire church, including the laity. Through time, church discipline became formalized and private. "Between the second and sixth centuries the system became increasingly formalized. Until the sixth century, the congregation was involved in reconciliation of the lapsed, but there was a gradual shift from the laity to the bishop, and eventually to the Priest."[50] This system of private confession is what is practiced in the Church of Rome today, when the penitent goes before a priest and confesses his sin in order for the priest to pronounce absolution.

The Reformers, Protestant churches, and Anabaptists practiced biblical church discipline. John Calvin said, "As the saving doctrine of Christ is the soul of the church, so discipline forms the ligaments that connect the members together, and keeps each in its proper place. Whoever, therefore, either desires the abolition of discipline, or obstructs its restoration, they certainly promote the entire dissolution of the church."[51] They believed that church discipline was so vital to the church that its loss resulted in the loss of the true church. One of the reasons for the absence of church discipline from the contemporary church is that it was abused in the past. George Davis's comments on past abuse, "The fact that church discipline has received so little attention in recent years is indeed lamentable. If the sin of earlier generations was abuse, the sin of today is sheer neglect."[52] Undeniably, there were some abuses in the past, but that alone cannot explain the multi-decade omni-hush, which has befallen all of Christendom concerning church discipline. Further, the answer to abuse in the past is not neglect but correction.

The Anabaptists also practiced church discipline, which was customarily known as *the ban*. The Anabaptists believed in the ban because the New Testament was their sole authority. Out of that presupposition, they established the essential marks of the true church. Some of these *essential marks* are the same distinctives held by other Baptist groups, as well as other Christian groups who have been influenced by the Baptist emphasis upon New Testament authority for the church and Christian life. Three of these marks relate to their belief in the indispensableness of the practice of church discipline. The Anabaptists believed that the first mark of the church was a regenerate membership. This means that the local church can be made up of only those who have put their faith in Jesus Christ as their Savior. The second mark was that of believer's baptism by immersion. Baptism "became for the Anabaptists the door into the visible church."[53] The third mark of the church was church discipline. These flow from the New Testament and enjoy an inseparable relationship.

The first mark, the new birth, or regeneration, was viewed as "a radical renewal of one's entire person; it is an eschatological event; it is a decided change in one's existence which is possible only by faith in Christ as the New Man."[54] The second mark of believer's baptism by immersion was viewed as an essential sign of the New Testament church, without which the church could not exist. Baptism identified the believer as a follower of Christ and served as the entrance into the local church. The relationship between baptism and discipline is that, "by it the believer becomes submissive to the discipline of the church. Baptism, while necessary as the initial act of obedient discipleship, is also the indispensable sign of incorporation into the visible fellowship of believers. The significance of baptism as subjecting one to the discipline of the church was clearly set forth in the Schleitheim Confession. . . . By this means the Brethren intended to maintain the integrity of the Anabaptist witness in life and deed. They succeeded so well that they were accused by their enemies of teaching sinless perfection."[55] The accusation of teaching sinless perfection was false and categorically rejected in Anabaptist writings. Would to God, that in today's church the emphasis on holiness was so intense that people accused, although falsely, the church of teaching sinless perfection. It seems that the avant-gardism de jour is to assuage the carnal and lost. Holiness in practical living, holiness within the church, and for many in doctrine as well, has become nothing more than a spiritual dinothere and deserving of the same attention.

The third mark of the church, church discipline, was also viewed as essential for the church to be the church. The logic flows accordingly; the church is to be made up of only born again people, whose lives evidence this undeniable eschatological change into a new being, who have been baptized, signifying their identification with Christ and their submission to the corporate body. If the church was going to maintain this New Testament testimony, discipline was essential because they knew people would slip in who were either unregenerate or acted like they were. Practically speaking, either one has the same impact upon the church, her mission, and the world. Thus, to maintain the church as a true uncorrupted New Testament church means there must be a mechanism to remove an unrepentant member. To fail to do so is for the church to prevaricate, which makes this church no better than the church of Rome. They believed the Church of Rome was so corrupted that reformation was an insufficient remedy, only restitution would restore the true church. "To the Anabaptists, the fall of Rome was absolute. . . . Reformation was out of the question. The Anabaptists saw their task as building anew on the original foundation."[56]

An integral component of their view of discipline was an inestimable and inviolable relationship between church discipline and the Lord's Supper. This understanding is the basis for Conrad Grebel's statement to Thomas Muntzer, "But if one should be found who is not minded to live the brotherly life, he eats to his condemnation, for he does not discern the difference from another meal. He brings shame on the inward bond, which is love, and on the bread which is the outward bond."[57] They did not see discipline as harsh but rather as an act of love and fitting for maintaining the meaning and sacredness of the Lord's Supper. This close relationship between discipline and the Lord's Supper can also be seen in statements like that of Balthasar Hubmaier who viewed the Lords Supper as, ". . . a public testimony of love, to which one brother pledges himself to another, before the church. They say that just as they now are breaking bread and eating with one another, and sharing the cup, so each will offer up body and blood for one another, relying on the power of our Lord Jesus Christ."[58]

Anabaptists were accused of being harsh and playing God in determining who would be cut off, as will any church today that seeks to follow the Lord's instruction about church discipline. Menno Simmons responded to such charges with these words. "Wherefore, brethren, understand correctly, no one is excommunicated or expelled by us from the communion of the brethren but those who have already separated and expelled themselves from Christ's communion either by false doctrine or by improper conduct."[59] They viewed the discipline as a temporary remedial act, believing that a true Christian seeking to walk with God will repent when confronted with his sin. So they believed that church discipline was indispensable to maintaining a New Testament regenerate church, holding the Lord's Supper in proper esteem and preserving the testimony of Christ and His church.

In the twentieth century, Baptist churches in particular, and other churches who believe in a regenerate church membership, sought to maintain a regenerate church membership, the testimony of the church, and holiness of the church along with the love and beauty of the Lord's Supper, while simultaneously disencumbering the church of the burden of church discipline. In so doing, the church lost not merely discipline but lost the ability to maintain the visible and true church; thus, in a very real sense, although not an absolute sense, lost the church. This loss was avoidable and is correctable, but only if the contemporary church grasps the teaching of the New Testament about discipline and the understanding of the inviolable relationship between discipline and the church as did the reformers, Anabaptists, and our forefathers.

In the 1800s, churches had such high standards of membership that the number of people attending Sunday worship was more than the total membership. Many attending who were not members were considered *constituents*. Because of the confusion over the definition of church membership today as compared with the pre civil war days, people inaccurately conclude that more people were unchurched then, than is actually the case.

Winthrop S. Hudson explains that the misunderstanding lies in the relaxing of membership requirements in the twentieth century from what they were in the nineteenth century. "The point at which misunderstanding occurs is when early nineteenth-century church membership is compared to post-civil war and twentieth century church membership, for they are not comparable. The American people were not as 'unchurched' in 1800 as the statistics would seem to imply. The confusion has been introduced by a progressive relaxation of membership requirements. The number of people attending Sunday morning worship in the 1830s was usually three times the membership of a church. Furthermore, churches customarily computed their 'constituency' (those nominally related but not members) as approximately twice the number of attendants. In terms of twentieth-century definitions of church membership (when what was once 'constituency' had become 'membership') . . ."[60]

What a contrast with today's church where there are at least three times as many members as people attending on Sunday morning, the exact opposite of the recent past. It is all the result of lowering the standards of what it means to be a member of the body of Christ, which is directly related to the abandonment of church discipline. Since, if you are going to lower the standard of membership to allow nominal or uncommitted members, church discipline must necessarily be relegated to the primitive times of the past. The best way to simply ignore the teaching of Scripture on church discipline or accomplish this feat is to develop a seemingly plausible and palatable list of supposed reasons why de-emphasizing church discipline is reasonable and right. If that does not work, some have gone so far as to attack those who practice it as mean spirited or legalistic.

When the modern church has three times as many members as worshippers, and we can't find thirty to fifty percent of the members, and open and flagrant sin is ignored in the church, it is evident that the contemporary church is out of touch, tragically out of touch, with the New Testament and our forefathers. Through the lenses of modernity and postmodernity, the past is viewed as Neanderthalish, and any mention of the Puritans is an emblem of shame and a reminder of something to be avoided at all cost. It is no secret that the impact of the enlightenment upon man, society, and the church inevitably leaves a wake of disdain upon the pursuance of holiness. That disrespect for the beauty of holiness necessitated the internment of church discipline. The disdain for the Puritans' and separatists' emphasis upon holiness, inside and outside of the church, is telling of the intensiveness and extensiveness of modern man's pride.

Modern man may gloat about how far we have come, and thrust his verbal stiletto into the Puritan and separatist image at each opportunity; but that will never erase the historical reality that God used them to found the greatest nation in the history of man. Conversely, the modern church is so anemic that at best it fails to stem the demise of the greatest nation, and in many ways is complicitous in her ruin. The contemporary church has exchanged the purity taught in Scripture, as sought by the Puritans and others, in order to bow before the gilded icons of modernity. On these philosophical kitsch al-

tars are sacrificed discipline, holiness, community, accountability, and ultimately the perceived spiritual viability of the
gospel, whose practice proclaims the very certain death of
modernity and every other man-exalting philosophy.

When the issue of church discipline is mentioned, there
are several arguments launched against the proposal. In order
to expose the weaknesses of these potential death threats to
discipline, we will spend the rest of this chapter and chapter 5
evaluating their plausibility before we move on to discuss the
reasons for church discipline. Regardless of their lack of cogency and reliability, these excuses have proven successful in
making the Bible and church history virtually the only place
where church discipline can be found. I divide the reasons
that have led to the banishment of church discipline to the
annals of history into two categories, theological and practical. The theological will be examined in this chapter and the
practical in chapter 5.

The theological reasons for church discipline are as follows:

The Misinterpretation of Various Passages

When man seeks to do ". . . what is right in his own eyes"
it is rarely without some biblical justification, no matter how
convoluted and warped it may be. Following are the primary
passages used to demonstrate that the church is not supposed
to practice discipline. Anti-disciplinarians do not deal with
the passages that directly relate to church discipline or how
their interpretations fit in with all of the teaching of discipline. They simply elevate their misinterpretation of Scripture to the place of unchallenged supremacy while allowing
no exposure to other verses that would contradict their interpretations. Those verses are ignored in the sincere hope that
they will go away or at least go unnoticed. Unfortunately for

the gospel, they have and do go unnoticed, but unfortunately for anti-disciplinarians they will never go away.

Matthew 7:1 says, "Do not judge so that you will not be judged." This verse serves as the omni-present *mantra* against church discipline. The mantra's explicit intent is to stop Christians from judging anyone; therefore, church discipline cannot be practiced. However, it should be no surprise to anyone that this interpretation, upon closer examination, does not fit contextually or logically. Nor does anyone, or can anyone, live according to the mantra of absolute non-discrimination.

Contextually, the non-judging of anyone cannot possibly be what Christ is teaching. This verse can only be seen as providing full discretionary power for never judging anyone when it is extricated from both its immediate context of the first twelve verses of chapter 7, and its larger context of the whole Bible. For example, Matthew 7:2 goes on to say, "For in the way you judge, you will be judged: and by your standard of measure, it will be measured to you." In other words, if you use human standards, you will be judged by those standards, and if you use the Word of God, you will be judged by that. Therefore, it is safe to make judgments as long as they are the same as God's, which is tantamount to Him making the judgment; we are simply following His judgment. Christ made the judgment to command the church to exercise discipline, and the church had better follow lest she become guilty of erecting another authority by which to judge Christ. Note again, verse 5 says, ". . . then you will see clearly to take the speck out of your brother's eye." This is a judgment about a brother, to note the speck in a brother's eye, and action is called for, taking the speck out. Then verse 6 says, "Do not give what is holy to dogs, and do not throw your pearls before the swine, lest they trample them under their feet, and turn and tear you to pieces." It is undeniably obvious that in order for someone to avoid casting his pearls before swine, he must make a judg-ment of what pearls are, what a swine is, and who the swine are—swine is clearly a metaphor for people. This passage is actually a strong warning against hypocrisy, of using standards other than the Scripture, and judging a brother's speck, while ignoring one's own log. Verse 1 is not a prohibition against all judging, for that would cause us to have to disobey the rest of the passage, and Christ does not communicate in such mean-ingless and contradictory ways. Consequently, this is a con-demnation of pharisaical, self-righteous judging and not of judg-ing in general.

Logically, this passage cannot be forbidding church disci-pline since the same One who spoke these words, explicitly and emphatically, also commanded the church to practice dis-cipline. Believing in the inerrancy of the Scripture necessi-tates that this passage refer to other than a prohibition or limitation of biblical church discipline. However, it is appli-cable in any situation where hypocrisy is present. A further exposure of the invalidness of the anti-disciplinarian's under-standing of this verse is if Christians are not to judge anything or anyone, how can we evangelize? Evangelizing includes mak-ing judgments about whom to evangelize. How do we help the alcoholic if we cannot judge who the alcoholic is? How can we help anyone if we can't make judgments about who needs help?

The idea of absolute non-discrimination may be politically correct, but it is an idea that has no validity outside the class-room or political demagoguery. One prime example of the pro-motion of an egalitarianism view of all lifestyles is the disgust that some display toward anyone using labels like: alcoholic, retarded, lost, troublemaker, etc. While labels can be abused, the use of labels is not in and of itself abuse, and for those who complain vociferously about the problems associated with using labels, let them try operating without them. Even the distinction between labelers and non-labelers is the use of labels. Thus, they cannot even talk about removing labels, or judgment, without making judgments and using labels. The fact is that we make judgments everyday, without them, we would fail to act like beings who are created in the image of God, and we would perish. Again, this passage is not about ceasing all judging, but about judging according to God's standard and allowing it to judge us first. When Christians proclaim that something like divorce or stealing is wrong, we are not judging people; but merely telling them what God's judgment is.

Matthew 13:24–30 provides those who do not want to practice church discipline another place to take refuge, albeit only for as long as someone does not look more closely at the passage. This passage is known as the parable of the tares among the wheat. The parable tells us the man sowed good seed, and then while he was asleep, the enemy sowed tares among the wheat. The slaves then ask, "'Do you want us, then, to go and gather them up?' But he said, 'No; lest while you are gathering up the tares, you may root up the wheat with them. Allow both to grow together until the harvest; and in the time of the harvest I will say to the reapers, "First gather up the tares and bind them in bundles to burn them up; but gather the wheat into my barn."'" (verses 28–30) Those who view this passage as being antithetical to church discipline conclude that no discipline—disfellowshiping—is to happen until the end of the age when Christ comes back. This interpretation is based on the assumption that the field is the church. However, there is a fatal flaw with equating the field with the church, and that is this, Jesus plainly states that the "field is the world" (verse 38). Thus, the parable is not about removing erring brothers from the church, but unbelievers from the world. Further, inerrancy demands that this passage is not prohibiting church discipline, since Matthew 18:15–20 clearly commands it, and the Scripture cannot contradict itself.

John 4:6–45 records Jesus' encounter at the well with the woman from Samaria. The argument against church discipline based on this passage is as follows: this woman had been married five times, and she was presently living with a man who was not her husband; Jesus did not cast her aside, but He witnessed to her. That is exactly what happened, but the inference that this has anything to do with church discipline is in error. This lady was a Samaritan. She was not a believer at the beginning of her encounter with Jesus, although she became a believer and a great witness for Christ among other Samaritans. The reason Jesus dealt with her the way that He did is precisely because she was not a believer, and church discipline is only for believers. Paul makes this clear in 1 Corinthians 5:10–13, where he says, "I *did* not at all *mean* with the immoral people of this world, or with the covetous and swindlers, or with idolaters, for then you would have to go out of the world. But actually, I wrote to you not to associate with any so-called brother if he is an immoral person, or covetous, or an idolater, or a reviler, or a drunkard, or a swindler—not even to eat with such a one. For what have I to do with judging outsiders? Do you not judge those who are within *the church*? But those who are outside, God judges. Remove the wicked man from among yourselves." This is the clear and consistent teaching of the Scripture—that we witness to unbelievers who are not supposed to be a part of the church; but we remove believers from the fellowship who act like lost people. Both cases are for the same reason, unbelievers, or those that act like them, are not to be a part of the church.

John 8:1–11 records Jesus' encounter with the woman who had been caught committing adultery. This is one of the primary passages referred to by anti-disciplinarians. It is also an interesting passage, because it evokes numerous and some-what entertaining interpretations and ideas about what Christ wrote in the sand. The passage says, "But Jesus went to the Mount of Olives. And early in the morning He came again into the temple, and all the people were coming to Him; and He sat down and *began* to teach them. The scribes and the Pharisees brought a woman caught in adultery, and having set her in the center *of the court*, they said to Him, 'Teacher, this woman has been caught in adultery, in the very act. Now, the Law of Moses commands us to stone such women; what then do You say?' They were saying this, testing Him, so that they might have grounds for accusing Him. But Jesus stooped down and with His finger wrote on the ground. But when they persisted in asking Him, He straightened up, and said to them, 'He who is without sin among you, let him *be the* first to throw a stone at her.' Again, He stooped down and wrote on the ground. When they heard it, they *began* to go out one by one, beginning with the older ones, and He was left alone, and the woman, where she was, in the center *of the court*. Straightening up, Jesus said to her, 'Woman, where are they? Did no one condemn you?' She said, 'No one, Lord.' And Jesus said, 'I do not con-demn you, either. Go. From now on sin no more.'"

Notice several things that are relevant to our discussion. First, according to verse 6, the Pharisees' real interest was not in seeking to have a more holy nation, but rather they were "testing Him, so they might have grounds for accusing Him." They believed that regardless of how Jesus answered, they had Him in their web of destruction. If He said she should die, the Pharisees could say that He was trying to usurp the power of Rome since at this time only Rome had the power of life and death. They would present it not as an answer to an ab-stract question, but a challenge to the authority of Rome. If on the other hand, Jesus did nothing; they would have alleged that he denied the authority of the law, and that it was His intention to abrogate it. Either answer seemed to seal the fate of Jesus as someone who could not be trusted, and they would have Him right where they wanted Him.

Jesus' response did neither, and rather than placing Him where the Pharisees wanted Him, He placed them where they did not want to be. Jesus said to them, "He who is without sin among you, let him *be the* first to throw a stone at her" (verse 7). Then, after they had all left, Jesus said to her "Woman, where are they? Did no one condemn you? She said, "No one, Lord." And Jesus said, "I do not condemn you, either. Go. From now on sin no more" (verses 10–11).

Those who see this as in conflict with the idea of church discipline argue that Jesus did not condemn her, nor could anyone else since everyone has sinned. Thus, the inescapable conclusion is that we should not judge anyone because all have sinned. This lays the groundwork for not judging a sinning brother or sister in Christ, but simply *loving* them because we all are sinners. This interpretation would be a great one if there were not numerous Scriptures to the contrary. Since there are copious Scriptures to the contrary, this interpretation is latent with insoluble problems. The most obvious is that it clearly contradicts the Scriptures relating to church discipline (Matthew 18:15–20; 1 Corinthians 5:1–13; 1 Thessalonians 5:14; and 2 Thessalonians 3:6,15).

Anytime an interpretation of one Scripture contradicts the clear teaching of another Scripture elsewhere, it is obviously inaccurate. The law did prescribe death as the penalty for adultery (Leviticus 20:10 and Deuteronomy 22:22). Consequently, the Pharisees were not wrong in what they said about her deserving death. For the law was given by God, and Jesus never contradicted the Old Testament. That they were commanded to recognize adultery as sin and worthy of death is another reason we know that this passage is not an absolute prohibition against judging. For the Jews (these Pharisees) were commanded by God to do such. Further, it is important to note that when God commanded the Jews to judge those who broke the law, they were sinners then also. In other words, if the phrase "He who is without sin among you" means that they could not have ever sinned, then they could have never carried out the commands of the law; for they were sinners then also. Clearly, Jesus was not contradicting the Scripture, and any interpretation that implies that He was is null and void. The same thing that has been said about other passages that have been misinterpreted to prohibit judging is also true here. If the Jews could not discriminate, how could they know whom to accuse of adultery or breaking the Sabbath, or whom to help? How will we know whom to help with the sin of stealing if we cannot determine who the thief is?

Since adultery was a sin worthy of death, and they were commanded to make such judgments—even though they were sinners as we are today, Jesus cannot possibly mean that a person has to be sinless before he can obey the Scriptures and judge someone according to the Scripture. Then what did He mean? The Scriptures, which command death for adultery, hold the key to properly interpreting this passage. Leviticus 20:10 says, "If *there is* a man who commits adultery with another man's wife, one who commits adultery with his friend's wife, the adulterer and the adulteress shall surely be put to death." Deuteronomy 22:22 says, "If a man is found lying with a married woman, then both of them shall die, the man who lay with the woman, and the woman; thus you shall purge the evil from Israel."

What the Pharisees in typical pharisaical fashion ignored, and others fail to notice, is that both the man and the woman caught in adultery are to die. In this pericope, the Pharisees brought only the woman. They were asking Jesus to receive their judgment on her for breaking the law in one area, adultery, while they were simultaneously breaking the law in a closely related area, punishing adultery. This is a classic example of hypocrisy and Phariseeism. With all of the facts and sanctified common sense in place, it is easy to see that Jesus' statement, "He who is without sin among you," did not refer to sinlessness, but rather sin at that very moment concerning the very issue at hand. They were violating the very law that they were demanding the woman and Jesus obey. Jesus did obey the law, although not in the way they were anticipating, for if both were not to be judged, as the law required, Jesus would not oblige the sinfulness of the Pharisees and play chauvinistic Pharisaism. Therefore, the passage has nothing to do with not recognizing sin, much less prohibiting the practice of church discipline.

Another important feature of this passage that is often overlooked, and I think many times intentionally, is the importance of the last statement Jesus said to her, "Woman, where are they? Did no one condemn you?" She said, "No one, Lord." And Jesus said, "I do not condemn you, either. Go. From now on sin no more" (verses 10–11).

The Old Testament passages quoted make it clear that she had sinned and the phrase, "Go. From now on sin no more," confirms that Jesus well understood that she had sinned. Jesus did not ignore her sin, nor act like what she had done was not sin, and it is wrong to conclude that He did. Whether or not she sinned was not the question posed by the Pharisees; the question put before Him was whether He would agree to her death because she was caught in adultery. This He refused to do because they were asking him to obey only part of the law, which is the same as disobeying all of the law. That she had sinned is never denied by Jesus, nor did He ever make light of her sin.

Jesus' final statement reflects the perfect and inflexible standard of God, "go and sin no more." Many focus on the former part of this verse and fail to acknowledge these daunting words. Further, it is not necessary or possible to know what Jesus wrote in the sand since everyone who was there is gone.

After looking at the most prominent verses in the anti-discipline arsenal that can be marshaled against church discipline, one must conclude that they have nothing to do with precluding Christians from judging, much less church discipline. Actually, the contrary is true. They all teach a very clear message; Jesus was very committed to keeping the law of God to the infinitesimal degree. In each case, the Word of God was followed precisely—what an example for the church. Jesus' example, as one would expect, actually strengthens the case for following the Scripture concerning church discipline, since He followed the Word to the letter.

Apathy Toward Holiness

The English term holy or holiness comes from the Hebrew word, "*kaw-dash*, (and) Greek *Hagios* which means to be set apart, be consecrated."[61] This is not some human attainment, but something given by God. "Holiness belongs to God as divine, and he would not be God without it. In that respect, 'there is none holy like the Lord' (1 Samuel 2:2). The ethical quality in holiness is the aspect most commonly brought to the forefront when the word is applied to God. It is basically a term for the moral excellence of God and His freedom from all limitation in His moral perfection (Habakkuk 1:13). It is in this respect that God alone is holy and the standard of ethical purity in his creatures."[62]

"A Christian is someone who has been made holy because he is set apart by God (1 Peter 2:9). He made us a new creation (2 Corinthians 5:17), and that includes creating a new person in holiness and righteousness (Ephesians 4:24). He lives within us (Colossians 1:27). Thus, the whole of the Christian's life is to be lived in such a way that the reality of holiness is reflected in every day living. Christians are to offer themselves as holy sacrifices (Romans 12:1). Those sanctified in Christ sanctify their family circles (1 Corinthians 7:14). Holiness here has a moral content and stands opposed to impurity."[63]

Because of who Christians are and what God has done for us, we are to live lives which are set apart from the world's standards, morals, ways, spirituality, etc., and live set apart to God. Peter states this emphatically, "As obedient children, do not be conformed to the former lusts *which were yours* in your ignorance, but like the Holy One who called you, be holy yourselves also in all *your* behavior; because it is written, "You shall be holy, for I am holy" (1 Peter 1:14–16).

Church discipline is an act that only makes sense in the context of a genuine pursuit of holiness. Minimizing church discipline is birthed out of a decreased desire for holiness. Clearly, the loss of the desire to pursue holiness, hold holiness up as esteemed, and see a mutually accountable relationship to one another as necessary to help each individual and the corporate body be holy and set apart from the world to God, precedes and assures the de-emphasizing of church discipline since church discipline is one of the primary ways of maintaining corporate holiness. In other words, discipline falls into disfavor because the pursuit of holiness has already fallen into disfavor. Once discipline is set aside, its absence tells new Christians that holiness is of marginal importance. This life message is so commanding that all of the spoken messages on holiness will be overshadowed by the resounding declaration of the life message that says no to holiness.

Holiness, on a practical level, is only obtained by Christians obeying the Word of God above mere reason, emotions, trends, or our fallen nature. Jesus said, "Sanctify them in truth, thy word is truth" (John 17:17). The word sanctify is from the same root word as holy. Salvation not only provides forgiveness, but it makes a person ontologically different via the new birth. Consequently, the church is something that is ontologically different from anything in the world, and she is to appear different from the world, categorically different. The world can never be holy, produce holiness, or share in holiness, and the true church cannot become what the world is, although she can be heavily influenced by it. Therefore, whenever the church is seeking to court the world, which is evident by de-emphasizing the tough Scriptures, it is never godly, Christlike, or God honoring. It is quite obvious that a local church can become very worldly or even become a congregation made up of one-hundred percent lost people, but this is not the true church. For the true church cannot become, ever again, like the world. The world simply moves into the building and displaces the true church, which produces a church like the church at Laodicea, which is a church out of the night of hell, a hideous phantom.

The reason for this is, the world and the church are ontologically mutually exclusive, and integration of the two is not really possible. When the church allows the world to infiltrate, rather than becoming partly worldly, the church becomes totally worldly in the area in which the world has been allowed entrance. This is because the world and the church do not actually assimilate; but rather they displace one another. It could be stated that, to the degree that the church embraces the world, the church ceases to be the church.

The same case exists when someone says something is "partly true." In reality, something is not partly true or partly false. That which is true is one hundred percent true and that which is a lie is one hundred percent false. The reason for this is, a truth and a lie are mutually exclusive, and when they come together they do not integrate but rather they displace one another. So that part of the statement that is true is all true, and that part of the statement that is false is completely false.

The same is true of the nature of light and darkness. Light and darkness do not integrate, but rather they too displace one another. When light comes in, to the degree that it comes in, the proportionate degree of darkness is displaced. The opposite of this is true also. When darkness comes into an area of pure light, the amount of darkness accepted is exactly proportionate to the light that is displaced.

This truth is well illustrated when someone says that the Bible is partly true. They usually mean for this to be taken as a positive affirmation of their faith in the Bible. However, it is actually a euphemistic way of saying that the Bible is also partly false. The problem with the Scripture being partly true is that it must also be partly false, and the part that is false is totally false, a complete lie. Since the Scripture is God's Word, the inescapable conclusion is that God lied or at least perpetuates a lie. Yet, the Scripture declares "God who cannot lie" (Titus 1:2). Therefore, when the euphemism is exposed for what it is, it is a blasphemous denial of God since if God ever lied, He must necessarily cease to be God.

Simply put, truth and lie, light and darkness, and the church and the world do not amalgamate. They displace one another. Thus, the part of the church that accepts the world becomes totally the world; the world that is hostile to God and salvation, and bows at the throne of Satan. This must be understood and embraced by the church for her to appreciate the need to remain on guard against worldly influence. For

where the world comes in, it comes in totally displacing the
church and the lordship of Jesus Christ. That part of the church
now belongs to the world. For the church and the world are
ontologically exclusive. This is a nefarious aberration of the
first order, with eternal consequences.

The downgrading of holiness within Christianity should
not be taken as synonymous with saying that holiness is not a
hot topic in the church. Holiness, as understood through the
dark shaded lenses of modernity, is in fact very much in vogue.
Contemporary holiness has been made synonymous with integrity. In much present-day preaching, the call for integrity
has replaced the call for holiness. While integrity is a good
word, it lacks the theological content and specificity of holiness. Holiness comes only from God and means to be set apart
unto Him. A Christian's inherent holiness is from God living
within the Christian. Our practical holiness is attainable only
because of the indwelling Holy Spirit. Holiness focuses upon
God and being rightly related to Him. The only persons who
can be holy are those rightly related to God.

In contrast, integrity means "adherence to moral and ethical principles; soundness of moral character; honesty; the state
of being whole, entire, or undiminished: *to preserve the integrity of the empire;* a sound, unimpaired, or perfect condition: *the integrity of a ship's hull.*"[64] If a person lives in adherence to moral or ethical principles—regardless what those principles are—he can be said to have integrity; in contrast to
holiness, which is a relationship with God based on a standard that is set by God.

Consequently, only those in right relationship with God and
living according to His Word can be said to have holiness. Integrity without the basis of holiness can mean a hedonist can
have integrity if he lives true to what he espouses. If a Christian
has integrity, then he will be godly, but another person could

125

have integrity and not even believe in God. Gang members can have integrity as long as they live according to what they profess. While integrity is a fine word, it is a woefully inadequate replacement for holiness. The primary impetus for using the term *integrity* in lieu of *holiness* is that people do not know what holiness means anymore, but they are familiar with integrity. It is true that people in our culture—and in the church to a large degree—are more familiar with the term integrity and often are at a loss concerning the word holiness.

But for the church to replace the word *holiness* with the word *integrity* because of the lack of familiarity is neither logical nor biblical. First, the words do not have the same meaning or application. Second, the cure for the lack of familiarity is not to discard an essential word of Christianity, but to use it all the more. One must ask how did such a prominent biblical word become so misunderstood? The answer must be, by one of two ways; either the church failed to communicate the gospel or she has failed to communicate it in the context of holiness, which is actually to fail to communicate the gospel since there is no other context. That people are not familiar with the word holiness is even more reason to use it. The reason they are not familiar with it is that they do not hear it.

There has been a concerted effort to rid the church's message of religious jargon so that the lost can understand it. This is a good and noble undertaking, which I applaud and practice. If holiness were in the same category as words like invocation, convocation, or benediction, then it should be replaced with words that are understood by more people. However, holiness is not some fringe concept to the teaching of Scripture and the gospel. It is at the very heart of it. Without the idea of holiness, the Bible becomes meaningless. Man was created in holiness—separated unto God. Then he sinned and is now unholy—separated from God. The whole plan of redemption, the gospel of the death, burial, and resurrection, is the plan to make man holy again and in relationship with God. Simply put, integrity is something man can obtain whereas holiness is not. The only integrity that God calls for, or accepts, is based on holiness. Thus, the preaching of integrity in lieu of holiness leaves man forever lost in his sin.

Holiness is still preached about, and there are several books on holiness, although compared to the number of self-help books there is a pitiful paucity of them. There are some within modern Christendom who place holiness in its rightful place; teaching about it from a biblical perspective and leading Christians to live it in their daily lives. For others, the preached message is all there is. However, there is a great gulf between preaching about holiness, which we must do and do boldly, and leading a church to pursue and practice it. Basically, every Christian appreciates a good message on holiness, but the amens heard during the preaching become deafeningly silent when you begin to act on the message and implement things like church discipline. Church discipline is one of the essentials whereby the church keeps herself set apart from the world. Without a doubt, the world will creep into the church, and without a way to remove those of the world from the church, the church will inevitably become another social organization.

This nefarious process begins with a subtle loss of desire for holiness, then an equally slight emphasis on something else that is spiritual, which seems to balance the scales from the injustice of selectively ignoring sections of the Word of God. In time, this is followed by faintly and implicitly equating holiness with extremism or legalism, and moderate libertarianism with grace; and then comes the openly disparaging remarks concerning church discipline. Eventually the world's ways of selfishness and relativism are no longer resisted, but rather they are welcomed, and the world lays hold of every aspect of the church and does so with a death grip.

By this time, the church no longer wants to be different from the world because it sees being different from the world as a threat to the lost receiving the church and her message, or maybe viewing the church as anachronistic—the cardinal sin to the church of modernity and postmodernity. The result is that the church becomes half-church and half-world, which neither God nor the world has much use for. Tragically, the church is the last to understand this final fate awaiting all churches that dine at the table of the *kosmos*. This is all done of course by basting the delectables of the world with *sanctified* Christian clichés until it appears scrumptious, but the end is the same as the world's only with greater deception. The idea of separation from the world is not meant that Christians are to separate from the world, lost people, or living life in the world. Christians are not called to live in monasteries. Rather, it has to do with the world (*kosmos*) as a system of ideas, values, goals, and methods. Thus, the *world's ways* mean adopting the system of the world as opposed to the system of Christ's kingdom.

The attribute of holiness is considered the overarching attribute of God. Theologians have consistently agreed that if God loses any attribute, He ceases to be God. So in that sense, no attribute is more important than another, for each are essential characteristics of deity. However, holiness is seen as overarching in that everything God does is holy. "Since holiness embraces every distinctive attribute of Godhead, it may be conceived of as the outshining of all that God is. As the sun's rays, combining all the colors of the spectrum, come together in the sun's shining and blend into light, so in His self-manifestation all the attributes of God come together and blend into holiness. Holiness has, for that reason, been called 'an attribute of attributes,' that which lends unity to all the attributes of God."[65]

As stated previously, if Jesus had tolerated sin in his life, he could not have had the power of God upon Him. As a matter of fact, if God tolerated sin in Himself, He would not have the power of God nor be God. Holiness and the power of God are inextricably united to one another. First and foremost, true holiness can only come from God and is given by God in the new creation. When He imparts His nature to a new believer and thereby the church, she is enabled by Christ to walk in and pursue holiness; unless there is practical holiness and pursuit of holiness by the Christians and the church, the church can no more expect God's power upon her than Christ could have if He would have courted sin. This is not to imply that Christians can attain perfection in this life. That does not come until the glorification, but the Scripture is equally clear in regard to its commands for believers and churches to follow Him and be holy now (1 Peter 1:14–15). Our ability to follow Christ and walk in holiness is because of His gracious provision and our diligent pursuit (John 14:15,23–24; Philippians 2:12). Without fellowship and holiness, there can no more be the reality of God's power upon the church than it could have been upon Christ without fellowship and holiness.

You may be thinking, if God's power does not abide upon the lives of people or churches unless they are holy, how do we explain the obvious saving power operating through churches and peoples' lives who are in sin, or later are exposed as wallowing in long-term and gross sin. The answer is God does work through sinful things, which is a manifestation of His grace and sovereign power. This can be seen not only in God working through someone who may be hiding sin from people, but also in God working with and through the lost and

129

the government, and giving sinful man the ability to live, all of which are manifestations of His power (Acts 17:25,28).

Neither the lost nor the carnal derail the sovereign power of God. The power that both the saved and the lost experience is not the power that is being discussed, nor is it what is needed by the church in order to be what Christ desires her to be. The power granted to all men falls under general grace. Sadly, God is quite accustomed to working in spite of peoples' lack of holiness rather than in concert with it. The answer to how God can accomplish His perfect will in spite of sinful man lies in the reality of the power of God and the power of the Word of God. The power which God manifests upon lost and carnal alike is not the power the church must have in order to fully represent Christ and experience the kind of power that He desires to bestow. It is still the power of God, but it is not the *pleasurable* power of God. The power that Christ experienced and the church must have is the power of God that is otherworldly and pleasurable. It is otherworldly in the sense that it is not a part of the display of God's power for the natural world through *natural* means, and it cannot be confused with natural phenomena. It is pleasurable to God in the sense that it pleases Him to empower and bless those who love Him, follow Him at all cost, and seek His honor and glory above everything. Isaiah says, "But to this one I will look, to him who is humble and contrite of spirit, and who trembles at My word" (Isaiah 66:2).

John says, "But an hour is coming, and now is, when the true worshipers will worship the Father in spirit and truth; for such people the Father seeks to be His worshipers" (John 4:23). Each of these passages emphasizes those whom God seeks. There are those who seek God, and then there are those whom God seeks to use and to worship Him. We should all desire to seek God, but what a wonderful thing to be the ones God seeks out to worship Him and to be used by Him. The Scripture is unambiguous; there are blessings and empowerments that are withheld from those who do not walk with God in practical holiness. If a person does not pursue holiness, he will never experience the power of God upon his life in the way that he would have had he walked in holiness.

This relationship between holiness and the power of God means that the loss of holiness necessarily results in the loss of power. Therefore, maybe the church should spend more time practicing church discipline than just praying for power. For where there is holiness, there will be the power of God. Maybe this is what missionaries are referring to when they visit American churches and make the following repeated observation, "It is amazing what the churches in America can do without God." What an indictment. The power that Jesus offers to the church is exchanged for a pot of naturalism.

Church discipline will remain disaffected from the church until the church once again hungers and thirsts after righteousness. It is impossible, though many never tire of trying, for a church to become more hungry for holiness while keeping church discipline on the sidelines of church life. Discipline is the Coat of Arms of a church's genuine pursuit of holiness. Conversely, there is no way for church discipline to regain its rightful place in the church, nor is it even necessary, unless there is a genuine quest for holiness.

This is the quandary of the modern church. Neo-holiness promises that church discipline is unnecessary or no longer works, clearly implying that Jesus is enveloped in a first century time warp. Neo-holiness equates speaking publicly on holiness, or amening a message on it, with holiness. However, church discipline is an integral ingredient in the quest for true holiness within the local church. The menace of neo-holiness arises when germane passages are ignored or distorted, or the belief that holiness can be proclaimed enough, so that it alone will lead to real holiness. Even worse is that this verbiage will be accepted as a replacement for biblical holiness.

Discipline is the precise and indispensable procedure that Christ gave for maintaining holiness in the local church. This is why a church's willingness to practice church discipline is the undeniable testimony that the church loves holiness, and the lack of discipline is the unalterable evidence of the opposite. Obviously, the preaching of Scripture is the primary way to teach about holiness, but without living it, a church is consigned to drown in her corporate self-deception and hypocrisy. The undershepherd of Christ is to preach the truth, and then lead the people of God to act upon it. It is highly improbable that people will ever lead the pastor to practice church discipline.

Also, as stated before, the inviolable relationship between the church's zeal for holiness and her passion for evangelism is both biblically and historically demonstrable. This is not a fortuitous relationship. For if the church is not concerned about her own holiness, she will likely not be concerned with transforming the unholy lost into a holy follower of God. Sin's sinfulness is only fully appreciated with the light of holiness illumining it. Evangelism is in its very essence an effort to make that which is unholy, holy. This can only be done by abhorring unholiness, loving God, and loving people. When the church reenthrones holiness to its biblically mandated position, a heart for evangelism will concomitantly increase.

I remember teaching the deacons of the church where I once pastored about what they were supposed to be and do as deacons. After teaching on those things, and raising the standard to the level of biblical fidelity, questions began to surface about men who had been ordained by the church but were not living a life befitting a deacon, and about what to do with them. They began to ask, "How can we let those men remain deacons when they do not even try to live the life?" This led to a unanimous decision by the deacon body to rescind the ordinations of three deacons. Once the deacons saw God's standard and realized they were required to live it, they did not want the deacon name to be besmirched by those who did not desire to walk with God. They knew to be a deacon of that church required practical holiness and consecration. But, notice that the desire and will to remove unfit deacons came only after they were taught the standard of what a biblical deacon was to be and were led to embrace it as the accepted standard of the church. Then and only then did they embrace the call to holiness. The same is true with church discipline. Only after the church's desire to be holy becomes real will discipline be sought and embraced as good.

The significance of this is, the desire for holiness is really the desire for Christ. While the subject of holiness and loving Christ can be distinguished between for the sake of discussion, they cannot be separated. Authentic love for Christ will thirst for holiness. The greater a church's love is for Christ, the greater risk will be taken to practice holiness. The pinnacle of that desire and risk for the local church is found in church discipline. This we all know to be prima facie truth.

Narcissism

In Greek mythology "Narcissus was a beautiful youth who rejected all admirers, including the nymph Echo. As punishment, the goddess Artemis caused him to fall in love with his reflection in a pool. Killing himself in despair, he was transformed into the flower that bears his name. From this legend comes the term narcissism, meaning exclusive love of self. Psychoanalytic theory considers this a normal childhood phase. In adults it may become narcissistic personality disor-

133

der."[66] Today narcissism denotes self-love, a preoccupation with self, self-centeredness, or selfishness. Self-love is man's basic problem and the source of all idolatry. "In the final analysis, every sin results from preoccupation with self. We sin because we are totally selfish, totally devoted to ourselves, rather than to God and to others."[67] The offense of the gospel of Jesus Christ is that, "It undermines the gospel of self-esteem, self-love, and high self-image, which appeals to man's natural narcissism and prostitutes the spirit of humble brokenness and repentance that marks the gospel of the cross."[68]

Due to Christianity's influence upon western culture, narcissism has been regarded as sinful for two millenniums. But with the burgeoning love affair with secularism birthed in the enlightenment, rather than considering narcissism an exhibition of sinfulness, it is viewed as an asset or quality. This distinguishes modern man from the backward and superstitious man of the past who believed in God, right and wrong, and loving others more than one's self. Conversely, humility is seen as debasing and ignoble. Nowhere is narcissism esteemed more than in America. Although some secularists repeatedly try to distinguish the self-love they preach from narcissism—which remember means self-love—it is a hollow and illusory distinction. Even an infinite number of disclaimers will never divest today's psychological self-love of its inherent narcissism, since to do so would strip it of its essence. That today's self love or self-esteem is nothing but yesterday's narcissism can be clearly seen by the ideas that are associated with today's self-love. It exalts the individual and minority status to the point of subverting the majority or common good.

Narcissism, as today's self-love, redefines freedom and tolerance, which used to mean that you were free to believe what you want even if you were dead wrong. Now, under the sway of narcissism, neo-tolerance means no one can judge your ideas as wrong, immoral, or less valuable than any other view; for to do so is to trample on someone else's self—esteem and assume that there is a standard outside of one's self by which to judge. Narcissism allows for another person's views to be illegal, but not good or bad as judged by a standard outside of man's law.

In most cases, good and evil, and legal and illegal are now synonymous. The golden rule, Do unto others as you would have them do unto you has been replaced by the rule of self-love, Do what is best for you at all cost albeit in a way that appears as altruistic as possible—though the golden rule is still invoked for purely pragmatic reasons of the narcissist. Clichés like, Look out for number one or If you don't look out for yourself, no one will, typify the philosophy of life that characterizes an alarming proportion of politics, law, education, relationships, work, sports, and virtually every area of American life, and to a daunting degree, the attitude of the church. The days are limited that a self-governed culture can survive the normalization of selfism.

The acceptance and the entrenchment of self love into the psyche of the average American is graphically demonstrated when you try to teach someone the grammatical rule of speaking of yourself last, like "you and me" or "you and I" instead of "me and you," or naming yourself first in a sentence. This is not difficult because of a sweeping ineptness in English, nor is there some kind of insufficient dexterity of the tongue to reverse the order. Rather, putting yourself last even in our spoken language flies in the face of the selfism philosophy of life that is now embedded in the human and American psyche, which always places self first. It is contrary and foreign to the thoughts and behaviors which so characterize people's lives that it takes a concerted effort to remember to place themselves last; an effort usually seen as too difficult and purposeless to warrant the trouble since it is evidently contrary to their perceived reality.

The exchange in emphasis from personal responsibility to individual rights, and doing for others before self to the pursuit of what is presently self-satisfying, are all characteristics of narcissism. The normalization of self-actualization was promised by men like Abraham Maslow and Carl Rogers to make us greater and more free. It is supposed to be modern man coming of age, and being unloosed from the shackles of religion, humility, and common good. Buzzard rightly says, "This quest for individualism promised a glorious autonomy. It is Maslow's 'self-actualized,' creative, and autonomous man who is the modern adult. But something has gone wrong."[69] Thus, narcissism has been promoted through the teaching of self-love and self-esteem. Although, it has been heartily embraced by much of the church, it has no real biblical support, and actually, the entire warp and woof of the Bible is vehemently against it. This is why all self-love proponents in the church must resort to a gross distortion of Matthew 22:39, and parallel passages, to legitimize this wolf in sheep's clothing. That narcissism can be accepted into the church even though it has no biblical support is actually one of the characteristics of full-blown narcissism. It dulls the senses to any kind of objectivity, especially that which tarnishes the wonder of love of oneself supremely.

The church's adoption of narcissism is not without an incalculably high cost. It carries a glaring and devastating impact on the church in general and church discipline in particular. The very act of church discipline collides head on with narcissism because in order to practice church discipline biblically, a person has to humble himself for the benefit of others—whether we are talking about the one being disciplined or the one implementing it. Narcissism seeks immediate gratification, self-aggrandizement, compliments, approval by all, comfort, and to look good, none of which are associated with church discipline. Church discipline requires loving holiness, God, His Word, and others more than self, all of which are adversaries of narcissism. Humility and narcissism are mutually exclusive attitudes, although narcissism manages remarkable success in parading itself as humility. This veneer is only undetectable because of our biblically illiterate culture and church, which understands humility as merely a personality type, basic demeanor, or disposition, a mindset that actually emasculates the biblical meaning of humility.

For the church to love discipline, she will have to abandon every nuance of spiritualized narcissism and embrace what Jesus said to His disciples, "If anyone wishes to come after Me, he must deny himself, and take up his cross and follow Me. For whoever wishes to save his life will lose it; but whoever loses his life for My sake will find it." (Matthew 16:24–25) The call is simple, to forsake self-esteem and embrace Christ-esteem.

A Distorted Understanding of God's Love

One of the most prevalent, if not the most ubiquitous, ideas used to derail any attempts at church discipline is the determined effort to demonstrate that church discipline is in some way contrary to the love of God. The argument is based on wonderful truths like, "God is love" (1 John 4:8) and "For God did not send the Son into the world to judge the world, but that the world might be saved through Him" (John 3:17). The argument is stated something like this: God did not come to judge sinners, but He loves them and seeks to save even the worst of sinners. Church discipline is judging, unredemptive, and unloving, therefore church discipline is wrong and should be avoided. This places discipline in the position of being equated with not being godly and/or loving. Regardless of the hermeneutical gymnastics that have to be utilized to arrive at such an unbiblical position, its popularity is instant and unquestioned by the spiritual narcissist.

I remember a pastor who once said to me, "I have never had to exercise church discipline on anyone, but just love that person with the love of the Lord." His statement lucidly sets forth the fashionable idea that loving and discipline are mutually exclusive. It is true that a person can implement discipline without love, but it is equally true that you cannot have love without discipline. This trendy definition of love, which excludes discipline as being a contradiction to real love, is clearly not from the Scripture since the Scripture makes discipline a loving thing to do and avoiding it synonymous with arrogance and not caring (1 Corinthians 5:2).

This all too common juxtaposition of God's love and discipline is born out of a prevalent misunderstanding of God's love and what God's love seeks to accomplish. Biblically, God's love is characterized by the desire to make the object of His love holy. The love of God never comes on a person and winks at his sin. The love of God envelops a person in order to make him holy. If the love a person claims to have will not sacrifice to help another person be more holy, it is not God's love. With those whom God loves, He seeks a relationship; and that relationship is always built upon holiness. God's infinite love spares nothing to make a person holy, even His greatest sacrifice of giving His own son. Of God's children, Hebrews 12:6 says, "For those whom the Lord loves He disciplines," and Revelation 3:19 says, "Those whom I love, I reprove and discipline; therefore be zealous and repent." It is human love or self love that keeps a person from exercising discipline to bring about holiness.

Love that does not discipline is simply not biblical love. Anti-disciplinarians emphasize all the passages on forgiveness, bearing one another's burdens, and love to prove their anti-disciplinarian position. However, then one must ask, is it really loving to withhold all of the truth of Scripture concerning discipline? Is God really a loving God since He is the one that gave all of the church discipline commands? The modern understanding of love is closer to what the Bible calls lust. The anti-disciplinarians' use of love, as an antidote to discipline, is an intentional distortion of the Scripture because they love themselves more than they love God. When love and discipline are positioned as antithetical, and the doctrine of church discipline is relegated to the ash heap of the Neanderthal church, other doctrines will inevitably be minimized or discarded. That is the uncontrollable direction of self-love.

The cross serves as the pinnacle of the compatibility of discipline and love. God poured out His discipline and judgment upon Christ whom He eternally loved. This was not done out of hate, except for sin, but out of infinite love for you, me, and the rest of the world. Had God said, "I love you," but did not give what it took to make us holy, we would be no better off than if God hated us. God's love always seeks to make the object of His love holy. Further, to separate the love of God from the doctrines of the Bible precludes the possibility of actually knowing what true God love is. It is only when sin, judgment, holiness, justification, imputation, hell, guilt, *imago dei*, propitiation, sanctification, glorification, resurrection, etc., are comprehended that God's love can be fully understood and appreciated.

The current trend toward the downgrading of doctrine as divisive, unloving, and irrelevant in exchange for just loving one another is not really love at all, at least not biblical love. Concerning the separation of love and doctrine, John

MacArthur warns ". . . that position is untenable, because many who call themselves Christians are deceivers. For that reason the apostle John began the chapter from which our text is taken with these words: 'Beloved, do not believe every spirit, but test the spirits to see whether they are from God; (1 John 4:1)'. And since an important body of doctrine underlies what scripture teaches about divine love, it is a fallacy to think of divine love and sound theology as in any way opposed to each other."[70] Martyn Lloyd-Jones says it succinctly in reference to 1 John 4:9–10, "people who thus put up as opposites the idea of God as love and these basic, fundamental doctrines can, in the last analysis, *know nothing whatsoever about the love of God.*"[71]

Discipline, biblical discipline, is born out of love, whether it is the discipline of a child by a parent or the church member by the church. Love in the Bible does mean that forgiveness must be offered, but it does not mean that discipline, or any other biblical mandate, is to be abandoned. When an interpretation of Scripture undermines another part of the Scripture, the interpretation is patently invalid. When a person skirts practicing discipline, which is so clearly enunciated in the Scripture, his understanding of the Scripture is flawed just like someone who practices discipline but does not love and forgive.

I remember an incident involving a young couple in our church. They appeared to be a solid couple. Sadly, the man eventually committed adultery, and he did it in a rather public way. His wife was hurting immensely, and we reached out to her in love, compassion, and support. We also reached out to him through the process of church discipline. We saw a side of him that up to this point was well hidden. In each attempt to approach him, he refused to accept any blame or help. After several months of working with him and praying for him, we had to officially remove him from the church. It is always immeasurably sad when this point finally comes. It is also incalculably difficult. This is the part that is deemed unloving by anti-disciplinarians. Actually, it takes an enormous amount of love, biblical love, which treasures the spiritual life of the erring brother, more than it does its own self. It is an existential, narcissistic, indefinable, meaningless, uncaring, immature love that polarizes love and doctrine or love and discipline.

A couple of years passed, and I received a phone call from the young man who had been disciplined. Since the last time that I had seen him, he had remarried, and he and his new wife were going to church regularly as he sought to get his life right with God. During this time, he realized that what he had done was wrong, and he accepted the responsibility for it. He was really trying to walk with God and be involved in the church he was now attending. As he relayed it to me, there was only one problem; every time he went to church, God convicted him about what he had done while he was a member of our church, and that he needed to publicly repent before God would bless him. He told me, "The whole time we worship and the preacher preaches, all I hear is God telling me to go back and make it right." He said, "I can't go on with God until I come before the church and repent." Then he asked, "Can I come back to the church, apologize, and ask the church's forgiveness for sinning against God and the church?" To which I immediately responded, "Yes."

We chose to do these types of things on Sunday nights when those present are more likely to be committed members. He came to the church, and I had him come to the front of the church and relay what he had said to me. When he did, there was hardly a dry eye in the house. After he shared, publicly apologized, repented, and asked the church for forgive-

141

ness, I asked the church if they were willing to forgive and invite him back into the fellowship and love him. The vote was enthusiastically unanimous. Then we had him stand at the front, and the members came by and hugged him, telling him of their love for him, and welcoming him back into the fellowship if he so desired. If you hate getting emotional, sensing a cloud of holiness settling in on the church, and experiencing the love of God in a way that never leaves you the same, don't try this. It is an overwhelming experience.

Our church had grown numerically since the last discipline case, and there were people in our fellowship that had never seen church discipline practiced; some of them had reservations about it as we began the process. However, by the time it was over, they were committed to it. They shared how it had helped them to grow as a Christian and understand how holiness and the love of God coexist. Joy comes only after the commitment to follow at all cost. Discipline is often portrayed as unloving, which signifies one or more of the following. They have never practiced church discipline for then they would know the love of discipline. They are implicitly calling God unloving since He commanded that we do it. They do not base their decisions about right and wrong on the Scripture. They may have their own sin that they are unwilling to deal with, and they cover up their fear of potential fallout by abusing the word love.

The Pervasiveness of Sin

This issue is pertinent to the present discussion, but it is also dealt with extensively in chapter 9. Thus, I will deal with it here briefly. The pervasiveness of sin is one of the most intimidating issues that must be faced when one begins to contemplate the task of church discipline. Sin is so familiar in the church, even in high places of leadership, that the thought of implementing church discipline is enough to cause retreat before the charge begins. At the mention of church discipline, the question inevitably arises, where do you start? However, the pervasiveness of sin, with its concomitant devaluing of holiness, should not serve as an excuse not to employ church discipline but a clarion call to implement it. Christ is never pleased with His house becoming a "den of thieves" (Matthew 21:13)—a den of iniquity.

The church must shed the fallacious idea that she can only reach the world by becoming like the world, because the church will never reach the world by becoming like the world but by becoming like Christ. Sin is so commonplace in many churches that implementing church discipline could result in a return to missions status—because of the onset of a backdoor revival. Although discipline is never a toothsome experience, clearly the lack of discipline for years and the acceptance of sin makes the task of executing discipline far more difficult and risky; however, it makes it no less mandatory in order to follow Christ. Christ commanded all churches to practice discipline, not just some churches.

The answer to the question, "Where do you start?" is somewhere. You simply start with child-like obedience to Jesus. If something is not being done which needs to be done, you must start somewhere. Somewhere is the beginning place where everything is started. If you don't start somewhere, you will never start. Simply put, the lack of certainty of where to start cannot become an excuse for disobeying the certainty associated with the mandate to practice discipline. If it does, it is also an adumbration of future compromises.

Deciding where to start is not as difficult as mustering the courage to start something and see it through. It is like two people who are going to start a diet. One is four hundred pounds overweight and the other is forty pounds overweight. Even though the size of the task is far greater for one than the other, they must each start at basically the same place; stop taking in more energy than is being expended. Regardless of how long your church has disregarded the teaching on discipline, you must start at basically the same place as any other church which is not practicing discipline.

The way to start discipline is slowly, after training and helping leaders understand their obligation to Christ. Then, and only then, the place to start is by addressing the most obvious, glaring, irrefutable case of flagrant sin. Do not start with a debatable case, but begin with the most glaring—I assure you it will arise.

Remember, as you contemplate whether to lead your church to understand and implement church discipline, that selective obedience stripped of its facade is really just plain old rebellion and disobedience. Far worse than anything that can result from employing church discipline in the right way is to fail to start discipline at all. Accept that it will take some time, training, and probably some rough going, but it must be done. Pastors facing the need to apply church discipline are tempted to procrastinate in hopes that the perfect church, which needs no discipline, will call. This is a mirage that keeps pastors from following Christ now, and ultimately disappoints and disillusions the pastor. Because of that, it is not only a mirage, but it is an intensely cruel mirage. For if the grass was as lush as it appears to be at the dream church, the last man would not have stopped grazing there.

The greener pasture is a callous illusion. People are people, and sin is everywhere. It serves as a well needed reality check for pastors to remember that Satan was in the garden, paradise. Thus, we can rest assured that he is in our present church and waiting on us to arrive at the next church also. Granted, he is more obvious, comfortable, and enjoys more free reign at some churches. I once heard it said, "If you can't do it where you are; you can't do it." I took that challenge to heart, realizing that if I cannot follow Christ where I am, I will not follow somewhere else.

We Have Disassociated Worship from the Word of God

It is common today for people to gather for *worship times* where proclamation of the Word of God is intentionally left out of the program. This may be stated as, "We are going to worship and not just listen to some preaching" or "There will be no preaching just pure worship of God," or a similar phrase which sets apart singing and music as an independent worship act, separate from the proclamation of the Word. Whichever way it is stated, the implication is that worship and a message from the Word of God are separable, and that somehow preaching is not worship and may even take away from worship.

People often choose a church based on the style or time given to worship—singing, etc. Even the time allotted for worship and preaching speaks of this separation. The twenty-minute sermon has become common—for some preachers preaching even this is too long. This is said to be done in order to allow more time for worship. We are told that people want to be more actively involved and since listening to preaching is purportedly passive, and worshipping—singing—is active, there needs to be more singing. As a result, worship is now viewed as needing to stand on its own—apart from the teaching of the Word of God.

Worship in song, prayer, and serving can be distinguished from teaching the Word of God, but disaster lurks in the shadows when they are separated. This new mega-trend of separating worship from the Word does not see preaching as worship. The question will inevitably be asked, "Is it always wrong to have a time where people gather for just worship—meaning singing—without allotting a time for preaching during the same meeting?" The answer to that question can only be given in the context of the follow up question, "Why?" Why does someone want just singing and no preaching? What is the motive for excluding God from speaking to His worshippers through His Word during worship? The answer to this question is the issue and the deciding factor in determining if it is right or best to have singing without the Word. Usually the answer involves a misunderstanding of what preaching and/or worship are, in which case the worship event will be flawed. When I speak of separating worship and proclamation of the Word, I am referring specifically to a group of people meeting for worship and intentionally excluding the proclamation of Scripture. This does not apply to extended events where the same group spends times in forums of preaching, teaching, business, and singing, as might be found in conventions or conferences.

The debates over worship today are primarily, and almost exclusively, about styles; contemporary versus traditional, choruses versus hymns, and whether the organ will dominate or not. Succinctly put, it is the question of to drum or not to drum. These discussions—I use that term broadly—are usually about preferences rather than biblical prescriptions. This is not the place to go into a full exposition of worship, but to note that there is a great need to keep all discussions of worship primarily centered within a biblical and theological framework. Without this, preferences will define worship, and unavoidably define it incorrectly.

This separation between worship and the Word is indeed a new phenomenon. Its consequences leave the church feeling good, but not being good. Whether it is serving, worship, prayer, evangelism, etc., the Word of God must be central. Separation of the Word of God from any aspect of Christianity can only lead to paganism—deification of man and his ideas. Man's bent is toward corruption not perfection, and even his euphemistic putsch, resulting in the compartmentalization of the Word of God, is a manifestation of this bent. It is the Word of God, as administered by the Holy Spirit, that exposes corruption; when the Scripture is de-emphasized in any area of reality, the outcome is inevitable and spiritually tragic. This truth is explicitly taught in the Scriptures (Proverbs 14:12) and graphically demonstrated in history. The outcome is always corruption without the consistent declaration of the Word. The immediate experience of godly felicity will eventually degrade into Babelic confusion.

The Scripture is often referred to as being foundational to everything, and this is true, if properly understood. It can lead to error when misunderstood or misapplied. The correct understanding is that the Scripture is foundational, but it is not merely foundational. We do not lay the foundation of the Word and then move on to bigger and better things. The Bible being the foundation is not analogous to the foundation of a building that is laid, then buried out of sight, and then more beautiful and enjoyable things built on top of it. Thus, the requirement for a building's foundation is that it be strong, level, and out of sight. If a building's foundation is done right, it will never have to be revisited again.

That concept of foundation being applied to the Scripture will lead only to paganism and distortion because the Scripture is the foundation, structure, and infrastructure for everything. How does someone know what to pray, to whom, when, where, and how if he does not know the Scripture? We may call our endeavors evangelism, but if the Word is

147

not central and the ever-present standard, it will eventuate in heresy. Without the Word of God, how do we know what evangelism is, who needs it, how to do it, where, when, by whom, ad infinitum.

The issue of worship is no different. How does someone know whom to worship, when, where, and how, if the Scripture is not preeminent and the central guide during worship? It is always man's propensity to warp worship so that he takes center stage rather that God. This was true in the garden, and it is true today. The error that brought Adam and Eve to self worship, worshipping God the way they wanted to, was that they did not heed the Word of God, and the same is true today. The Word of God is not something that you come to know, and then move on. Unless there is a constant balanced diet of the Scripture, and implementation of it in our lives, we are doomed to forget the Word and follow our flesh.

Further, the idea adopted by many, which implies that you can study the Scripture for a while and learn enough to assure future fidelity to God, is deceptive. We spend twelve years or more, eight hours a day, teaching children temporal things like math and English, and then suppose that we can hear from the Word of God thirty minutes a week, and be sufficiently equipped for the noblest of spiritual assignments. How can someone recognize the need for twelve years of school to learn finite truths, and then believe that the infinitude of God and His work can be grasped with a little time here and there? This is impossible—not only because of the infinity of the knowledge of God, but also because of man's sinfulness and bent toward corruption. For what is clear at one time because of hearing the Word of God eventually becomes weakened or distorted during times of silence from God's Word. Anyone who walks with God and has spent years in dedicated study knows how true it is; we never stop learning about God, the

things we once learned we later forget, and that only continued exposure to the sharp-edged sword of the Word of God
can expose error and restore fidelity. Yet, the church has been
hoodwinked into courting the thinking that an occasional devotional is sufficient, deep doctrine or theology is outdated,
and that preaching potentiates diminished worship.

In this kind of milieu, the Bible becomes little more than a
multi-step manual that answers the how-to questions that will
get you through the week. This is spiritually ruinous because
man's problem is that he thinks he knows how to do more
than he really does, and consequently he does not ask the
questions that really matter. Thus his real needs, well below
the tide of felt needs, are not dealt with. It is only when confronted by the probing light of the whole counsel of God that
man's true needs are exposed to him. Man is deceived and he
deceives (Jeremiah 17:9–10). Once the Bible is viewed as no
more than a practical guide for life's malaise and a ready reference to answer everyday questions, man's spiritual life will
be malnourished because of man's sinfulness. He thinks he
knows how to walk with God, but he does not, and therefore
he fails to seek the truth that really matters.

The predilection of man to worship God in an unworthy
and unacceptable manner is lucidly portrayed by two facts.
First, half of all the Bible says about worship is exposing and
condemning false worship. Much of this false worship was being practiced by the people of God who chose not to closely
follow the Scripture. God never accepts worship that deviates
from what He says worship is supposed to be because everything else is a form of self worship. Second, the words which
Jesus said to the Samaritan woman, "You worship that which
you do not know" (John 4:22) reminds us that Jesus did not
accept any other kind of worship, regardless of the sincerity,
etc., of the worshiper, as anything but wrong and unaccept-

able. These two facts alone should indelibly etch upon our heart man's predisposition to worship wrongly and to do so while feeling that everything is great. She was sincere[72] and dedicated, but she was wrong. She was wrong, and her worship was simply unacceptable. All the sincerity in the world does not make a wrong right.

The emphasis in the past on the centrality of the Word of God can be seen in the common expression used in past days like "we are going to preaching" which was synonymous with "we are going to worship." Baptist churches have always placed the pulpit in the center of the worship center. This is not because of aesthetics or the practicality of it, nor did that tradition develop fortuitously. Baptists have always been known as people of the book. They placed the pulpit in the center to symbolize that the Word of God would be central to everything they did. Each departure from that centrality has proven to be to the church's peril.

This tradition is grounded in Scripture. The New Testament makes it clear that preaching and teaching played a central role in the early church. It is noteworthy that the only functional qualification of an elder is that he is "able to teach" (1 Timothy 3:2). Historically, teaching of the Word has been central to evangelicalism because of the scriptural example and commandments. Also, the reason preaching and teaching have such a central role in the church is that Christianity is objective truth. David Wells says, "It is precisely because Christian faith presents itself as objectively true that it has always exalted teaching. Unless truth is objective, it cannot be declared to others, cannot be taught to others, cannot be required of others. Wherever biblical religion has been recovered, the recovery of the teaching office is never far behind."[73]

Baptists have always made preaching central to the worship time. Our Baptist ancestors would never have thought of decoupling preaching and theology or preaching and worship. "Theology was as important to them as business and entertainment have become to us. As a result, the sermon became a time for active mental participation."[74] Worship without the Word of God was basically unheard of. When they gathered for worship, the teaching of Scripture was prominent. "Despite the discomfort, the maximum length of sermons ranged from two to four hours. Members of the congregation went to church expecting to be physically uncomfortable but spiritually and mentally blessed."[75]

What a contrast with today where many come to church to be physically comfortable and psychologically soothed. For them, "The sermon, therefore, became the primary means of interpreting and understanding current events."[76] The idea of the time of worship being essential and something that is mentally challenging in order to be equipped to interpret world events is quite foreign to the vast majority's idea of worship time.

The sermon has become a devotional, or a how-to for numerous temporal or faddish puzzles rather than a means of developing a Christian world-view; and thus, about twenty minutes is sufficient. However, if developing Christians with biblical world-views and teaching Christians how to think Christianly in order to be able to engage the culture is the priority of the worship gathering, then preaching will once again be enthroned as an indispensable part of true worship. Dr. Fasol states concerning what the people thought about long messages in the past, "The people demanded the preaching of long sermons that established the intellectual base for all of their beliefs, especially their dissent. A brief sermon would not have challenged the minds of our forefathers."[77]

I think that same thing is true today. Brief sermons do not sufficiently challenge. When preaching is viewed as an extrinsic part of worship, the understanding concerning both becomes an aberration. When preaching ceases to come from the God-called man of God, filled with the Spirit and Word of God, declaring eternal, objective truth with an undying passion, then the message will become no more important than a song.

Martyn Lloyd Jones rightly stated, "preaching is delivering a message."[78] He believed that "The preacher must see himself as a witness. This will make his ministry compelling, giving it passion, fervor and persuasiveness."[79] If our messages are mere recitations of endless illustrations, chronicling the woes of our day, pop psychology, and void of passion about truth from God; then it probably is best to show videos or create a sort of sanctified vaudeville and *preach* twenty minutes—or less, much less, would be preferable. If the pastors are not passionate about the message they preach then I doubt anyone will be passionate about hearing it or seeing it as a time of worship. Jones exclaimed, "Preaching is theology coming through a man who is on fire."[80]

Lest I be misunderstood, let me state emphatically that I am not arguing against using dramas, videos, PowerPoint presentations, CDs, tapes, sensitivity to guests, or a host of other modern techniques for disseminating truth or enhancing the communication of the message and worship. I believe that all of these things can be utilized for the glory of God. We practice all of these at the church where I pastor. Rather, I am arguing against the error of decoupling theology from preaching, and biblical exposition from worship.

Don Whitney speaks forthrightly about this vital issue, "We normally think of worship as something we do, and since preaching is done by the preacher (and not us), many fail to think of preaching as worship. But *listening* to preaching *is* something you do, and it *is* an act of worship when you listen with an eager mind and responsive heart. The reason it is an act of *worship* is that you are listening to *God* speak (through His word)."[81] Martin Luther wrote, "The highest worship of God is the preaching of the Word."[82] J.I. Packer wrote, "Congregations never honor God more than by reverently listening to His Word with a full purpose of praising and obeying Him once they see what He has done and is doing, and what they are called to do."[83]

Biblical preaching is worship because it is God speaking to His people, and His people *actively* listening with the intention of obeying. Biblical preaching cannot be separated from biblical worship anymore than it can be separated from evangelism, prayer, growth, etc. Granted, what is being advocated today by some—and some of what has been called preaching in the past—is simply not biblical preaching. It is more of a contemporary communication about whatever is newspaper worthy couched between a couple of slices of Scripture. One advocate of this style of preaching explains the rationale behind it as he delineates the principles for how to have an effective message for our day. He says, "Limit your preaching to roughly 20 minutes, because boomers don't have too much time to spare. And don't forget to keep your messages light and informal, liberally sprinkling them with humor and personal anecdotes."[84] This man and many others have simply redefined preaching to the point it can no longer be considered worship or biblical preaching. This kind of preaching can never be a form of worship since it begins and ends with man.

Further, the continued emphasis on the necessity of preaching short messages because people are busy or have a short attention span is a theory birthed in the recesses of hell. It is a ploy of Satan to undermine and marginalize the Word of God in Bible believing churches. In liberal, humanistic churches, he has undermined the Word by seeking to discredit its reliability. In conservative churches, he seeks to undermine the Scripture by diminishing the amount of exposure it gets. The result is less prominence, less understanding of its essentialness, and less communication of the real message of God. Either method results in the same outcome. The argument would be laughable if it were not for its ineradicable consequences.

It is wise to remember, these same busy or brief attention spanned people spend hours in front of a television set to watch soap operas or sporting events, or spend fifty minutes in class several times each day. They go to football games and sit in inclement weather on metal benches—which must have been designed by an entrepreneurial chiropractor assuring himself of ample and continued business. It is true that everyone is busy, but everyone makes time for what is important to him. The fact is that God, His truth, and worship are not as important to some people as television or football. Rather than the church coming to grips with this reality, she continues to accommodate carnality and contemporary excuses. A church that honors Jesus Christ cannot be built on the lowest *carnal* denominator.

It is a glaring error to try to frame the church's worship according to the needs of those who don't really want to worship in the first place. Can you imagine sports events doing that? I have yet to see a football game go to three quarters because people are busy or cannot pay attention for four quarters. I have watched parents sit through long hours of their children's baseball, gymnastic, or soccer practices and games— and some of these give incalculable breadth to the word *boring*. Often these same parents say they do not have time for church. The fact is that I, along with other Christians, have done the same thing with our children and are still active at our churches. It always gets back to priorities, not time. When people say they are too busy for church or sermons longer than twenty minutes—that implies that those who are faithful servants of the church have nothing else to do, which is simply not true.

All churches should seek to be sensitive to those who are visiting, but there is a danger in creating our church to suit them. "Preachers who concern themselves with user friendliness cannot fearlessly proclaim the whole counsel of God. Those who aspire to preach a timely message will find themselves at odds with the timeless truth of the Bible."[85] Dr. Albert Mohler Jr., President of Southern Baptist Theological Seminary, speaking in conjunction with Southern's 39th Annual Church Music Institute said, "Too often churches divorce the Word of God from the songs they sing in worship. The prerequisite for worship music is the Word of God. This means that a biblically illiterate congregation is automatically going to fail the test of singing God's song God's way."[86]

When the contemporary church separates biblical preaching from worship or exchanges biblical exposition for twenty minute devotionals and contemporary communiqués, the church not only loses truth, but it also loses true worship.

CHAPTER 5

They Say Church Discipline Is No Longer Practical: The Practical Reasons for the Banishment of Church Discipline Answered

1 It Was Abused in the Past

When the subject of church discipline surfaces, someone will inevitably point to the abuses of the past as reason enough to squelch the whole conversation and move on to something more palatable. It is an undeniable fact that there have been abuses in the past. George Davis writes, "A perusal of old church minutes would tend to justify the claim that in the past church discipline was often wrongly motivated and sometimes concerned with petty matters."[87] A classic example of abuse is when Pope Gregory VII (1073–1085) forced Henry IV to stand as a penitent in the snows outside the castle at Canossa begging the Pope to cancel his excommunication.[88]

To deny the abuses of the past is to deny reality, but to not practice church discipline because it was at times abused is to be unfaithful to our Lord Jesus Christ. There is really no logical reason to not do something because someone did it wrong or abused it. We can safely say that everything gets abused by someone, and everything is done wrong by almost everyone at some time. Thus, this same argument would do away with eating, dating, marriage, evangelism, offerings, ad infinitum. The abuse of something is not a plausible reason to abandon it, but rather it is a reason to do it right. George Davis comments, "Abuse in the past, however, can never justify neglect in the present."[89]

The antidote to abuses in the past and the negative connotations that now are associated with church discipline is to revisit the biblical teachings concerning it and implement it accordingly. It is like child abuse; the answer to child abuse is not to do away with discipline but to exercise good discipline. The worst form of church discipline is no church discipline, because that leaves the church powerless, the gospel corrupted, and God dishonored.

2 Fear

It is beyond question that we have become a society of fear rather than a society of faith. Fear always becomes more prominent in secularized societies. When faith is diminished, the void will not remain long; fear will rush in as a mighty river. The first time that we see fear in the human race is immediately after the fall of man. Speaking about Adam and Eve, the Scripture says, "They heard the sound of the Lord God walking in the garden in the cool of the day, and the man and his wife hid themselves from the presence of the Lord God among the trees of the garden. Then the Lord God called to the man, and said to him, 'Where are you?' He said, "I heard the sound of You in the garden, and *I was afraid* because I was naked; so I hid myself." (Genesis 3:8–10, italics added). Apparently man had never experienced fear before, but now after sin, which separated him from the presence of God and innocence, he is afraid, even of God.

158

There is a godly fear that is a reverential awe of God. Such fear characterizes the godly like Noah and Abraham. It results in worship and obedience to God. The fear talked about here is the fear associated with everything but the reverence of God. This is seen in the ever-increasing types of phobias of our day. These fears are the result of sin, separation from God, and not fearing God as man should. Fear is an ever-ready substitute for faith. When man's faith in God is diminished, the prevalence of phobias increases proportionately.

Fear keeps many pastors and Christians from facing the issue of church discipline. These can range from the fear of losing a pastorate, income, friends, a family's love, respect from peers; to diminished chances of getting another church, failure, family being severely hurt, being misunderstood, splitting the church, being severely criticized, and being denominationally ostracized, to name a few. In all truthfulness, these things are some of the realities that must be faced, and they loom ominously and dauntingly over the challenge to practice church discipline. In other words, the fears are well founded. These things do happen, and no one can guarantee that they will not. Each of these, not to mention multiples happening at one time, poses a sufficient deterrent from practicing church discipline for the vast majority. Again these fears are well founded, and their becoming a reality can exact an enormous price from those who dare to traverse the grounds of church discipline. This is especially true for the pastor and his family.

Nothing can remove these potential hurts or their concomitant fears. The only way to overcome them is the same way that we overcome every other fear, and that is by faith. Just as fear fills the void left by the absence of faith, faith also casts out fear. Some believe that you must have all faith and no fear before you can really follow God. I suppose that is the goal, but I must admit that I have never been involved in church discipline where I was not afraid. Some may say, "Well, if you had more faith you would have no fear," and that may be very true. Two things seem to make the fear a reality with me. First, I know I have a long way to grow as a Christian, and I do believe when I have reached a certain place I may fear no more; but regretfully I am not there, and my Lord has commanded me to obey now, so I go ahead with some fear. My faith in the Word of God is what I follow, but I must admit that fear stalks the heels of my faith. Second, I have personally experienced all of the previously mentioned potential fears and hurts; consequently, I know firsthand how difficult it can be. When the potentials become realities, and they cease to be an abstraction, they become exceedingly more intimidating. This is particularly true when you see your family having to endure so much suffering because of the vengeance of narcissism.

I do not think you have to be fearless to be faithful, but rather have faith greater than your fear. Our fear of failing God must be greater than the fear we have of anything else. That is the combination of humility and obedience. In this light, some fear becomes an asset.

3 The Demand for Perfection

This argument can be stated thusly: if church discipline cannot be done perfectly then it should not be implemented. We know that church discipline cannot be done perfectly. Therefore, we cannot practice church discipline. This argument includes two requirements. The first one is the requirement to be able to implement and complete the process perfectly; the second is that the people need to be perfect before the church practices discipline. Either of these, if followed, would preclude the possibility of ever practicing church discipline since there will inevitably be mistakes in the process and because no one is perfect, nor will they be this side of heaven.

Concerning the first requirement, Dr. Davis states it succinctly, "Some critics have argued that since church discipline cannot be implemented with absolute perfection, it ought not even be attempted."[90] There are two fatal flaws with this type of reasoning. First, we don't hold this standard anywhere else; if we did, we would not allow anyone to preach, evangelize, pray, etc. Ultimately, man could not even die since he surely does not die perfectly. The second flaw is, it undermines Scripture with the tyranny of the perfect. The reality is that God commanded the church to practice church discipline knowing that she would not be able to do it perfectly. Remember, when a church practices discipline it does it much more closely to perfect than when a church chooses not to even attempt it.

The second requirement postulated says, "Since no one is perfect, and we are all sinners; we cannot practice church discipline;" or "No one is perfect, you know." They may refer to the words Jesus said when the woman caught in adultery was brought to Him. He said to the Pharisees, "He who is without sin among you, let him be the first to throw a stone at her." Then He spoke to the woman and said, "Did no one condemn you?" She said, "No one, Lord." And Jesus said, "I do not condemn you, either. Go. From now on sin no more" (John 8:7,10–11). I have already shown that to interpret this passage as forbidding anyone from judging another or exercising church discipline is against Scripture and reason, and incapacitates anyone from living.

The idea that church discipline cannot be exercised because no one is perfect is based on a misunderstanding of church discipline—among other things. If a person, or everyone for that matter, was perfect then there would be no reason for church discipline. It is the very fact that no one is perfect that makes church discipline essential. It serves to correct an erring Christian and protect the Christian society.

Church discipline reminds us that we are all subject to like passions and should not ignore that reality or minimize the damage that can be wrought to the kingdom. The requirement of perfection further misunderstands not only the application of church discipline but also the breadth of church discipline.

Church discipline is not just the formal process of disfellowshipping an unrepentant brother or sister, but it is a brother holding another brother or sister accountable; this includes things like praying for someone or going in private to help a brother or sister who is wandering off the path of righteousness. It also misunderstands the recipient of formal church discipline. It is not for the brother who is seeking the Lord and yet failing, but it is for the person who chooses to walk in open sin and defiantly disregards the Lord and His Word. Formal discipline is primarily for dealing with rebellion—not slipping. Handling a Christian who was a drunk in the past and now has been faithful to Christ for years, but slips every once in a while is handled quite differently than the person who claims to be a Christian but makes no progress in leaving the alcohol and following Christ.

I have counseled people with basically every conceivable problem. These were done in confidence and without the need for implementing formal church discipline. Although I do consider biblical counsel within the purview of church discipline, the difference in whether or not formal church discipline is implemented is not necessarily determined by the sin that is committed, but rather by people's view of and response to their sin. If they are seeking to confess, repent, and work on it, I believe we ought to work with them with patience, love, understanding, and support. It is only when they refuse to deal with their own sin that the process of formal church discipline is warranted. Formal church discipline is implemented when people have already, in lifestyle, left the church; church discipline is the formal recognition of that with an earnest attempt to bring about repentance through the loving reproof of their brothers and sisters in Christ.

4 We Live in a Culture that Devalues Discipline

Our society has little appreciation for discipline of any kind. The last forty years have seen an unprecedented devaluing of every kind of discipline in both the American culture and the church. Our culture has experienced a cultural and moral meltdown. A mere cursory glance at any of the areas of discipline discussed in chapters 1 and 2 lucidly demonstrates this. Some examples of this meltdown are: the constant denigration of parental discipline, the lowering of standards of discipline in public education, decreasing the severity of penalties imposed for crimes, the lack of moral discipline of public officials, and the public's acceptance of these officials' abuses of essential morality. Even the military has been forced to lower its essential, stringent demands so that it could become a place of social experimentation.

What are preeminent in our society are personal rights. When rights become preeminent, personal responsibility and discipline will inevitably be minimized or relegated to a cliché status. It is not by accident that the avant-garde personal rights of today result in the demise of personal responsibility. Even in sports, we have witnessed a decline in the behavioral discipline of some athletes. What is now tolerated by referees, coaches and spectators would have not been tolerated in the past, but the exaltation of personal rights, privatization of morals, and the decreasing of team or community responsibility has made it unavoidable. These athletes model the deification of individual rights and demonization of personal responsibility to the youth of America. Thankfully, some athletes live at a higher plane and model true sportsmanship built upon personal and corporate responsibility. They stand as welcomed icons of personal responsibility. Added to this obvious theater of personal aggrandizement is the notion that many want every game to end with both sides winning and no one losing in order to protect the players' self-esteem, reinforcing the acceptability of the loss of any standards whereby actions can be judged as good or bad, win or lose—which consigns us to the pragmatic *common faith* of John Dewey.

I would like to say that we Christians are not affected by the cultural downgrading of discipline, but that would simply be naïve—or downright blindness. All of us are affected by our culture in varying degrees. An inadequate awareness of this fact leads to a de-emphasizing of the Scripture in order to integrate with the culture of the day. When contemporary America's culture of selfism makes its way into the church, church discipline becomes difficult, if not almost impossible, usually resulting in enormous fallout and requiring great courage. Since we are not disciplined in our own lives, we see little need to discipline others. In many cases, someone may be privately doing the very things that they are now being asked to discipline a friend for. They will then offer all kinds of excuses not to discipline even if that means attacking and seeking to discredit the one trying to lead the discipline.

When Jesus sought to bring spiritual discipline to Israel, and mankind in general, there was enormous rebellion against it. The only way to undermine His message was to attack Him, and that they did vociferously. Based on that reality, He said to His disciples (which also applies to all Christians) "If they have called the head of the house Beelzebul, how much more *will they malign* the members of his household" (Matthew 10:25).

Our society extols numerical growth, large over small, self, freedom, privatized religion, materialism, spiritual relativism, and avant-garde neo-tolerance. As mentioned earlier, I use the word neo-tolerance to distinguish between the historic meaning of tolerance and the way it is being used today. In the past, tolerance meant accepting the right of people to believe whatever they wanted to believe. One person might believe in God, and the other would not. It did not mean that the ideas could not be debated publicly or that both were inherently equal. According to the law of non-contradiction, opposites cannot be true in the same way at the same time. Consequently, both could not be equally viable although a person was free to believe and defend either one. Today, neo-tolerance teaches the inherent equality of all lifestyles and world-views. Thus, we are pressured to not only accept a person's right to believe what he wants, but we must accept that what he believes and every other belief is equally right. The end result is that there is no absolute right or wrong but only personal preferences.

Multiculturalism is a prime example of this egalitarian perspective. America is portrayed as the melting pot, signified by people coming from all over the world, from many cultures, and then being educated in the same language, values etc., which have made America a greater culture. America is obviously a better culture than the one they left, or else people from around the globe would not leave their culture to come to this one. This seems to be undeniably obvious—and it was undeniably obvious for centuries. This is what it means to become an American. In contrast, multiculturalism says all cultures are equal and when someone comes to America, they must bring their culture with them, and America must place the newcomer's culture on the same level as American culture. Rejection of this notion is a badge of bigotry and racism.

Consequently, we are rapidly approaching a time, and it is already here to a significant degree, when no cultural or personal expression or view can be challenged in the marketplace without the politically correct police demonizing you with every pejorative known to man. Nothing is right or wrong, better or worse, and to say that it is to be a bigot, racist, idiot, narrow minded, backward, etc. Neo-tolerance requires nothing outside the individual's experience to authenticate it, for the individual experience is unassailably self-authenticating, regardless of how aberrant it actually is. In this milieu of anti-disciplinarianism and neo-tolerance, it will appear to be supererogation to be called on to implement church discipline.

In order for churches to be willing to implement church discipline, members must be taught the biblical view of all forms of discipline and taught to prize discipline. If this is done, they will see discipline for the wonderful and loving thing that it is. Not only has the church been unsuccessful in stemming the tide of the diminishing of culture's support of responsibility and discipline, but she has also been contaminated by the devaluing of discipline and thus has been complicitous in the decline. This is to the detriment of both society and the church, and considerably devalues church discipline.

5 The God of Growth Towers Above the God of Scripture

Why is that? Why is the quest for growth such a powerful force in the church today, and I mean beyond the godly desire

166

to fulfill the Great Commission? I believe there are several reasons. I speak as a pastor who, along with my fellow pastors, feels this pressure intensely. We may say growth does not matter, but every pastor knows that is not actually true. It matters, and it matters to everyone who loves God and people—and to most who do not. No pastor desires that his church not grow, and conversely, every pastor is ecstatic when it does grow.

The term growth, in a general sense, includes numbers, influence, acceptance, popularity, comfort, offerings, ecclesiastical unity, fellowship, peace, etc. Optimally, we would like to grow in all areas, but growth in any area will normally suffice. In a particular sense, the term growth is used to describe numerical growth. The profound pressure to grow has to do primarily with numerical growth. If this happens, everything else is perceived to be fine. If there is no numerical growth, nothing else matters. But why is there such an inordinate and relentless pressure to grow? Why does every pastor know that the church must grow numerically, or else he needs to be praying about where God wants him to move? It is not that there has not been a desire for numerical growth in the past or that growth is inherently evil; but rather, why does growth seem to be the insignia of faithfulness to God today?

There are a few reasons for this tremendous and inestimable pressure. First, growth in general is a good thing. Growth in knowledge, maturity, spirituality, love, etc., is good. Things that live grow, and we want to live, so we want to grow. As a matter of fact, the Scripture commands us to grow. "But speaking the truth in love, we are to grow up in all aspects into Him who is the head, even Christ" (Ephesians 4:15). 1 Peter 2:2 says, "like newborn babies, long for the pure milk of the word, so that by it you may grow in respect to salvation." Peter also commands, "but grow in the grace and knowledge of our Lord and Savior Jesus Christ. To Him be the glory, both now and to the day of eternity. Amen" (2 Peter 3:18). Growth is good, and the lack of growth in living things is normally a sign of sickness or death. Thus, there is nothing inherently evil or wrong with growth; it is actually a good thing.

Second, every pastor lives with a profound awareness that his effectiveness as an undershepherd is almost always evaluated based on his ability to lead the church to grow numerically. Further, his holiness and love for God is, more often than not, evaluated by the same criteria since if he were really a holy and faithful pastor his church would be blessed by God and grow. A person in a larger church is usually perceived as somehow holier or more committed than a pastor serving in a small church located close to where the Great Commission ends. This is the same mentality the disciples demonstrated when they posed the obtuse question to Jesus about the man who was born blind—which they assumed must be a sign of God's displeasure. "And His disciples asked Him, 'Rabbi, who sinned, this man or his parents, that he would be born blind?' Jesus answered, '*It was* neither *that* this man sinned, nor his parents; but *it was* so that the works of God might be displayed in him" (John 9:2–3). It is obvious that this man could not have sinned before he was born, but when outward blessings of God become the litmus test of holiness, obtuseness knows no boundaries. The growth standard declares that growth equals a good pastor, and by contrast, non-growth equals a bad pastor.

All of the reporting data serves to support this notion since numerical growth is the easiest to measure. Consequently the significant areas of church life are indicated by statistics. Keeping records of these kinds of statistics does have value, but it is very difficult to find a spreadsheet that calculates the many important things that go on in a church like the members' spiritual growth, becoming a better witness, learning and applying the Bible to their life, engaging our culture, and following Christ in all things. Further, most people who complete these stats understand God and His ways and do not make the demeaning and inaccurate aforementioned false assumption, and even work on dispelling the harmful idea that growth equals godliness. Nevertheless, the message, whether subtle or not so subtle, is still the same—no growth means no good. Therefore, the size of a pastor's church is often the most popular barometer of his spiritual capability as unfortunate as that may be.

Third, we are Americans who are influenced, often more than we admit or even know, by the American culture. American culture is one of numerical growth whether one is talking about economics, the number of games won by a team, the size of a house, salary, power, etc.; the point is clear that growth is the Magna Carta for the American culture. It is the *raison d'etre* for businesses and becomes so for churches that lose their biblical moorings in the deluge of post modernity. An athletic coach is the greatest as long as his number of wins continue to grow or peak the chart; the CEO of a corporation is wonderful as long as the company sales increase, and the prevalence of that mentality in the church is painfully evident to pastors who are also considered the greatest as long as the church grows.

This enormous pressure, which can only be fully appreciated by a pastor and to some degree by a staff person, persuades pastors to focus myopically on those passages in Scripture that emphasize growth and avoid those areas that may dissuade people from joining the church because of a high commitment level. This is done either consciously or unconsciously, but it is done. This includes emphasizing things like evangelism, offerings, fellowship, revivals, attendance, etc. All of these should be emphasized, but the misfortune is that the things that potentiate a decrease in growth—even temporarily—are concomitantly avoided at all cost; and they must be if the god of growth towers above the God of Scripture. Even when there is an ungodly deacon or church member, and everyone knows it, that person will rarely be dealt with biblically if it jeopardizes numerical growth. Consequently, they thrive, unleashing their paralyzing venom from time to time right in the sanctuary of holiness, protected from all would-be challengers by the god of growth. This is a major reason that church discipline is held in such low esteem, because it inevitably leads to some loss of members—provided the disciplined does not repent.

Because of the enthronement of numerical growth as the decisive factor of success and faithfulness, church discipline is consigned to the Jurassic Park of church history; only unlike the movie Jurassic Park, the hope is that this dinosaur will never live again. The growth argument goes something like this: things that grow or help to grow are good and things that do not grow or help to grow are bad. Church discipline does not cause growth; therefore, church discipline is bad.

At this point, you may think that I am not in favor of numerical growth, or that I don't view growth as good and nongrowth as bad for living things. But that is not the case. I do believe that growth is good, but I also believe that church discipline helps churches to grow. It may not help you grow immediately, and you may even see a temporary decline. However, if done right, it also moves the church toward a growth posture as I related in chapter 1. While not all detractors are wolves in sheep's clothing, there is often someone in the church that is holding the church back from growing. Maybe they are an influential family who wants it their way, carnal deacons, or church members who really care nothing about reaching a lost and dying world.

As common as the spring rains is the reality of churches hiring a pastor and joyfully welcoming him, only to see the powers that be pressure him out after a couple of years because the wolves among the sheep have not been dealt with. The cycle repeats itself unabated until someone leads the church to follow the Lord in church discipline or else the church becomes a Laodicean social club. This goes on all over the country and goes on in the same churches for decades. Until someone stands against it, the church will never be under the rule of Christ, but she will remain under the damning domination of the self-appointed insurrectionist. Only when these people are dealt with can the church be unified in pursuing God because unholiness never desires an all out effort to pursue holiness, and it never will. When a pastor seeks to lead a church to be more evangelistic, prayerful, and faithful to the Word, and there is resistance to him, the church needs to see the spiritual warfare that is going on. The carnal will not be so naive as to say they are carnal, but spiritual people ought to be able to see beneath their veneer of euphemisms.

Churches, which have experienced growth over a number of years under the leadership of several pastors, can actually become more than one church under the same roof. This causes perennial divisions within the congregation about which direction the church should go because people came in under different pastors with somewhat different visions and styles of leadership. Leading these diverse groups to move in one direction can often be done with time, teaching, finesse, and prayer. However, when you combine these factors, that some of the members are carnal and there are two or three churches under one roof, it can become impossible to lead the church into experiencing New Testament church life without some fallout—translated as a decrease in numbers.

For example, suppose a very conservative preacher is called to a church that is liberal, and has had liberal preaching for twenty years. It is possible that the whole church will move to being a conservative Bible-believing church, but it is not probable. It may be that some will have to leave or be disciplined in order to become a New Testament church. In these types of situations, great patience, wisdom, and commitment to being there a long time are required. To go into that type of situation and think you will change it in a year or two is the infallible formula for a short pastorate, church split, undue hurt to the body of Christ, or all of the above.

There are times that church discipline does not lead to numerical growth within the foreseeable future. However, if church discipline does not lead to numerical growth through time, it still leads to growth the only kind of growth Christ called us to, which is faithfulness to His Word. The god of numerical growth has trumped the call to follow the Christ of redemption, and this to the beclouding and peril of authentic Christianity. The god of growth produces a porcine church and the God of Scripture produces a pure church. The test for whether something is good can include growth, as long as it is the right kind of growth. Faithfulness always leads to spiritual growth, which often leads to numerical growth. Mere numerical growth, not based on faithfulness to the whole counsel of God, merely leads to growth away from faithfulness and equating blessings of God with numbers rather than faithfulness. Remember, church discipline is not evil, but it will be opposed by evil people with evil agendas. Satan will make sure the detractors of the Word of God are there to taunt the faithful and derail their faithful pursuit of God; just as he was in the garden, so shall he be with the church.

I am presently the senior pastor of Trinity Baptist Church in Norman, Oklahoma. It is a very biblical church, including both the easy and the difficult things. However, I can really take no credit for that. Several years ago, Dr. Bill Elliff pastored this church. It was a large and growing church. All Bill had to do was maintain the status quo, and the church would have continued to grow numerically; but numerical growth was not really Bill's heart although he desired that also. Most of all, he desired to lead the church to be biblical and faithful to Christ. He led the church to practice church discipline and implement a plurality of pastors. These actions precipitated an eventual church split. The move toward New Testament Christianity would come at a high cost to Bill, his family, and all of the then members of Trinity who had a greater desire to be a New Testament church than maintain valuable friendships, comfort, and even family tranquility. After it was over, many had left the church. Eventually, God moved Bill to other ministries, and he is now a pastor in Little Rock, Arkansas.

Bill led the church to follow Christ at enormous personal cost, but he did not get to reap the benefit of his labor and sacrifice. For that is the way the Lord works at times. However, I can personally testify that what he led the church to do was not in vain. For, though I did not sow or water, I am reaping the benefit of that sacrificial following of Christ at all cost. The people who were here when I was called as senior pastor are here because they too made a choice to pursue faithfulness and follow the leadership of a godly pastor in establishing a New Testament church. They too did this at remarkable personal cost. This church is on the path that I have sought to lead the other churches that I pastored. We are presently pursuing the same direction that Bill led them to follow. The blessings that we now experience are because of Bill's leadership and the people who sought to follow God. Thanks for the faithfulness. Now may we be faithful with what God has given us. At times the benefit of church discipline is not experienced until later, and sometimes by others, but it will be experienced.

The church growth movement, which epitomizes an un-balanced emphasis on growth is not likely to be implementing church discipline any time soon. There are also many tradi-tional non-growing churches that do not practice discipline, but they act like only the church growth movement alone has embraced postmodernity. This is far from the truth. Some churches that are a part of the church growth movement—we all are for growth by the way—are more biblical than some who are not. However, there is an underlying presupposition that dooms the church growth movement to potential immen-sity in breadth and certain superficial depth. This lethal pre-supposition is the idea that somehow deep theology and ex-positional preaching—and their corollary non-devotional time requirement—hurts the church's ability to reach out. The consequence of this presupposition is the icon of the twenty-minute sermon and an emphasis on everything else but expo-sition and theology. Os Guinness relates this same sentiment, ". . . the church-growth movement has two common deficien-cies. On the one hand, its theological understanding is often superficial, with almost no element of biblical criticism. As a well-known proponent states, 'I don't deal with theology. I'm simply a methodologist'—as if his theology were thereby guar-anteed to remain critical and his methodology neutral. But in fact, theology is rarely more than marginal in the church growth movement and discussion of the traditional marks of the church is virtually nonexistent. Instead, methodology, or technique, is at the center and in control. The result is a meth-odology only occasionally in search of a theology."[91]

Even if no numerical growth is experienced when church discipline is invoked, and even if it results in loss of numbers permanently and the church never reaches its former size, it is still right because Jesus said so. And that must be enough. You can never follow Christ without growing spiritually.

6 Discipline Is Too Difficult

Let's face it. Church discipline is an immensely difficult task with no guarantee that the desired results will ever be realized. It is at best an extremely demanding responsibility to take on. This gives birth and life to the continual question, Isn't there a more productive and peaceful way to obtain the same results? Some view discipline merely as an instrument for creating problems that would not have come about without discipline. However, I would argue that the implementation of discipline exposes the already present problems rather than creating them. Friendships can also serve as a formidable deterrent to a person who otherwise might support the practice of church discipline since the person being rebuked may be a friend, and rebuking a friend is never a pleasant task; but it is seriously wrong to equate unpleasantness with unnecessary or wrongness. Further, it is playing God to predict the future and to do away with Him entirely by rewriting Scripture based on that prediction.

Church discipline, by most, is clearly viewed through the spectacles of pragmatism. They will say, as we all know, there is only so much time, and there is more ministry to do than there is time for already. What about ministry to widows and orphans? Shouldn't we be taking care of them instead of going on witch hunts? However, these kinds of discussions are purely spiritual pragmatism, which always opts for the least difficult and most acceptable enterprise. Jesus knows all about the widows and orphans and cares more about them than any human being, and the Scripture commands the church to minister to them; but it is the same Scripture that also commands the church to practice church discipline. If our churches function as New Testament churches, we will be able to do both. If we do not function as New Testament churches, the problem may be the lack of discipline. The discussion should not be about which command to follow and which to ignore, but rather how to follow both for the honor of our Lord Jesus. He is honored by our unrestrained obedience not by our compartmentalized obedience.

I cannot argue that church discipline is not difficult nor guarantee that the desired results will be realized. I cannot guarantee safe passage through the shark-infested waters of church discipline, where sometimes the innocent becomes dinner for the insatiable appetites of carnal carnivores. I have personally found the process of church discipline to be emotionally draining, time consuming, and an all-around demanding task. On the average, the church discipline cases that I have been involved in that went to the point of disfellowshipping took about six months. Needless to say, you're doing all of the other normal work of the church simultaneously. This is why it is essential to have others trained to help in carrying out church discipline.

Having said that, I personally do not regret following Christ in any of the discipline cases that I have been involved in regardless of their outcome. I have grown enormously through these times in a way that I do not believe is available to those who skirt the issue. I have also watched other Christians grow through the process. Most of all, there is a peace in my soul, beyond measure, that I sought to follow Christ just like I preach. This reward is immeasurable and cannot be gained in any other way.

There have been a few times when a deacon's behavior warranted discipline. On one of these occasions, a deacon was not coming to church regularly, which necessitated that he be approached—yes it may sound odd, but I believe deacons ought to come to church. I talked to the chairman of the deacons about the situation, and while we were praying about the circumstances, a new chairman was elected; and so I approached the new chairman with the same concern, which he had also noticed. It just so happened that the new chairman and the deacon of concern were longtime friends. However, the new chairman was more a friend of Jesus than of any man, which is crucial in these types of situations. After we had prayed for several weeks, we determined that it was time to meet with the deacon privately, express our concerns, and see if we could help.

We asked to meet with him, and he agreed. When we all sat down, I started to relay the purpose of the meeting. He immediately responded, "I know why you want to meet, and I am glad you called the meeting. I just wish you would not have waited so long." He then explained that he was struggling with whether to stay in our church and serve as a deacon or to go to a church in a neighboring community. What brought about his dilemma, and his absence, was that his children went to a school in another area, and their friends went to the church located in that community. Consequently, his wife and he were torn between whether to stay at our church, which they loved, or go to the church where their children had more friends—I am not evaluating the rightness of this decision but merely relaying the circumstances as it relates to this case of church discipline. At the close of our meeting, we agreed to pray for a few weeks in order to determine the Lord's will for his family and him.

At the conclusion of two or three weeks, they had decided that God wanted them to transfer to the other church. We all still remained friends, and our blessings were upon his decision. Two important things came out of the willingness to confront a brother who was not fulfilling his responsibility as a deacon. First, he was glad we came to him because he was a spiritual man and knew he was not giving the church all that he should. He was relieved when we came and helped him process what was notably a difficult decision. Second, the deacon chairman, who later became a lay pastor in the church, spoke some words at the conclusion of the discipline; words I shall always treasure and never forget. He looked at me and said, "This experience has caused me to grow significantly in my spiritual life." That is the nature of following Christ, particularly in the difficult things like church discipline.

7 Metropolitan Anonymity and Rural Relationships

This could be called the *where I live you can't practice church discipline* argument. Whether someone lives in a rural, semi-rural, urban, or metropolitan area, they claim the peculiarities of their area make discipline highly improbable if not impossible.

The rural peculiarity is the reality that almost everyone in the church is related or lifelong friends, and the pastor is an outsider; and more than likely he always will be and probably will be gone soon—one way or the other. I admit this does make for a difficult task of getting people to support discipline. It is only possible with serious preaching and discipleship, and this will take time. However, the fact is that this closely-related church would also closely approximate much of how it was in the New Testament and almost all of church history. If family and friendships kept church discipline from being practiced in the early church, it would have never started. In some ways, it does make it tougher, but that can actually be good in that it makes us be more aware of being loving and patient. The important thing to remember is that Christ commanded discipline to be carried out as long as the church is upon the earth, no matter where she is, even in the rural areas. Sometimes the interrelatedness of the rural community, and the fact that everyone knows everything that goes on, is more of a reason to practice church discipline if the church is serious about the lost in the community. Non-Christians who live in rural areas are, odd as it may seem, some of the most gospel hardened. This is not because the gospel is necessarily repugnant to them, but rather that they have watched firsthand hypocrisy go on unchecked for years. They refuse, often ever so kindly, to be told about their sin when they know the church has its own fair share of nefariousness, which she readily winks at, while remaining unflinching in the call for others to repent. This type of situation, which is repeated over and over, serves as a thunderous example of how the lack of church discipline over the years has undermined the credibility and desirability of the gospel. It is not uncommon to witness to a longtime resident of a small close-knit community and hear the lost person remind you that they live more faithfully to the Scripture than some within the church. Regrettably, many times they are telling the truth; what difference do they see that would serve as an incentive to become a Christian? It does not take him long to reason that if sin was that serious to God, He would surely deal with the sin among His own people first (1 Peter 4:17). Therefore, God has looked over their sin, and he will surely look over mine. That is not good theology, but then neither is ignoring church discipline.

The other end of the spectrum is the metropolitan area and the peculiarities associated with it. Not only is it difficult to know what the members do during the week because they are so spread out; but also the nature of city life and the pervasive urban attitude extol the privatization of religion and individualism. There also are significantly more churches to choose from, and there are fewer historic or family ties with a particular church. These particulars pose some different obstacles for the implementation of church discipline than found in rural life, but just like addressing the unique difficulties of rural life, these too can be solved. It takes better organization. For example, the church can be organized into small groups that everyone must belong to, which either meet on campus, in the community, or both; these groups minister to and keep up with their members. This would often be the first point of disciplinary contact. The members must be taught the value of community. The early church "had all things in common" (Acts 2:44). In addition, the option of people having many churches to choose from, along with not having any traditional ties to a particular church, can actually be a blessing as far as church discipline goes. If you raise the standard of the church to the level of authentic Christianity, troublemakers often will either get saved or leave, and people looking for a social club will look elsewhere; thus eliminating much of the need for church discipline.

The fact is, wherever a church is located, there will be peculiarities about the environment that are not conducive to church discipline. That is the nature of a fallen world and not so much the issue of rural verses urban. The Scripture is absolute, not relative to the situation. When we seek to do God's will, we are not dependant upon the correct environment, but the presence and power of God; He has promised that to us. "Truly I say to you, whatever you bind on earth shall have been bound in heaven; and whatever you loose on earth shall have been loosed in heaven. Again I say to you, that if two of you agree on earth about anything that they may ask, it shall be done for them by My Father who is in heaven. For where two or three have gathered together in My name, I am there in their midst" (Matthew 18:18–20). That is a promise that is given specifically to those who practice church discipline. The church is a place, regardless where it is located, of a spiritual family and eternal friendships. Therefore, if the members are so disassociated from some accountability to the church, or if church discipline cannot be enacted because of family or friends, then discipline cannot be enacted except in a church of non-family and non-friends, which itself is not a church. The end result of this thinking is church discipline has no place in this life, and Jesus' teaching is a bunch of to do about nothing. However, Jesus' teaching is forever true and forever relevant.

8 The Size of the Church

This last issue is closely related to the previous one in that it has to do with size. Only now it is not the size of the community but the size of the church. The small church is difficult because often one family can make up twenty-five percent of the church. Thus, to discipline one of them is nothing less than monumental, and without their support, the likelihood of successfully disciplining anyone else is highly improbable. The larger church has a much different problem. No one family has enough members to influence a vote, but it is extremely difficult to communicate the truth about a particular incident of discipline without it being distorted a thousand times. The very nature of a large church prohibits the entire church from being as close to everyone as in a smaller church.

However, as with the other scenarios, the size of the church does not absolve us from the command of Scripture. It just means that we must do things that facilitate solving the problems associated with implementing church discipline in our particular situation. In chapter 10, I will mention several things that can help.

Prevaricators continually seek to portray church discipline as a witch hunt, but nothing could be further from the truth. Church discipline is brothers and sisters in Christ seeking to obey our Lord Jesus Christ in everything. But if someone is bound and determined to cast church discipline into that light, I would quickly respond; if there is in fact a witch among us, the best thing that can happen is to have a witch hunt.

CHAPTER 6

Can the Church Be the Church Without Discipline? The Biblical and Practical Reasons for Church Discipline

This chapter presents biblical reasons for the necessity of church discipline along with two practical reasons. It appears that more than a few people believe they can get along fine without church discipline. The facts in favor of that conclusion seem irrefutable. The following is often touted as such proof, "people are being saved, the church has grown, and the budget is up." However, as we all know, appearances can be deceiving and in this case damningly deceiving. Any time the church looks to experience for validation of her actions, she will normally be able to justify herself because humans are impressively apt at interpreting empirical data to support a favorable conclusion; social psychologists call this "self-serving bias."[92] Also, the god of growth will allay any doubts about the church's viability as long as the numbers are increasing; but experience cannot determine the justifiableness of the experience because the question is whether the experience is justified. Philosophers call this *begging the question*. In other words, when someone seeks to prove the rightness of their experience, they need something other than the experience itself to validate that the experience is right; true justification comes only from the Scripture.

We will look at the practical reasons why the church needs discipline and then the theological. The first of two practical reasons is to maintain a viable organization. The church is an organism, but it is also an organization, and for any organization to remain viable, it must have rules along with the means to implement and enforce them. The opposite of this is anarchy. As G. K. Chesterton wrote, "When men are weary they fall into anarchy; but while they are gay[93] and vigorous they invariably make rules."[94] The nature of a church necessitates the need for organization. Os Guinness says, "There is clearly a need for an organization whenever one person does not have the strength, talents, time, or resources to accomplish a desirable end result by himself or herself."[95]

It is inevitable that some will make their way into a local church that either are not saved or eventually live as if they are not. If the church does not have a means of dealing with them, the spiritual life of the church will inevitably be downgraded. That being the case, there must be rules. Further, for rules to be effective they must have two associate components: first, a disciplinary consequence for infraction of the rules and second, an effective means of carrying out the discipline. Without these, rules become mere clichés.

Imagine that your local school passed a rule that it is a violation to skip school. People were even warned not to skip school since it is against the rules. However, after establishing this rule and elucidating it so that it was well understood by all, the school did not establish a consequence. There existed a well-articulated and clearly understood rule, but it lacked any discipline for those who defied it. Even with a superficial understanding of human nature and the nature of organizations, one would be forced to admit that the rule would have little effect upon the overall problem of truancy with the possible exception of some Kantians who would seek to obey for duty's sake.

An equally unmanageable situation would arise even if it was against the rules to skip school, and the penalty of being expelled was firmly established, but the school could not enforce the penalty. The outcome is the same as the first scenario. There would be little or no effect upon the problem of truancy.

For rules to matter, the rule and the consequence must be clearly articulated and the means and will to follow through must be present. In the church, we know the rule of church discipline. Preachers preach on it, or at least some do who dare to be so bold. We know the means for carrying out discipline and the concomitant consequences, for they are spelled out by Jesus in His second mention of His beloved church. What is lacking is the will to implement what Jesus has ever so clearly stated. Thus, the end result for the local church is the same as not having any rules. Only in the spiritual realm, this lack of will carries infinitely more severe consequences because it undermines the integrity of the church and her message. As with any organization, the church loses her moorings, effectiveness, and identity with the loss of discipline.

The second practical reason for discipline is to maintain a legitimate church membership. When a pastor is asked what size church he pastors by someone who is not church savvy, and he is seeking to impress them a little, he will—in those weak moments of pride—tell how many *members* the church has rather than how many attend, unless there is the possibility they may actually visit his church. However, when he deals in reality, he speaks of how many come on Sunday morning. The difference in these two figures is dramatic indeed. The figure is often two to five times more people on roll than in attendance. This reality redefines what it means

185

to shepherd the flock and devalues church membership. Add to this the fact that the pastor does not even know—and has not even seen—two-thirds of those on roll. Now add to that the difficulty of shepherding a few wolves mixed in with the sheep, and the task is not only impossible but also nonsense. Anything anyone can belong to and not have to do anything to remain a member is probably not worth belonging to. It is also true, "If one cannot be 'out' then one never knows whether one is really in. The community of faith is not a limitless community."[96]

The local church is a community of people called out by God, regenerated by the Holy Spirit, and baptized in obedience to our Lord Jesus Christ. Church discipline is a vital ingredient in maintaining that community. The church must decide, "What does belonging mean? One observer noted that the requirements and expectations at any of the local civic or social clubs exceed the expectations of the church. Does it make any difference to identify with a body of believers and join the 'ecclesia'? Church discipline tells us that membership means something. It says that membership is a commitment. It teaches that membership is participation in a community with shared values and common, mutual obligations. It informs us of the obligation of membership to spiritual responsibility. Our churches expect, and often get, little."[97] Sadly, in the name of love, openly rebellious people are often overlooked or even placed in positions of leadership in hopes that they will do better if the church just *loves* and trusts them; even though that process is unbiblical, and they create havoc in the church. This thinking and action quenches the work of the Holy Spirit and bridles the church to the hand of the carnal rather than to the hand of the Lord Jesus Christ. Actually, the most beautiful Christian and loving thing that can be done is to confront the *brother* with his sin and the harm he is

186

doing. Prayerfully, he will repent. Even if he does not, those in the church who really want to walk with God and are being held back by the leadership's unwillingness to deal with a carnal member, deserve a real community of believers to mature in. For the church to experience real church, there must be a cessation of coddling the carnal and snickering at sin, along with intentionally riveting our energies upon building up believers, feeding the flock, and protecting God's people from wolves in sheep's clothing.

If a farmer has a fox in his hen house, he does not just pray for him to leave. He does not congregate all the hens together to pray for the fox to leave, or for him to become a chicken. No! He gets the fox out of there as soon as possible to protect the hens. There are some things that we should pray that God will do, and there are other things that He has commanded us to do that we simply need to be obedient and do. Church discipline is one of those things. We need to pray that He will help us, but not whether to do it or not. We have His answer if we are willing to accept it.

Following are ten theological reasons for church discipline:

1 To Acknowledge Christ's Lordship

The Scripture is clear in declaring that Jesus is the head of the church (Ephesians 1:22, 5:23; Colossians 1:18). Undeniably, this teaching is obfuscated and circumvented when a local church chooses not to follow Christ in church discipline. When Christians choose to exclude following Jesus in the more difficult areas and emphasize only the more palatable or exciting, they are actually enthroning themselves as lord since they are the ones choosing what to obey and what not to obey. It is true that Christ is still Lord over the church, but the church, unwilling to seek to follow in everything, is deliberately not acknowledging that reality. This diminishes the power of God in the church, distorts the testimony of the church, and dishonors Christ. The message of the gospel, the simple gospel, becomes so entangled with confusion that it is like watching a show on cable television without the cable. The church is declaring to the world that people must obey Jesus and accept Him as Lord; and yet, the people watching the church wonder if obeying Christ is really that important since the church doesn't obey Him in everything. This is not referring to a church seeking to obey Christ and failing, for which there is understanding, but rather this is a state of affairs in which there is a willful failure to even attempt to obey Christ.

Church discipline is an effort to get a wayward brother to acknowledge the lordship of Christ in his life. In order to accomplish this, he must see the seriousness of his sin and the importance of pursuing holiness at all cost. If the church that is telling him these things is not living a message that reflects this reality, it will dilute the much needed life message and further deceive upon the sinning brother.

It is hard to imagine how Christ is pleased and honored by people who are supposed to follow Him but are selective in what and how they follow Him. If a child obeys his parents' commands only when it is easy, or only in what the child already wants to do, but fails to obey in the areas which are difficult or the child does not enjoy, the child is considered self-centered and rebellious. How can it be any different with God's spiritual children who choose not to obey? The most vivid display of the lordship of Christ is found in the martyr's choice to die rather than disobey Christ. We see this same kind of devotion and honor in the lives of saints in the past and present who live daily for Christ and often at great personal cost. Lordship is most clear and undeniable when people follow Him in the face of great personal loss. This always brings

188

us back to the very basics of what a Christian and a church are. "Is the church a leisure time activity, a sort of 'hotel' where strangers occasionally gather on their travels through life, or is it a unique community of persons who bind themselves both to one another and to the lordship of Christ as holy and redeemed people? Does its character imply commitments that are not options but must be kept, values that are to be cherished, conduct that is normative?"[98] The answer to these kinds of questions will determine to a large degree our response to the commands to practice church discipline.

2 To protect the church

One of the primary responsibilities of a pastor is to protect the flock from predators and dangerous infiltrators. As the apostle Paul was preparing to leave Ephesus, he warned the elders of the church, "Be on guard for yourselves and for all the flock, among which the Holy Spirit has made you overseers, to shepherd the church of God which He purchased with His own blood. I know that after my departure savage wolves will come in among you, not sparing the flock; and from among your own selves men will arise, speaking perverse things, to draw away the disciples after them. Therefore be on the alert . . ." (Acts 20:28–31).

Richard L. Mayhue forcefully declares, "Guarding Christ's flock of believers from spiritual danger is one of the most neglected pastoral duties in today's church. In addition to commissioning spiritual sentinels to watch over His flock by directing them into truth and righteousness, God has charged these sentinels to protect the flock from doctrinal error and personal sin . . ."[99] Paul makes it clear that threats to the well-being of the flock are not only from external persecutions of the flock but also from the danger that arises from within when he states in Acts 20:30, "from among *your own selves men will arise*, speaking perverse things, to draw away the disciples after them" (italics added). Jude likewise warns, "For certain persons have *crept in unnoticed*, those who were long beforehand marked out for this condemnation, ungodly persons who turn the grace of our God into licentiousness and deny our only Master and Lord, Jesus Christ" (Jude verse 4, italics added). It is undeniable that in America the greatest harm to the church comes from within. The world creeps into the church, which according to Scripture is inevitable, and when the church does not remove the leaven, the church loses her churchness.

As long as there is a devil, the need to protect the flock from internal and external foes must remain one of the shepherd's chief responsibilities. In addition, while the care of each individual is scripturally important, the actions of one should never predominate over the protection of the flock. In other words, no individual should be able to consume enough of the leader's time or strike enough fear in his heart to deter or hinder him from protecting the flock because "What is often either overlooked or misunderstood is the fact that every church has a responsibility for the 'ninety and nine' as well as the wayward 'one.'"[100] Leaving the flock to search for the one who has gone astray is not the same as sacrificing the flock for the sake of one whether he is a wolf in sheep's clothing or a rebellious sheep. For the church to remain honoring to her Lord, she must be protected against those who desire to either sway her from without or corrupt her from within.

Rarely, if ever, is the church's integrity toppled in a day or an event. The infiltration and corruption of the church always begins with the acceptance of the thoughts or worldview of the world, which are in rebellion to the lordship of Christ. It is in the area of thinking—the heart, mind, and soul—that the contemporary church needs protection. While this is always true, there are times when the church's most obvious threats come from physical persecution, but when that is absent, the war is in the mind of the church for the soul of the church. The problems do not begin with overt or covert action, which normally captivates much of the church's attention, but they begin in the thought life of an individual, then move into the church, and by the time the aberrant behavior is evident, the corruption of the mind is substantial. The de-emphasization of the role of teaching in the church is one of the results of the failure to realize that corruption infiltrates the mind before the life of the church. The Holy Spirit makes it clear that when Ananias and Sapphira sinned with their offering in Acts 5, their action was the result of sinful thought. "Peter said, "Ananias, why has Satan filled your heart to lie to the Holy Spirit and to keep back *some* of the price of the land? . . . Why is it that you have *conceived* this deed in your heart" (Acts 5:3–4, italics added). Before there is immorality, false doctrine, or divisiveness, there is always corrupt thinking. Thus, vigilance must be given to the constant nourishing of the mind and soul on the Word of God. This is essential to protecting the flock from corruption.

The church has not gone untouched by the victim mentality of contemporary society. Troublemakers in the church are often excused with words like "that is just the way they are, or we don't pay so and so any attention." This is far removed from the teaching of Scripture, which teaches that mankind is created in the image of God and is thus capable to choose and be responsible for those choices. While the church does have a responsibility to the individual, it also has a responsibility to the flock at large. These two are not in conflict but rather work in concert. The troublemaker should not be protected at the expense of everyone else. The church should bend over backwards to help an erring brother, but when he chooses to live by his choices over Christ's commands, he must also be allowed to live with the consequences of his choices.

The two societal influences that have affected the church's attitude concerning church discipline are determinism and individualism. Determinism places an undue emphasis upon the impact that various factors like biology, sociology, and psychology have upon behavior; thus influences become determinants. Consequently, the person is not held accountable for his actions because of the non-controllable determinants from his past or his biological makeup. As demonstrated in chapter 2, this undermines the very basis for the gospel, and if there is no gospel, then Christianity is just another man-made religion. As a matter of fact, the entire Bible must be categorically rejected if man is not self-determined. For if man is not self-determined,[101] he is a mere machine or animal, not culpable, and God is capricious and self-serving for treating him as though he is a free moral agent.

Individualism is an undue emphasis upon the individual. In American society, individual rights have trumped the idea of the common good. While there should not be an abuse of any human being or unalienable right because every human being is created in the image of God, neither should there be a trampling upon the common good since it is exponentially more evil than trampling upon the individual—as evil as that is. Abuse of the common good results in trampling on many individuals rather than one, all of which are created in God's image rather than one, and if it is wrong to abrogate individual rights, then it is all the more evil to abrogate the rights of a community of individuals. It also elevates the individual to an undeserving status of demigod. Evangelicalism, of which I am a part, has a strong emphasis upon the individual, which is known as pietism. This is in fact a strength of evangelicalism and characteristic of its biblical fidelity. However, the importance of the community, and our responsibility to each other, is a biblical truth that must be kept in balance with the truth concerning the importance of the individual; this is to avoid deification of the individual along with the degradation of the community. The New Testament teachings on spiritual gifts, communion, fellowship, teaching, ministering, corporate prayer, church discipline, caring for widows, the one another passages, the church, etc., all emphasize the cooperative nature of Christianity. This New Testament emphasis on community resoundingly declares that no Christian can honor God who is not actively involved in a local church.

Where determinism says you cannot hold the individual responsible for his actions, individualism—extreme pietism—says I am not accountable to anyone other than my self for my actions, and it is no one's business what I do as long as it just involves me or *consenting adults*. Unbridled individualism is an exaltation of subjectivism, which results in the elimination, or at least the marginalization, of objective truth and the community. Os Guinness warns, "Whenever evangelicals have an experience of direct, personal access to God, we are tempted to think or act as if we can dispense with doctrine, sacraments, history, and all the other 'superfluous paraphernalia' of the church—and make our experience the sum and soul of our faith."[102] But Jesus said, "Why do you call me Lord, Lord and do not the things which I say?" (Luke 6:46). The truth is, that with the loss of community go the loss of the church herself and the loss of Christianity.

The church will be penetrated by those who are Satan's messengers. While there are safeguards that help minimize the penetration, there is no way to preclude it entirely any more than Adam and Eve kept Satan out of the Garden of

Eden. Therefore, the church must exercise church discipline to remain a church and not become a social club. The Scripture warns, "a little leaven leavens the whole lump" (1 Corinthians 5:6). This warning must be heeded or the lump becomes so permeated with evil that it no longer desires purity enough to exercise discipline.

3 For Evangelism

Previously, we laid the groundwork for understanding that church discipline, the gospel, and the Great Commission are eternally and inextricably bound to one another. Without the clear and correct teaching on the *imago dei*, responsibility, and man's accountability, there simply is no need for a gospel that calls people to die to self (Matthew 16:24–25). Three specific and practical areas lay in peril because of the demise of church discipline in the local church.

Evangelism is the carrying out of the Great Commission as found in Matthew 28:18–20. This is the intentional and deliberate spreading of the gospel in order to see men and women accept Christ as Savior and Lord. In doing this, they become disciples and followers of Christ. We then teach them to follow Christ in all things, so that they will go out and teach others to follow Christ in all things. To be about this heavenly mandate with supernatural effectiveness, three things must be right in the church, and they are, at least in part, dependent upon church discipline. These three things are: purity of the local body, testimony of the church, and the perceived credibility of the Scripture.

First, the local church body must be pure although not perfect. The lack of purity, or concern for purity, in the local church not only limits the experience of supernatural power, but it also blurs spiritual vision and dulls passion. When sin is tolerated in the church, the church loses a clear sense of the seriousness of sin and its consequences. Sin may still be preached about, members may shake their heads in shame as they watch the world sink deeper into sin or hear the pastor chronicle more of the debauchery of our day, but something has happened. An inescapable corollary of the loss of church discipline is an ever decreasing real, as opposed to merely espoused, belief in the evilness of sin and existence of hell. The inevitability of this results from an intolerable incongruence that develops in the human mind when contradictory positions are embraced for the sake of appearance. The mind can only be deluded so far, and then it seeks congruency concerning thought and action. Someone well said that people live more consistently with what they really believe than they usually are willing to admit. When sin is said to be damning, an affront to God, and summoning the wrath of God, yet the church simultaneously refuses to deal with the sin in her midst, which everyone is painfully aware of, the mind soon realizes that it is important to espouse a belief in the sinfulness of sin, for whatever the reason, but it is not really real or something that warrants action at all costs. There are many contributors to lethargy in evangelism, but one of them is surely the lack of church discipline which says that sin is not that serious; and God is not that concerned with it. Evangelism is always a casualty of impurity in the church.

A pure body means a body of born again believers walking in obedience to the Scripture. The makeup of the average local church screams out, "We are not all saved." Without discipline to remove those who have not been saved, the church will never have a unified sacrificial passion to reach people with the gospel since many in the body have not seen the gospel as appealing enough to embrace it themselves. A substantive emphasis upon evangelism necessitates an equal emphasis upon purity. For if evangelism and the result of evangelism, which is salvation, are about anything, they are about holiness. God is seeking to bring men and women into a holy relationship with Him like Adam and Eve had in the garden prior to the fall. It is only a transformed life that will consistently desire to see other lives truly converted. Unless a person has experienced being born again, he cannot see the lostness of the world or the need for sacrificial evangelism. These people can infect a church, which results in evangelism becoming something that is done from the pulpit by a *professional*, or not done at all. Even Christians are susceptible to the temptations to avoid these spiritual endeavors. But when wolves in sheeps' clothing are among them, the susceptibility is immense.

Secondly, the public testimony of the church is also at stake. While it is possible for the gospel to be received from a church that is seen as corrupted, it is not likely or practical. When it does happen, it is the sheer grace of God and the reality that the person probably is not aware of the excessive hypocrisy of the church. How much damage has been done to the gospel by the exposed sin and hypocrisy of the church is only known by God. If we knew it, we probably could not handle it. For then we would be forced to stand face-to-face with spiritual carnage of gargantuan proportions and a hellish villain, and the villain is an unholy church. The world will always be hostile toward the church's message of holiness, but its justified disdain and ridicule comes from the church preaching the message of holiness while wallowing in sin.

The damage done by the fall of an internationally known television evangelist is not only far reaching, it is long-term, and for some eternally so. The godly pastors and Christians across America who seek to practice authentic Christianity three hundred and sixty five days a year will not be the model

196

the media replays; rather it will always be the one that most effectively characterizes hypocrisy, and this until it becomes etched upon the American soul. This may not be fair, but then again who promised that life would be fair; but it is reality. This should not cause despondency in the heart of the church but a greater quest for holiness.

Local scandals cause the same kind of damage, and although they lack the breadth of national scandals, the scars are equally as deep. People who live in a community where churches split over silliness and ignore members who practice the things that the lost are called on to repent of have little regard for the church, her message, and her Lord. At times, the lost have seen enough duplicity to vehemently determine to have nothing to do with the church. Often these thoughts are spoken loudly and repeatedly to anyone who will listen. Disappointingly, many churches consider their rejection of the gospel as the prima facie evidence of how gospel hardened they are, when in reality, they may in fact be more hypocrisy hardened than gospel hardened.

This is one of the reasons why we hear so much about the effectiveness of relational evangelism, small groups and the like. How many times have we heard a new convert say, "I never wanted anything to do with Christianity, and I thought everyone was a hypocrite. Then, I got to know some Christians and watched their lives and desired what they had." In this is found a wonderful truth. The only reason he desired what these believers had is because he was able to see what they had because they lived it. He did not witness perfection but authenticity. It usually takes Christians living up close with an unbeliever to convince them of the authenticity of Christianity and the truth.

When Christianity goes into a new area where they have not heard the gospel, people have to be convinced of the truthfulness of the gospel. Often throughout history, as is today, this resulted in a great outpouring of souls being saved. Although the credibility of the messenger is always important, when the gospel goes into uncharted waters, the credibility of the message is foremost in the mind of the hearer; because at this time, he probably does not know the messenger or enough about the message to be able to evaluate the messenger's fidelity to the message. However, an undisciplined church will eventually undermine its credibility as a messenger and with that, the reality of the message in the minds of the listeners. People will become hardened, but they are not necessarily hardened to the gospel per se, but to the hypocrisy of the church and the messenger. Actually, very few people have any problems with Jesus Christ. "Even Friedrich Nietzche, who pronounced the death of God and lamented the decadence of the church, spoke of Jesus as a model of the heroic."[103] In addition, Baruch Spinoza viewed Jesus as "the greatest and noblest of the prophets."[104] He believed "the ethics of Jesus are almost synonymous with wisdom: in reverencing him one rises to 'the intellectual love of God.'"[105] Voltaire "accepts gladly the theology of the Sermon on the Mount, and acclaims Jesus in tributes which could hardly be matched even with pages of saintly ecstasy."[106] "George Bernard Shaw, when critical of Jesus, could think of no higher standard than Christ Himself. He said of Jesus, 'There were times when he did not behave as a Christian.' We cannot miss the irony of Shaw's criticism."[107] These are words from some of the great infidels of history. That they did not recognize Him for who He really is is not the point being made. That knowledge does not come from man (Matthew 16:15–17). The point is that, on a human level, they are turned away from Christianity not by the Jesus of the Scripture, but by the Jesus Christ they see through the church which scorns discipline, coddles the carnal, and winks at its own hypocrisy while castigating the world for her sin. It is a long road back for churches that have lost their trustworthiness, but it is a road that must be traveled and is worth traveling.

The most vicious attacks and criticisms toward church discipline come from within the church. This is much of the basis of the world's bias against it. This is an appalling shame. Church discipline is not only misunderstood by the world, but it is also shamefully misrepresented by the contemporary church. If the church gave a unified voice in its support of biblical discipline, the external criticisms would be marginal.

A person can dislike your message but respect your conviction and consistency. There are liberals whom I respect because of their sheer honesty and forthrightness about their aberrant beliefs and goals, even while I loathe their adulterated message. They may be wolves among the sheep, but their disguise is exceedingly gauzy; and that is something to be thankful for. Their heresy is undeniable. We disrespect their views, but if they are honest about them, we can respect their honesty. The ones who deserve no respect are those who say one thing and act to the contrary. These elicit nothing but distrust. I must admit, from a phenomenological perspective, the world's hesitancy to bow before the words of Christ when they see the church refuse to bow before them makes sense to me. Maybe we should remind ourselves of the words of the Holy Spirit through Simon Peter, "For *it is* time for judgment to begin with the household of God; and if *it begins* with us first, what *will be* the outcome for those who do not obey the gospel of God?" (1 Peter 4:17).

This is not to say that we are seeking to please the world, far from it. We are seeking to please God and demonstrate to God, the world, and ourselves that we take our message seriously; then our call to repent will be substantiated by our obvious "fear of the Lord" (2 Corinthians 5:11, 1 Peter 2:17, Ephesians 5:21). It is a truism that once the message bearing entity loses its credibility, the validity of the message itself will eventually be called into question. It has been often and well stated that the reason the church is having so little influence upon the world is that the world is having so much influence upon the church. This seems to be true not only contemporaneously, but historically as well. When the church remained pure from the world's influence, she turned the world upside down. When she did not, the world turned the church upside down.

We cannot correct all of the distortions that the church has sent out about what the real nature of the gospel, the church, and the Word of God are, but we can work to see that reality in our own churches. It is possible that if enough churches followed church discipline, others would be encouraged to, and only God knows what He would do in response to that kind of courage and love for Him. By the way, obedience out of love is what God holds us responsible for, isn't it?

When discipline is first implemented, the immediate fallout may appear to be all negative. However, in time the church will benefit by pleasing God, and the credibility of the church and her message will experience a renaissance. This is not to say that everyone will then believe our message, but whether they believe it or not, they will know that we do. That is the assurance that is lacking today. It is obeying the really tough things that signal to the church and the world, but most importantly to God, that we take every word of God seriously. Inerrancy is not a theological abstraction existing in a vacuum disassociated from real life. Rather, it is a belief that has very practical and necessary corollaries. When the world sees the church living out her message in the exacting areas of Christianity, it may prove to soften the hearts of those who are now called gospel hardened—whom I believe, at least in part, are hypocrisy and disingenuousness hardened.

People, who are allowed membership in a church while living like the lost, inflict incalculable harm on evangelism, and we facilitate that unholy alliance by allowing it. We fail to sufficiently evangelize them by exercising discipline and thus confronting them with their sin, and concomitantly hurt the evangelization of everyone else by allowing them to undermine the credibility of the entire church.

For example, let us say a well-known lost man dies that we will call Bob, and a local preacher is called upon to preach his funeral. When he preaches, out of a misdirected compassion, he preaches as though Bob went to heaven. However, everyone knew the evil life he lived. Hence, the conclusion is clear to all who are present, whether they get it consciously or unconsciously, if a wicked sinner like Bob was a Christian, then we all must be Christians no matter how bad we live; thus, the gospel is undermined. Why would someone desire a message that calls him to "deny himself" and "take up his cross" (Luke 9:23) and yet receive the same eternity as his now deceased friend who lived like he wanted? Whether the message is corrupted by embracing evil in order to make it acceptable, or a church coddles evil in order to be perceived as more tolerable and in touch, both result in negating the cogency and perceived relevance of the gospel. An organization does not lose its credibility through the actions of a wayward member; this merely tarnishes the image. It is what the organization does in response to the member's aberrant behavior that determines whether the organization loses its credibility.

Third, closely tied to the testimony of the church is the perceived reliability or trustworthiness of Scripture. The Scripture is always reliable, but the perception of that reliability fluctuates rather significantly. Scripture claims many times and in many ways to be truth in its entirety, and given by God (John 17:17; 2 Timothy 3:16; Psalm 19:7–14). This being the case, man is not free to pick and choose which parts he will believe and obey without undermining all of it. You cannot minimize one part of Scripture without ultimately degrading the sufficiency of all Scripture. The church may invent creative ways that appear to justify skirting parts of God's message while embracing other parts, but she cannot do that without doing exactly what the world does and undermining the message of Scripture. The message of Scripture is not many messages each complete in and of itself, but it is one message: the message of redemption, which has many parts to it. Thus, God does not accept embracing one part without embracing the whole, for to do so is to abrogate the whole. One cannot merely embrace the Sermon on the Mount without embracing the totality of Scripture. For the well-loved Sermon on the Mount continuously points to man's need of redemption and the rest of Scripture.

The final words of Jesus are a warning against changing the Scripture, "I testify to everyone who hears the words of the prophecy of this book: if anyone adds to them, God will add to him the plagues which are written in this book; and if anyone takes away from the words of the book of this prophecy, God will take away his part from the tree of life and from the holy city, which are written in this book" (Revelation 22:18–19). A similar perversion is when portions of the Scripture are elevated, and the demanding sections are ignored.

It reminds me of people who profess to place themselves under the Mosaic law, as though we live under the old covenant, or that the new covenant is inadequate or incomplete and needs the old covenant to prop it up, which is clearly contrary to the teaching of Scripture. They emphasize the essentialness of keeping the law, condemn everyone who does not, and yet they actually only seek to practice part of the law. They take the aspects they want and leave the rest, and not unexpectedly, they leave the difficult. For example, they say we are under the law and are to keep the Sabbath. Thus, no labor is to be done on the Sabbath. However, they conveniently omit the penalty for violating the Sabbath, which was to put to death (Exodus 31:14). This leaves their message of the necessity of keeping the law severely handicapped since their life message is the essentialness of keeping *part* of the law, and apparently there is some discretion in which part of the law a person may choose to keep.

What makes the early church seem so stellar is not that they were perfect, or even had as much as we do, but that they sought to teach and live the gospel. What they knew, they were called on to live even at great personal cost. This is exactly what makes any Christian or church admirable. Granted, it is historically naive to believe that the early church had everything just right, but the Scripture is also clear about their great sacrifice to follow God. Before the world can be expected to take the message of Scripture seriously, the people of God must take it seriously. Then the world may disagree, and this they will surely do, but they will see that the Scripture is an indissoluble unit that cannot be approached cafeteria style. When the church willfully neglects certain teachings of Scripture, that life message of selective obedience is present and rivals the truth of the gospel every time it is shared. This reality is simple and automatic; if the Scripture, like the ones about church discipline or the ones which tie one's love for Christ inextricably to obeying His Word, can be ignored without consequence, then maybe the Scriptures that teach about repenting of sin, hell, and judgment can be handled the same way.

It is a grave error to assume that the lost do not make this association. The only time it is not made is when the selective obedience is unknown. However, history reminds us that the church's hypocrisy is always known by the world—even if it is embellished. Conversely, even the most ardent critics of Christianity have lauded those who exemplified true surrender to Christ. For Christians in America, the awareness of the media's insatiable appetite to expose the church's hypocrisy should behoove us to labor arduously for the church to live consistent to her message. Then we can say, "Do as I do" rather than "Don't do as I do, but do as I say." Then, we will have the power of God upon us and our message and life will be congruent, which always strengthens the message. Peter mandated this emphasis for early Christians, "Beloved, I urge you as aliens and strangers to abstain from fleshly lusts, which wage war against the soul. Keep your behavior excellent among the Gentiles, so that in the thing in which they slander you as evildoers, they may on account of your good deeds, as they observe *them,* glorify God in the day of visitation" (1 Peter 2:11–12).

The inevitable result of spiritualized relativism is the loss of desire for evangelism and credibility of the message and the messenger. The eternal result is the church failing at her primary mission of spreading the gospel and making disciples. This deontological loss leaves the church impotent and catapults her into an identity crises. An organization's lifespan is extremely short without a clear and valuable purpose. Thus, the church begins looking for herself in all the wrong places like social movements, faithism,[108] organizations, ecumenicism, political caucuses, etc.

Because this book is focused on discipline in general and church discipline in particular, most of the examples of disobedience relate to these two areas. This is not intended to elevate obedience in these areas beyond what they merit nor to de-emphasize the significance of disobedience in other areas. But since discipline is the topic of the book, it is used liberally as an example. However, I do believe that our response to the difficult areas like discipline tell us, and the world for that matter, more about our true surrender to Jesus Christ than obedience in the easier and less costly areas. I also believe that while discipline is not the only truth to be maintained, faithfulness to Christ cannot be fully realized without it.

4   To Glorify God

The objective of every Christian and every church is to glorify God. To fail to understand or accept this is to fail and to fail completely and comprehensively. Nothing can supplant this as both the immediate and ultimate objective of every Christian and church. "Whether, then, you eat or drink or whatever you do, do all to the glory of God." (1 Corinthians 10:31). One may even ponder that if even the most mundane of activities are to be done to the glory of God, how much more those things that are beautiful, noble, and eternal? This is ultimately why everything exists, including the church. The church is here not to be popular, or valued as relevant by a fallen and narcissistic society, nor even by the professing church, but to glorify God. This is the sum of our call. Rather than seeking the world's affirmation of the church's significance, "The object of the church is to see that the world acknowledges the glory which is God's (Romans 15:9) and is shown in his deeds (Acts 4:21), in his disciples (1 Corinthians

6:20) and above all in his Son, the Lord of glory (Romans 16:27)."[109] The simple truth is, when we obey God, in both the spirit and the letter, we honor Him, and when we don't, we dishonor Him. It is that simple. Jesus said it unambiguously, "why do you call me 'Lord, Lord' and do not the things which I say" (Luke 6:46). This passage speaks of the lost that really do not know Christ as Savior and Lord, demonstrated by the fact that they do not follow or obey Him. A corollary passage is 1 John 2:4 which reads, "The one who says, 'I have come to know Him,' and does not keep His commandments, is a liar, and the truth is not in him;" conversely, true believers are known by their obedience, "whoever keeps His word, in him the love of God has truly been perfected. By this we know that we are in Him" (1 John 2:5).

When we seek what He seeks, we honor Him. When we seek purity, to be like Him, and the lost to be saved, we honor Him. Holiness is one of the indispensable pursuits that flows out of a love for God; as Peter well said, "but like the Holy One who called you, be holy yourselves also in all *your* behavior; because it is written, 'You shall be holy, for I am holy'" (1 Peter 1:15–16). Since the glory of God is the peerless priority of all of our pursuits, one should ask what is glory, and what does it mean to glorify God? How does the church know if she is glorifying God or actually dishonoring Him? The following quotes should shed light on the meaning of this all-important concept. "In relation to God it denotes that which makes God impressive. Since God is invisible, it necessarily carries a reference to his self-manifestation. We find some instances of the meaning "splendor" (which merges into "honor" as in Isaiah 17:4), and the use of *doxa* for other Hebrew words for God's power (Isaiah 30:30; 40:26). The primary sense, then, is the divine glory that comes to expression in God's acts in creation and history. *Doxa* is the divine nature in its invisibility or its perceptible manifestation, as at the giving of the law, or in the tent or temple. God is the God or King of glory (Psalm 24:7 ff.; 29:3). To give him glory is not to impart something he does not have; but to acknowledge the honor that is his due (Isaiah 42)."[110] It is a term that means, "to express something that is absolutely objective, the reality of God."[111] "In God's case, his glory is his nature. The glory that God grants to rulers or to those who fear him is no more than power or dignity."[112] Man was created in the image of God and "the first man had a part in God's glory, and if this was lost at the fall, its restoration is the goal of salvation history (expositions of Daniel 12:3)."[113] Man, now fallen, still retains the image of God although it is corrupted.

"In the New Testament, giving God glory means acknowledging (Acts 12:23) or extolling (Luke 2:14) what is already a reality. New Testament doxologies, then, presuppose an is, *estin* (Galatians 1:5; 1 Peter 4:11). In the Old Testament the stress lies on seeing the divine *doxa* (Leviticus 9:6; Isaiah 6:1; 35:2). In the New Testament, however, the emphasis shifts to participation."[114] When man sinned he fell, and his fall made him come "short of the glory of God" (Romans 3:23). Redemption is the restoring of that glory. In the resurrection, "The righteous will shine, as in Daniel 12:3 (Matthew 13:43). The body is transformed in the resurrection into a body of glory (Philippians 3:21). We are glorified together with Christ (Romans 8:17; Colossians 1:27; 3:4). This is part of the parallelism of Christ's resurrection and ours. Participation in *doxa* is by participation in Christ. Eternal glory is the goal of our calling (1 Peter 5:10) but glory is to be revealed to us, and we are to enjoy the glorious liberty of the children of God (Romans 8:18, 21). What is sown in dishonor is raised in glory (1 Corinthians 15:43). Yet the future glory has its roots in the divine purpose and action, so that we may be said to be already glorified (Romans 8:29–30; 1 Corinthians 2):"[115]

Considering all of this, we can conclude that in one sense God is intrinsically glory. This is His ontology, and it can neither be increased nor diminished. It is who He is. He is "the King of glory" (Psalm 24:7). Glory cannot be given to God in the sense of adding to His nature. He is infinite and intrinsic glory. However, in another equally biblical sense we give God glory and are commanded to do so. "Ascribe to the LORD the glory due His name" (1 Chronicles 16:29). We give God glory, but not by increasing the glory of His nature since that is impossible because he is infinite glory. By giving God glory, we mean that we proclaim His glory to the world, or give Him praise, recognition, and honor for what only He can do. Thus, in this sense we glorify God. The only way man can glorify God is through obedience. We set His glory on display before the world by honoring Him through obedience of living in the glory that has already been given to us in Christ and in anticipation of the glory which shall be restored to us in the glorification (Romans 8:30).

Following Christ in willing obedience to all of His commands, including discipline, honors, glorifies, and pleases Him. It demonstrates our love, commitment, surrender, and supreme trust in Him. It says that we seek His glory above every accolade of man, comfort, security of the world, and tendency of selfism that arises from within man. We dare to follow. Conversely, we dishonor Him through disobedience, shying away from discipline, demonstrating our measured love, guarded commitment, conditional surrender, and limited trust in Him. This demonstrates that we bow to the accolade of man, the comfort and security of the world, and the passions of selfism. We dare not follow. No amount of rationalization or spiritualization will produce another reality. It is that simple.

5 As a Deterrent for Becoming Cavalier About Sin

As the old saying goes, "out of sight, out of mind." When an appropriate penalty is assigned to a wrong, it is not only inherently right and maintains the balance of justice, but it also heightens the awareness of the wrong and the wrongness of wrong. Conversely, the opposite has the contrasting effect. The lack of penalty, or sufficient penalty, not only violates justice, but it conceals the wrongness of the wrong. It desensitizes man's sense of justice. The human mind will normally conclude that the severity of the injustice is measured by the severity of the public outcry and punishment. Our laws, morals, and mores are even established along these lines. Seldom will every person who is a part of a particular culture understand the inherent injustice involved in a particular wrong that is committed. However, everyone associates a serious penalty with a serious crime. People who live on the edge of the law know full well where misdemeanors become felonies. There is an inherent tutorial aspect to all laws. The law speaks of the rightness or wrongness of an action, and the penalty bespeaks of the degree of seriousness of the violation. Consequently, the penalties attached to wrongs teach the wrongness of the wrong, keep the reality and cost of the wrong before the culture, and thus have a deterrent effect. This in turn, gives people an appreciation for doing right.

Either the church has forgotten that little truth, or she simply failed to grasp it, because she often seeks to live in a wonderland where she can declare to the world that sin is deadly serious, to be shunned and repented of, fleeing to Jesus as fast as you can; and yet sin within the camp goes without any penalty or consequence at all. Thus, the absence of discipline and penalty for the wrong undermines the message of the gospel to the world. If the paucity of examples of church discipline are any indicator, man does not need to fear that God will judge sin. The truth is that what we know by Scripture, the world also knows intuitively, that judgment must "begin at the household of God" (1 Peter 4:17). No organization can effectively call others to do what it does not do, at least not after the hypocrisy is known, for duplicity wins out over every message except simplicity—genuineness. The dominant life message of this age is *cheap grace*. The wonderland mentality says that penalties for wrongs, at least in the church, runs people away and tolerance draws them in; but shouldn't we take notice that, in the age of the greatest tolerance of the American church, we see what most have had to accept as the final tolerance is the tolerance of empty buildings. When it does not mean anything to be a member, it simply does not mean anything to be a member. The church's wonderland is becoming increasingly empty and unchristian. Because everyone knows, if the wrong is serious, there must be a consequence, and if there is no consequence, then the wrong may just as well be a right.

Only the sick "need a physician" (Luke 5:31). However, if our sicknesses have no symptoms, then sickness is not so bad and we will not seek a physician. Technically, being sick never bothered me, but I have found the symptoms of sickness to be most miserable. Without symptoms, one will not seek a physician or a cure; for one will not even know he is sick, which clearly demonstrates that without symptoms, sickness has no terror. Equally as clear is sinners, in part, know they are sinning because of the penalties; without penalties and consequences, wrongs are nearly indistinguishable from rights—at least on a phenomenological level, and that is where most people live. As far as distinguishing right from wrong, the penalties serve the same relationship to right and wrong as symptoms do with health and sickness.

210

When a church embarks on the path of church discipline, she finds herself alone, sometimes profoundly alone. The pastor begins by looking for books on the subject, and finds that they are as sparse as ducks in the desert; for there is no room for them on the bookstore shelf unless we commit the appalling act of de-shelving the overflow of self-help books. The pastor then seeks to talk to other pastors who successfully practice church discipline. He finds that a meeting with of all of them could be held in a phone booth. This must change. I pray that it will. If you understand the lateness of the hour for America, the chasm between the contemporary western church and holiness, then weep over and pray for the church, and lead out with courage.

The presence of church discipline precludes the potential for the church to ignore and/or become cavalier about sin. Without the consequence of sin, sin loses its perceived sinfulness. Sadly, knowing that there are behaviors and sins that can result in the removal of a *believer* from the fellowship of believers is, to most, beyond the pale of compassion and reason. People who have never seen discipline practiced before have concluded *a priori* that it must be cold and harsh. If this *a priori* rejection can be surmounted, and they walk through this pursuit of love and holiness called church discipline; sin will become more sinful and holiness more priceless to them. The mere process of walking through church discipline will heighten their understanding of the evilness of evil and the meaning of holiness more than years of holiness conferences; this is not intended to minimize the importance of conferences which emphasize holiness. Holiness to most people means loving Jesus, not murdering or stealing—excluding justified thefts from evil people like the IRS—or cursing at people, and sin means *dysfunctions*, biological determinants, and what other people do. When in reality, sin is actually not doing what

God says to do both in letter and spirit, and holiness is walking in intimacy with God according to His Word.

I recall a member of my former church, who said, "If I am ever going to start living in sin, I will join another church first because I don't think I could handle being disciplined." A nonchalant attitude about sin is inevitable if there are no consequences for sin. The church that practices discipline will be more keenly aware of sin in the church, the world, and their own life.

Church discipline makes purity and holiness something very real and relevant to everyday life rather than a mere sermonic anecdote. While purity and holiness are abstract terms, church discipline makes them become very concrete, which allows even the youngest of Christians or simplest of minds to understand holiness enough to seriously pursue it. Although all believers experience sin firsthand, without church discipline, the seriousness of it within the body of believers remains abstract. It is similar to the difference between knowing that we are going to die, and then coming to the brink of death with a life threatening accident or disease. The latter makes the awareness far more concrete, and normally has a marked influence on the individual. Facing it head on increases the perceived reality of it. The abstract becomes the concrete; the potential becomes the actual, and consequently, is felt acutely. It seems obvious that the church is not serious about the seriousness of sin and holiness or else she would see church discipline as the blessed grace that it is. Anyone who practices church discipline knows that the church at large sees discipline, and anyone who pursues it, as many things but blessed is not one of them.

6 To Prevent the Judgment of God

Church discipline is a means of preventing a more serious discipline from the Lord being inflicted upon the wayward Christian or church. God disciplines every true believer (Hebrews 12:4–11). The severity of that discipline varies. It may be disciplining in the sense of training. If there is sin in the life of the believer, then it will be according to the sin and the believer's willingness to deal with it. The church's discipline of its wayward members may help to avert the more serious, direct discipline of the Lord. For church discipline is the exercise of the Lord's discipline through His church.

There are illustrations in the New Testament of the Lord's discipline coming upon a church or person because the church was not disciplining herself. For example, the Corinthians were abusing the Lord's Supper—along with everything else; at least they were consistent, albeit consistently wrong. Because of that abuse, and their unwillingness to deal with it, God had to discipline many of them. The Holy Spirit says to them through the apostle Paul, "Therefore whoever eats the bread or drinks the cup of the Lord in an unworthy manner, shall be guilty of the body and the blood of the Lord. But a man must examine himself, and in so doing he is to eat of the bread and drink of the cup. For he who eats and drinks, eats and drinks judgment to himself if he does not judge the body rightly. For this reason many among you are weak and sick, and a number sleep. But if we judged ourselves rightly, we would not be judged. But when we are judged, we are disciplined by the Lord so that we will not be condemned along with the world" (1 Corinthians 11:27–32).

Apparently, the Corinthians were very open-minded, allowing for full expression and self-actualization. This problem is evident in chapter 5 as well. They knew that their brothers and sisters were sinning, but they did not love God or them enough to confront them. Consequently, God had to implement direct divine discipline, which apparently is far more severe than the discipline the church would have invoked since some of them died—sleep is a euphemism for the death of believers. I believe God still does this when the church fails to exercise church discipline. Individuals who are truly God's children and live in rebellion do suffer His discipline. The writer of Hebrews reminds us "For those whom the Lord loves He disciplines, And He scourges every son whom He receives. But if you are without discipline, of which all have become partakers, then you are illegitimate children and not sons." (Hebrews 12:6,8). The reason some can live like the devil and not suffer the discipline of the Lord is because they do not belong to the Lord, which is all the more reason to remove them. If they are believers, church discipline allows God to use Satan as an instrument to bring His people to repentance. This remedial aspect of church discipline is seen clearly in 1 Timothy 1:20, where Paul speaks of "Hymenaeus and Alexander, whom I have handed over to Satan, *so that they will be taught not to blaspheme*" (italics added).

When the church exercises discipline, she is offering an opportunity for the disciplined to repent and avoid the experience of more severe divine discipline. Again, contrary to the popular misconception, we see church discipline as a very loving thing. George Davis says regarding this, "Church discipline must be seen as only one aspect of God's overall design that His people be a disciplined people. A logical progression exists in the matter of discipline: (1) parental discipline, (2) self-discipline, (3) corporate or church discipline, and (4) divine discipline. A breakdown in any one of the first three will result in a demonstration of the fourth. Church discipline, then, is designed to reclaim a wayward believer before divine discipline becomes necessary."[116] I would add to that the potential danger of suffering governmental discipline. How many people are in prison for breaking the law, sometimes habitually, who claim to be Christians and are members of some church, probably in good standing? It would be telling, and potentially very depressing, to find out how many of these have ever experienced any church discipline.

We will never know how many may have avoided prison if their church had practiced discipline, or how many would have come to Christ if their church had disciplined them when they broke the law, but it seems safe to presume that more would have than without it. We do know that the perceived trustworthiness of the gospel and the church's credibility would have been greater before the eyes of the world. Once again, we see the gospel appearing emaciated because of the lack of church discipline.

We had a young man in my former church that was found guilty of a crime in a different state. This prohibited our going personally to him or him coming to the church. Therefore, we followed the teaching of discipline via letter. We wrote him a letter that described our love for him and brokenness over what he had done. Then the letter explained the biblical teaching on what is expected of a church member, and since he had let God, the church, and the testimony of Christ be dishonored, he needed to repent of what he had done, and ask for the church's forgiveness by letter. If he did, and if this was followed by seeking to live for the Lord as reported to us by the chaplain; we would forgive, love, and support him during his time in prison. Thankfully, he did repent and seek to live for the Lord. Later he was transferred to a prison in the state, and I was able to visit him. Neither distance, nor prison, nor any other circumstance should deter us from following Jesus.

If the church fails to discipline individual members, the church not only opens them up to divine discipline, but she opens the whole church up to the displeasure and discipline of the Lord since the nature of sin is to spread, gain respectability, and acquire as many adherents as it can (1 Corinthians 5:6). The seven churches of Revelation chapters 2 and 3 provide lucid illustrations of this truth. Each of these churches demonstrates a different problem and situation. For example, the church at Ephesus was called on to repent or lose her true nature as a church, "Therefore remember from where you have fallen, and repent and do the deeds you did at first; or else I am coming to you and will remove your lampstand out of its place—unless you repent" (Revelation 2:5). The lampstand is defined in Revelation 1:20 as the church. If the Ephesians' church did not repent, the discipline of the Lord would culminate in the church being removed. This either means the church in its entirety—people, building, services, etc.—will cease to exist, or the building, services, and many of the outward functions of the church will go on unabated, but Christ, the essence of the church, will have removed Himself. This means His person, power, and presence would be removed, but the externals would go on as usual. How many churches hang on this precipice today. How many have been at that crossroad in the past, and then called a liberal or ungodly pastor, or called a godly man who sought to lead them to fall in love with Christ again only to be hated or maligned. They are still meeting, singing, and giving talks, but Jesus no longer meets with them. They have lost their church and are no longer representatives of Christ in the world; only vast cisterns of religious activities to catch and hold the world's rubbish. Dr. Barnes says, "The meaning is, that the church gave light in Ephesus; and that what he would do in regard to that place would be like removing a lamp, and leaving a place in darkness. The expression, *'I will . . . remove your lampstand from its place,'* is equivalent to saying that the church there would cease to exist."[117] "The church continued and was later the scene of a major church council, but after the 5th century both the church and the city declined. The immediate area has been uninhabited since the 14th century."[118]

The church of Pergamum had apparently tolerated sin so long that it was in danger of Christ bringing swift and severe judgment, "Therefore repent; or else I am coming to you quickly, and I will make war against them with the sword of My mouth" (Revelation 2:16). This church and churches like the Corinthian church make it clear that God disciplines churches that do not discipline members. This alone should encourage any pastor to lead his church to practice discipline and lead his church back to holiness unless there is an unspoken distrust in the Scripture.

There are actually two other great lessons concerning the issue of discipline in Revelation chapters 2 and 3. This is only seen when the churches are viewed as a whole. Of the seven churches, there are two that received no condemnation: Smyrna and Philadelphia. These two churches were faithful to follow Christ, unwilling to compromise in the face of danger, and devoted to fulfill the Great Commission. The other five received some condemnation from the Lord, and there is actually a progression from unhealthy to rancid and repulsive. First, Ephesus is condemned for "leaving your first love" (Revelation 2:4). Christ was no longer the center of worship, doctrine, choices, and motivations. They were still Christians and by most standards a great church. They were persevering, and they would not tolerate false doctrine; but they had left their love for Jesus, His truth and His ways.

Second, Pergamum was characterized by tolerating the false teaching of Balaam. Third, Thyatira was characterized by accepting the false teaching of Jezebel and immorality. The acceptance of false teaching always eventuates in accepting or tolerating sin, tradition over the Word, immorality, and every sort of God disgracing deviation. However, embracing aberrant teaching begins with not maintaining the priority of the church, which is loving Jesus. If Jesus is not the love of the church, before long His Word will fall into disfavor as well—at least the difficult parts.

Fourth, this declension leads to the state of the church of Sardis. He said of her, "you have a name that you are alive, but you are dead." (Revelation 3:1). This is the state of many churches today. There is no life, and yet they claim to represent the resurrected living Lord; there is only spiritual darkness, and yet they claim to represent the light of the world. Notice that it did not happen in one step or one day. Most churches are born out of a revival of loving Christ and His Word. In time, they can become focused on other things rather than loving Jesus, which is characterized by keeping His Word. Then aberrant doctrine is tolerated, accepted, and embraced along with a declining moral standard; then they feed upon this spiritual arsenic, and soon they are dead. It is a dark place indeed when the light of the church no longer shines.

False doctrine begins with what I have designated as non-functional inerrancy. This is the idea that believing the right thing is sufficient to please God in contrast to believing and doing the right thing. For example, a non-functional inerrantist may believe, or ostensibly believe, that abortion is wrong, but they do very little if anything about it; they may say that purity is important but do not work to pursue it or lead a church to. The same could be said in many other areas. They agree with the teaching of the Scripture, at least ostensibly, but they always find an excuse for not actually obeying. Non-functional inerrancy is the first and somewhat subtle slip toward overt rebellion against the teaching of the Scripture. This slip begins with a loss of zeal for the greatest commandment, "'You shall love the Lord your God with all your heart, and with all your soul, and with all your mind.' This is the great and foremost commandment" (Matthew 22:37–38).

Once this is abandoned, and the abandonment begins in the privacy of one's own heart and also in the very heart of a church, it will shortly be followed by viewing false doctrines that were once abhorred as tolerable, then within acceptable limits, and finally normal. A church does not have to become a den of flaming liberals to become a dead church. There are many churches that are, as the old saying goes, "Straight as a gun barrel and empty as one too." If nothing is done to revive the dead church, she will continue the dreadful move toward the fifth and final phase of decline, that of the Laodicean church. The Laodicean church is the church that is not the church. The devolution is complete. The lampstand is gone. The church is enshrouded in a veil of darkness and spiritual death. Christ is on the outside of this church.

Some interpret the verses describing this church as meaning that this church was merely a materialistic church but still a church. I do not think that understanding takes into account the extreme severity of the language. What the Pharisees were to Israel, the Laodiceans are to the church. Their spiritual condition as delineated in Revelation 3:14–22 belies the possibility of being Christian. They are lukewarm verse 16; self-deceived and deceiving verse 17, and Christ is on the outside verse 20; the statement in verse 17, "you say, "I am rich, and have become wealthy, and have need of nothing" are not the words of even the most carnal believer. Christians know that they need Christ even if they do not pursue Him as they should. Further, Christ is never on the outside of His church or a believer's heart.

Following are the reasons given for understanding this to be an authentic church: being lukewarm is considered to refer to being backslidden. This is derived from viewing the Laodiceans as saved (hot) and then becoming worldly (cold), and thus they become lukewarm. But that is not the only way of arriving at lukewarm. You can take hot water and add cold, as the former interpretation concludes. However, you can also take cold water (spiritual death) and add hot (religion) to obtain lukewarm. In this scenario, the people, or the bulk of the people, who made up the Laodicean church at the time of this writing, were not truly born again. They were lost and had clothed themselves in the garb of religion. History is all too familiar with stories of churches that began with a heart full of love for Jesus and ended with a building full of people who did not know Jesus. Understanding this church as religious but not saved fits far better with what Christ threatens to do with them, "I will spit you out of my mouth" verse 16. The word spit means to vomit. This false church so nauseates Christ that He becomes sick and violently expels them. This threat would never be made by our Lord about one of His churches full of His people whom He promised, "lo, I am with you always, even to the end of the age" (Matthew 28:20). To make this anything but a revolting upchucking of that which is nauseating, never to take it back in again, is to miss the whole thrust of the imagery of vomiting them out. For no one redigests his own vomit except a dog.

Some see this as speaking to believers when it says in verse 19, "Those whom I love, I reprove and discipline; therefore be zealous and repent." Two things need to be noted. First, God loves even the lost (John 3:16) and seeks to bring them to repentance, through reproof, conviction, and discipline (John 16:8). The same Greek word *eleycho*, translated reprove in Revelation 3:19 is translated convict in John 16:8. Therefore,

God reproves both the saved and the lost. It is also notable that the word translated love here is not from the Greek word *agape* but *phileo* in contrast to Hebrews 12:6, which uses *agape*.

As the chronological order of these churches and order of aberrations are looked at holistically, there is an evident progression in the decline of a church. It begins with a waning love for Christ supremely, second, doctrinal errors are tolerated, third, doctrinal errors are embraced along with their corollary immoralities, and fourth, the church moves into the mortuary phase of being a church of the living dead. If there is not a revival, either front or rear door, the church will eventually lose all of the really saved people, or so many that their presence is virtually undetectable, and the church will become a phantom church. This phantom calls herself a church and appears outwardly to the unspiritual eye to be a church, but it is merely a phantom, a hideous damning phantom. The loss of love for Christ necessarily leads to a loss of love for His Word, which eventuates in following after the world until the church is engulfed by the world. The loss of love for Christ and His Word results in an unwillingness to exercise discipline, which ultimately and necessarily leads to dead churches like Sardis and non-churches like Laodicea. The devolution of a church from a place of resurrection life to a place of rancidness, rigor mortis, and death is an insidious process, not an earth-shaking event. The length of time, sometimes decades, that it takes for this to happen, all the while maintaining the shell of a church, serves as a potent ingredient for intensifying the deception necessary for a church to complete the downward spiral to the cesspool of Laodicea. This makes the passageway even more alluring and devious.

For a church to use her experience to determine her spiritual health is an inherently flawed determiner certain to per-

petuate the milieu of deception because as the church de-
clines, so does her ability to detect sin and spiritual disease.
Her evaluative acumen is as corrupted as her experience as a
church. When a church evaluates herself by herself, or other
churches that may be going in the same direction, she loses
the ability to detect the decline because the measuring rod
and the church are declining concomitantly or in tandem.
Thus, the descent becomes imperceptible. The only sufficient
measuring rod is the Scripture and that alone.

In light of this terrible future that looms portentously before every church that embraces a genre of neo-tolerance,
which is merely old-fashioned disobedience, church discipline
radiates with compassion and love for God, the church, and
lost man. Conversely, after the alluring glow of neo-holiness,
which does not require church discipline or even allow it, begins to fade under the thickening cloud cast by the ever increasing and demanding presence of sin, the lack of discipline
is seen to be the cruel insatiable tyrant that it is; a tyrant that
is not satiated by anything less than Laodicea. The warning
that must be heeded by all is, as Christ stood on the outside of
the church of Laodicea knocking to get in, so the spirit of
Laodicea stands just outside every church seeking to get in.

7 To Restore Genuine Freedom to the Church

Discipline is liberating and the lack thereof is bondage. An
Olympian can do what most people only dream about because
he has disciplined himself. The freedom that a champion ex-
hibits while performing is, in large part, the result of discipline. The church that is truly free to be what God wants her
to be is the church that exercises discipline. We have exchanged a disciplined body of believers walking in spiritual
freedom for libertarianism cloaked in Christian clichés,

wherein carnality is normalized and the church sports a spiritual Epicureanism. Then again, maybe it is not so spiritual. Further, it is an undeniable reality that the normalization of carnality in the church will ultimately result in carnality in the leadership of the church. Then, when God does send a man of God to shepherd His flock, the vision from God for the church is squelched; the man of God is undermined, and so shall it forever be until discipline is reclaimed as an integral part of a loving and faithful church. The incident recorded in Acts 5:1–11 concerning Ananias and Sapphira gives a vivid picture of the place of holiness and discipline in the early church; and how the presence of sin is what destroyed the unity of the church, and the expulsion of it resulted in immediate unity.

The Scripture says, "But a certain man named Ananias, with his wife Sapphira, sold a piece of property, and kept back *some* of the price for himself, with his wife's full knowledge, and bringing a portion of it, he laid it at the apostles' feet. But Peter said, 'Ananias, why has Satan filled your heart to lie to the Holy Spirit, and to keep back *some* of the price of the land? While it remained *unsold,* did it not remain your own? And after it was sold, was it not under your control? Why is it that you have conceived this deed in your heart? You have not lied to men, but to God.' As he heard these words, Ananias fell down and breathed his last; and great fear came upon all who heard of it. And the young men arose and covered him up, and after carrying him out, they buried him. Now there elapsed an interval of about three hours, and his wife came in, not knowing what had happened. And Peter responded to her, 'Tell me whether you sold the land for such and such a price?' And she said, 'Yes, that was the price.'" Then Peter *said* to her, 'Why is it that you have agreed together to put the Spirit of the Lord to the test? Behold, the feet of those who have buried your husband are at the door, and they shall carry you out *as well*.' And she fell immediately at his feet, and breathed her last; and the young men came in and found her dead, and they carried her out and buried her beside her husband. And great fear came upon the whole church, and upon all who heard of these things" (Acts 5:1–11).

To summarize the event, Ananias and his wife Sapphira had sold some land and chosen to give some of the proceeds to the church. This would have been fine and no sin would have been involved. They then decided to claim to give more of it than they actually did, apparently desirous to be seen as very committed, generous, and sacrificial and to receive the praise of the church. This hypocrisy is what brought about the confrontation with Simon Peter and the judgment of God, which resulted in their deaths. Peter encapsulated their sin in two statements, "Ananias, why has Satan filled your heart to lie to the Holy Spirit," and "Why is it that you have agreed together to put the Spirit of the Lord to the test?" (verses 3 and 9 respectively). They lied to God and put Him to the test, which means that they tested the limits of God to see just what they could get away with before God did something; they presumed on the grace of God. In promoting themselves, they were in effect saying what we are doing is not too bad, but is actually good and God should not judge us because we have helped the church. Apparently, Peter either had the gift of discernment or God revealed to him what they had done. Regardless how he came to know about the sin, when he did learn of it, he dealt with it immediately and decisively. Notice that this was not a brother or sister slipping into sin; if that were the case, Galatians 6:1–2 would have prevailed. This is someone knowingly and willingly using the church for his own ends; that demands immediate and decisive action. They were actually sowing the seeds of destruction of the church, because "a little leaven leavens the whole lump" (Galatians 5:9). They were destroying the purity, unity, and testimony of the church and thereby curtailing the power of God in and through them.

This is precisely the same scenario today. People seek to use the church for their own ends: recognition, comfort, social fulfillment, status, business, ad infinitum, and when they are allowed to get away with it, they chip away at the true unity, purity, testimony, and nature of the body of Christ.

When Ananias and Sapphira were removed from the church, the unity, purity, and testimony of the church immediately came back. The awesome display of God's holiness caused people to view the church with fear and reverence; "great fear came upon the whole church, and upon all who heard of these things" (verse 11). The unity also came back to the early church, and so it will in the local church today. The church was born in unity as described in chapters 1 and 2 of Acts. Unity is not something that had to be conjured up or added later to the church—nor can it be. It is a part of the ontology of the church. It is a repeatedly stated characteristic of the early church (Acts 1:14, 2:46, 4:24, 5:12, 6:5, 12:20, 15:25). This is why Paul says, "being diligent to *preserve* the unity of the Spirit in the bond of peace." (Ephesians 4:3, italics added) The church does not need to, nor can she, create unity, she only needs to maintain it. This is a vital point in understanding the irreplaceable role that church discipline plays in the life of the church. The unity of a local church is given by Christ and is intrinsic to the church, but it can be corrupted, distorted, or disrupted. However, it cannot be created by the church or anyone else, nor does it ever need to be. It is the church's responsibility to preserve the unity of the church, and a vital and indispensable component in effecting that is church discipline. Without church discipline, real spiritual unity is impossible to maintain, and in most cases it is

225

not even understandable because if the counterfeit is all a person has ever experienced, it will be difficult to detect it as such apart from a thorough knowledge of the Scripture. The unity that the church had enjoyed since its inception was still present just before this incident of disunity (4:24); then, the presence of impurity brought the corollary disunity, but immediately after the sin was expelled from the body; the unity returned (5:12). The reason that churches are so disunified when there is an attempt to practice authentic Christianity is because sin has never sufficiently been dealt with before.

The pursuit and experience of unity comes about by having a thorough understanding of and experience in practicing Philippians 2:1–11. Without going into a long exposition of this passage (which is the only kind of exposition this passage deserves because of its profound richness, meaning, and depth), let me say the Philippians, although a very good church, had some disunity within the fellowship, and this is Paul's prescription to deal with it. This passage is intensely Christological and theological, but the purpose of the passage is to guide the church to walk in unity. The presentation of Christ as Holy God (6a), Humbled Servant (6b–8), and Honored Savior (9–11) is to call the church to a life of humility (1–5). These verses contain the most moving and profound example of humility that can be found in time and eternity. This humility is to characterize the church. "Have this attitude in yourselves which was also in Christ Jesus" (verse 5). This attitude caused God, very God, to come and die for us. If this attitude prevailed in Christian's lives today, there would only be disunity when an Annanis or Sapphira slipped in; and they would be dealt with quickly for the sake of salvation.

In Acts chapter 5, when Ananias and Sapphira brought corruption into the church, it had to be dealt with if the unity of the body was going to be preserved. Therefore, they were exposed and dealt with decisively because God commands it, and because no individual or group of individuals is more important than the unity of the body. It is a confused, theological quantum leap from the New Testament's teaching on unity to the modern church's understanding of unity, which revolves around an idea that results in sanctioning, not dealing with, the sinful person. This convoluted idea was birthed in the pit of hell because it was clearly not birthed in the Scripture or by the Holy Spirit. When Ananias and Sapphira and their sin were removed, the restoration of unity was immediate "and they were all with one accord . . ." (verse 12). This passage gives a clear example of how the unity given by the Holy Spirit is disrupted and how to restore it again. It is an example of "preserving the unity of the Spirit" rather than trying to create it. It is clear from this passage that church discipline is not the cause of disunity in our churches, but rather the cause of disunity is the lack of church discipline. The lack of church discipline results in the lack of salubrity.

If a pastor seeks to lead his church to practice church discipline when they have never practiced it before, he will experience some disunity; in actuality the disunity has been there all along, and it will inevitably be manifested at some time whether it is at the time of church discipline or the implementation of some other biblical idea. This reality will become evident after the honeymoon is over. It either manifests itself by fighting, retarding the church's spiritual direction and desires, or by bringing about disunity. Unity is not as elusive as one might think based on experiences with the contemporary church; but unity will always elude the church's attempt to create it because real unity is not created but maintained. The truth is, the unity of the church is given by God at the beginning; it is a part of the church's ontology—essence (Acts 1:14; 1 Corinthians 12:13), and it is disrupted when sin comes in (Acts 5:1–11; 1 Corinthians 5:6). Once unity is replaced with disunity, disunity remains until the sin is dealt with (Matthew 18:15–20; 1 Corinthians 5:7; Acts 5:12), which requires the attitude of Christ (Philippians 2:5; 1 Corinthians 5:2,6).

Biblical unity is not just everyone getting along, or even everyone having the same mind on a particular issue or direction. Biblical unity is evident when the church is in one accord in following the words of our Lord Jesus Christ, the head of the church, in everything He said. Disunity is evidenced by the church's unwillingness to follow Him in everything He said. A group of lost people can be unified in opinions, directions, selection of candidates, etc., but they will not be willing to follow Jesus. A church that is immersed in a cesspool of carnality may very well be unified in their love of snorkeling around every Lord's Day, but if they will not follow the teaching of the Lord, they are biblically disunified. The more a church will follow Christ with one heart, the more unified she really is, but mere agreement on ignoring certain aspects of Scripture for the sake of unity is not unity but disunity and a cheap facade. To lead a church from equating unity with merely everyone being in agreement on certain issues or having good friendships in the church, to biblical unity, which means one accord in following Jesus, takes time, prayer, teaching, finesse, courage, and fellowship.

The church's ineffectiveness and impotence are directly related to the lack of church discipline; although this is not the only factor in the equation, it is a significant one. Pastors are well aware of the otherwise unexplainable problems they face in seeking to lead a church to really be a praying, teaching, discipling, and evangelizing church. It is bewildering to teach a church something that is undeniably biblical, which even they agree with, and then watch people oppose it. Of course, this apathy or rebellion against following the Scripture into uncomfortable areas comes on the heels of the last chorus of "O, How I Love Jesus" and "Wherever He leads I'll Go." This paradox doesn't make sense until you factor in the absence of church discipline, which eventuates in an environment conducive to the presence of the natural desires of non-Christians and carnal Christians, and the loss of passion for knowing and following Christ. That anyone would be against deacons having to come to church regularly—and I don't mean being regular at just the Sunday morning services, Christmas, or Easter services—be involved in following and assisting the pastor, prayer ministries outreach, or the church loving erring brothers enough to deal with them as prescribed by Jesus, is inexplicable unless they are carnal or lost. Yet, this goes on in local churches every day in America, and the backlash of leading a church to follow all of Scripture can be of gargantuan proportion.

Disunity never travels alone. When disunity is accepted, its corollaries of peacelessness, spiritual impotence, and spiritual retardation are also accepted, regardless of whether this is fully realized at first or not. When discipline is absent, the ability to disciple, evangelize, and emphasize other spiritual disciplines is severely handicapped. Therefore, discipline liberates the church to be the church.

Jay Adams refers to the liberating dimension of church discipline as preventive discipline because it maintains an atmosphere of good order, which is necessary for the church to be the church. He says, "Where there is righteousness (good order, in conformity with God's requirements and truth), there is peace, where there is peace, learning can take place. And when discipline is intact, God's name is honored, His church grows, and offenders against God and His righteousness are reclaimed in repentance. That is what discipline is all about."[119] He further states, "The positive effects of good order, peace, and purity in the church . . . promote the glory of God."[120] "Too often discipline is thought of only in a remedial sense; its promotional and preventive aspects are unrecognized or ignored. In most minds today, discipline means 'the way you get rid of troublemakers.'"[121] To fully appreciate church discipline, it is crucial to see it in all of its varied levels and forms, and all that it does for the good of the kingdom, the local church, and the individual believer.

Adams ties this together quite well.

"Preventive discipline, the promotion of good order and true belief, is both the formal responsibility of the leadership of the church—such as the elders, the pastor-teacher, and the deacons—and the informal responsibility of all of the members of the church. Ephesians 4:11–12 makes that clear. The leadership exists to build up the members in their faith and to help them discover, develop, and deploy their gifts for mutual ministry among themselves, so that the whole body builds itself up into the stature of Christ. All the 'one another' passages (e.g., Hebrews 10:24–25; Colossians 3:16), in which believers are exhorted to assist one another in various ways according to their gifts and their loving concern for each other, stress the informal aspects of positive, preventive discipline. It is good order, for instance, to love and do fine deeds; and it is informal preventive discipline for believers to 'stimulate one another' to love and do fine deeds (Hebrews 10:24). It is good order when believers regularly attend the meetings of the body; it is good informal discipline when they encourage others to faithful attendance (Hebrews 10:25). These are concrete examples of preventive, positive discipline. But the encouragement of one believer by another to good works does

not make the headlines the way that the excommunication of a gay song leader does."[122]

Peace creates an environment conducive for growth. Peace,
not just the absence of conflict, but the real peace of God that
desires holiness and is content in Him. Conversely, the absence of peace drains time, thought, and heart, and spiritual
growth is held hostage by unbridled carnality.

8 To Avoid the Fallout from Not Practicing Church Discipline

The would-be Olympian will only be a would-be with out
discipline. Like the undisciplined athlete who loses the gold
because of a lack of discipline, the undisciplined church loses
the "gold, silver and precious stones" and settles for the taw-
dry gilded icons of plaques for mere numerical growth, and
the ascending smoke from note burnings—the new burnt offering with a less than sweet savor. If these are attained by de-
emphasizing holiness, then they are mere "wood, hay, and
stubble" (1 Corinthians 3:12).

When you look at how God handled lying in Acts chapter
5, those who cause division in Romans 16:17, immorality in 1
Corinthians 5, heresy in 1 Timothy 1:19 and Galatians, you
have to be concerned over the dwindling similarity between
the early church and the contemporary church. The Scripture says that the early church turned the world upside down,
which is enormously convicting for the contemporary church
that can barely chronicle the decline of contemporary western culture much less turn it upside down. Does anyone truly
believe that a new strategy will emerge that will be able to
resurrect the vast majority of western churches? Could it be
that we have lost the holiness that enveloped the early church,

and with that the power of God? Could it be? If so, we should weep for our churches and our own cowardice.

It is common knowledge that new churches grow faster than old churches. We are told, and most have seen firsthand, that when most churches get established, they will cease to grow. The reasons given for this catatonic state are normally things like they become too bureaucratic or traditional, or they lose their vision. Consequently, we are told that we cannot depend on most older churches to reach our country and our world. If this is true, we are in serious trouble. Not only have we lost most of the established churches as resources for reaching the world, but also there is an ominous cloud of fate looming over every new church start. Thus whatever she does, she must do quickly because she also is headed toward that same gloomy state of stasis.

While I agree that churches, as well as small groups, tend to grow more when they are new than when they come of age, I also agree that much of this is attributable to factors such as premature satisfaction, bureaucracy, or traditionalism. It can also be attributed to demographic stagnation, facility limitations, and area saturation. However, I am unwilling to accept that most of the mature churches have to come to the point where they cease to grow through effective evangelism and discipleship. There simply is no biblical reason that necessitates this eventuality. While recognizing the aforementioned contributors, it still must be asked why tradition, bureaucracy, and pre-mature satisfaction are allowed to become so prominent as to trump Scripture. It seems that the most plausible answer must be that at some point sin became more tolerated, and with that tolerance came a concomitant loss of zeal for the Lord, holiness, and the things of the Lord. The difference between an old church and a new church is sin, which is at first shunned, is later minimized, then normalized or ignored. The new church has the fire of God burning in her soul, but in time, just like in Acts 5, sin slithers into the fellowship, and what the church does with it will determine to a large degree whether the church will grow as she matures. I wonder what the history of the church would have been had Ananias and Sapphira been tolerated. I wonder, but I also thank God I do not know. Today, they would not only have been tolerated, but they would have been given a time to share a testimonial at the next stewardship banquet. Even things like becoming satisfied, bureaucratic, or unhealthily traditional are sin when they cool the fires of evangelism and holiness.

Consequently, while we need to start new churches, we also need to reclaim the older churches. We know that older churches do not have to lose their evangelistic zeal because the Bible does not prescribe that; it actually prescribes the very opposite. Many older churches are reaching people for Christ; although if church discipline is not practiced, the church is eventually headed for a showdown with the sinful that have "crept in unnoticed" (Jude verse 4). In addition, the longer discipline is ignored, the greater the loss that will be suffered by the church when someone seeks to lead them toward holiness and fellowship. Countless pastors know this, and they learned it at incredible personal and familial cost. Further, as a matter of stewardship, those involved in new church starts must work diligently to make sure that the churches they start practice discipline from the beginning lest they create more of the very sickness they were intended to remedy.

Can you imagine the idiocy of the military only being able to use new recruits and not seasoned soldiers? This is a terrorizing thought as anyone who has served in the military would readily attest. What if only football teams with freshman could win games? The reason you would never witness this kind of bottom-up thinking in the military or sports is that they exercise discipline in order to keep all the troops and players ready. The church is the only place where the nonsense of no discipline would be considered, much less allowed. Discipline is essential to the continued vitality of the church. Therefore, we ought to be clear about all of the reasons which contribute to their paralysis, not just the more tranquilizing and affirming ones. It is better to have a few devoted men and women than to have enough people to fill ten Barnum & Bailey big tops and that be the sum of their commitment.

The loss of discipline in society and in our schools has produced an environment of Columbines and potential Columbines. The lack of personal responsibility has produced a record number of debts, bankruptcies, cases of obesity, broken families, ad infinitum. The initial devaluing of discipline promises liberation, which causes exuberant joy over the newfound freedom from fear and bondage as discipline fades into a distant and repugnant memory. However, in time, incipient anarchy sets in, and the numbers of potential insurrectionists multiply along with their own style of putsch. Then everyone is frantically searching for answers to the mounting problems, but they fail to find the answer because they look to man and the future when the answer lies in the past where discipline died. They dare not look to the past because that would mean that they may bear some responsibility in the demise of societal security and the stifling of progress; to make looking into the past even more improbable, is the fact that man, even Christian men and women, normally views the past as bondage and the present as freedom. Thus, mankind continues to seek to convince himself that it will all work out as he presses forward in this adult land of Oz; only to find out too late that unlike Dorothy's Oz, the wizard is not good but evil and offers no answers to the traveler's problems.

In our culture of immediate satisfaction, pundits continually spout off quick superficial answers to profound life-threatening problems. An all too familiar example is the epidemic of school shootings around the country. We now have children killing children with guns and bombs. Just thirty years ago, it would not only have not happened, the thought of such would not even have been seriously entertained. It was simply too improbable to believe that it could actually happen. Now that it is happening, at schools across the country, and no one knows where it will strike next; the most common answer for this epidemic is to blame those wretched guns. Otherwise intelligent individuals regularly proclaim, We must either decrease or get rid of all the guns to stop the school killings. They forget that some have used not only guns, but also bombs, which can be made out of a mixture of everyday items, and that they can use many other things to kill if need be.

It is maddening to watch the experts, psychologists, and pundits theorize in articles, books, and public appearances, but miss the whole source of the problem. It is not unexpected that they miss it because they miss many things that are readily apparent, if only one will open his non-politically correct eyes to see. Simply put, if it is the guns, then why were we not having this problem thirty years ago since guns were plentiful then also? In fact, years ago boys brought their guns to school. When deer season opened, they loaded them right in their truck so they could leave straight from school to go to the woods. No one worried about being shot. Guns have been around since long before there were public schools in America. Consequently, it seems appallingly weak to argue that guns are the problem since they have been around for centuries without the present day children-killing-children gangland style, or any style for that matter. It cannot possibly be the guns or else the school war zones would be nothing new.

So what is it? Could it be that morals have decayed, and we have made the daunting and consequential shift from viewing the world as created by God, to whom man is ultimately accountable, to a Darwinian world where the strong survive and the weak must be eliminated? We have moved from man being created in the image of God with choice and responsibility for those choices to a Freudian man who is not free but determined by biological and subconscious impulses and thereby logically not fully responsible for his actions; from valuing the absolute sanctity of every human life to the relativistic quality of a human life perspective which establishes the value of life based upon the value system of each individual? Could it possibly be that these brutal killings are merely the inevitable outcome of teaching children that they came from animals, there is no God, there are no values to be prized beyond your own, nothing is intrinsically right or wrong, and that human rights trump human responsibility? Could it be that this modern day barbarianism is merely the logical consequence of evolutionism? The answer is an unequivocal yes. World-views do not exist in a vacuum. They have necessary concomitancies.

The church faces the same moral dilemma when she views her problems, her lack of respect from society, and her impact on society. She often thinks her problems are primarily location, money, lack of staff, and countless other things, when the problem may be substantially deeper and long term. Consequently, the cure may be more than managerial or geographical; it may be theological. It may be in part because of the neglect of church discipline. It is clear that the absence of discipline in the church has changed the nature of the church by allowing lost people to be leading, and worldly ideas to creep in and eventually reign—of course always with sufficient religious garb to conceal this disobedience from the unsuspecting. Many reputable people, including Billy Graham, have made the statement repeatedly that they believe our churches are composed of at least fifty percent lost people—of course we can never know this for sure since we cannot find about two thirds of the members to ask them. Clearly, the lack of church discipline has been a major contributor in erecting the quasi-church of today. The church discipline that needs resurrected encompasses the full breadth of discipline, which includes everything necessary to provide houses of worship, love, prayer, fellowship, discipleship, and learning the Word through teaching, preaching, and obedience. Hence, the church will never regain what she needs until holiness is valued and sought, and that will necessitate the re-instituting of church discipline. This will take abandoning present ideas of what a good church is, and courage. What is lacking in the church is not vision, contrary to popular thinking; it is courage plain and simple. We don't have to have a vision, for God already has revealed His vision, and that is enough vision for a lifetime. What we must have is humility and courage.

9   It Potentiates Winning a Wayward Brother

This is a wonderful and very practical reason for exercising church discipline. The potential, not guarantee, of winning a brother is the most oft cited reason for attributing value to discipline. Remember that discipline is not always the official excommunicating of someone. As a matter of fact, a church that is practicing all the spiritual disciplines will seldom need to exercise full excommunication of a brother or sister, and will still be able to maintain a holy fellowship although there will inevitably be times when formal discipline is necessary. Nevertheless, most church discipline can be exercised on the private and semiprivate level.

Some say that they fear approaching a wayward brother who at least still comes to church because then you might lose him altogether. He might just leave. This misleading conclusion arises from viewing a spiritual situation with natural eyes. Actually, he is already lost, and that is implicit in the phrase "if he listens to you, you have *won* a brother" (Matthew 18:15, italics added). He already has sin in his life, and that makes time of the essence, like with a child. "Discipline your son while there is hope, And do not desire his death" (Proverbs 19:18).

Apparently there may come a time when there is not a place for hope. It is like a person who is swimming and begins to drown. If you throw him a rope, you are not causing him to drown. He is already drowning, but you are giving him a chance to come back to solid ground and live. How unloving it would be to see someone who was drowning and then not cast a life rope because you think he might get mad or blame you for his drowning. He may be so waterlogged that he does, but that does not make it true. It would be callously unloving not to cast him the lifeline. Similarly, it is equally unloving to not approach a brother walking into sin and rebellion, and even more so since the consequence is not for this life only but also the life to come.

10 To Practice Authentic Christianity

Authentic Christianity is following Christ in spirit and letter. This involves all of the spiritual disciplines including prayer, evangelism, fellowship, Bible intake, fasting, and prayer to name a few. Although each Christian will, because of the natural and spiritual gifts given by God, excel in some areas more than others, God does not bless those who become specialists in certain disciplines and ignore the others. Whitney says concerning this, "The Spiritual Disciplines do not stand alone. God will not bless

238

the practice of any Discipline . . . when we reject His Word regarding relationships with others."[123] Thus, the pursuit of authentic Christianity is a comprehensive pursuit.

For many, there is a wonderful and insatiable quest to practice authentic Christianity like that in the New Testament. This desire transcends denominations and is found within every Christian who earnestly desires to follow Christ. In stark contrast are those in the church who do not know Christ, or are not really living for Him, and they have no desire to pursue authentic Christianity, for the cost is clearly too high. Their quest is to see what they can get by with and yet remain within the general blessings of God just as Ananias and Sapphira did long ago. Thus, a church cannot experience authentic Christianity without practicing church discipline. Where church discipline is ignored, authenticity is raped and redefined.

Unless things change and change significantly, there will be a time in America's future where believers will choose between martyrdom and compromise. We will write with our own blood the kind of history we only read about now. Nevertheless, the choice then as now is the same. It is the choice of whether to compromise or not. It seems patently disingenuous to esteem the martyrs who shed their blood so that truth might be preserved and spread throughout the entire world while simultaneously compromising so that our lives will be less difficult or so that we will not lose friends. Further, it seems highly romantic to look into the future and see ourselves faithful to God in the face of being fired from jobs, jailed, or martyred when we choose unfaithfulness, although fully rationalized, in the face of a paucity of difficulties today in comparison to those of the real past or romanticized future. The time to learn faithfulness is now. If we are not faithful in facing the difficulties of this day, it is incredulous romanticism to believe that we will be faithful in the major trials to come.

CHAPTER 7

Church Discipline Requires a Tender Heart: Love Not Legalism

Abiblical attitude is crucial to the whole process of discipline. If the attitude of those implementing the discipline is not right, then what God designed to be a beautiful act of selfless love is transformed into an ugly act of power even if all the other instructions are followed to the letter. Without the right attitude, discipline simply cannot honor God because discipline is more than just the implementation of rules and consequences. This is one of the main reasons that there must be clear and comprehensive teaching on church discipline before implementation is attempted. To implement church discipline in a church where it has not been thoroughly explained, which takes time, will surely result in disaster. Even if the discipline process is completed and all seems well; if the attitude was wrong, the result will be evil. The offspring of that evil may surface as a disuniting and judgmental spirit in the fellowship, or it may lay dormant until the next attempt to lead the church in discipline and then surface with a vengeance.

Not only must the church be taught on church discipline specifically, but she must be taught the Word of God, in-depth and comprehensively, and led to respect and follow the Word of God in everything. Without this thorough maturing of the church, the potential for backlash increases because you would be asking an unspiritual church to do a very spiritually difficult task. It is of paramount importance that the pastor makes sure his heart is right prior to entering into the uncertainties of church discipline. The following characteristics that compose the right attitude are not listed according to priority since they are all essential for the biblical attitude.

First, the attitude of the church should be one of grief. Paul scolded the Corinthians for their failure to have the proper attitude concerning a sinning brother when he said, "And you have become arrogant, and have not *mourned* instead, in order that the one who had done this deed might be removed from your midst" (1 Corinthians 5:2, italics added). The word mourn is the Greek word *pentheo.* It means, "to mourn, to grieve . . . it is commonly used for mourning for the dead . . ."[124] This is true in both the Old and New Testaments. It was used by the Old Testament prophets in prophecies of disaster (Joel 1:9, Jeremiah 14:2; Lamentations 2:8) and in the New Testament (Matthew 9:15; Revelation 18:7–8). It is easy to see that mourn communicates an intense sadness and remorse.

The word embodies that inexpressible and profound sense of loss and grief that is experienced when a loved one dies. This level of grief is almost unfathomable because of the unbearable sense of loss and because death is unnatural. God created man to live, but man dies because of sin; although death is a conquered foe and one day will be done away with completely, for now, all of mankind must die. Man was not created to endure the grief of death. Death is an interloper. The pain of this type of intense loss and grief is only fully understood by someone who also has lost a loved one in death. For them, no communication is necessary for mutual understanding, but the attempt to explain this agony and darkness of the soul to someone who has not lost to death is indeed impossible. The loss of life, the most unnatural of all losses, casts a deep dark shadow over even the brightest of days.

I have preached many funerals over the years, and there is a time during the funeral that I find to be the most intense, nearly an unbearable moment of grief. That is when the guests have been dismissed from the sanctuary and only the family remains, and the family gathers one last time at the side of their departed loved one. As I stand at the head of the casket during this deluge of anguish and emotional upheaval, it is all I can do to remain composed enough to carry out my responsibilities. The summarization of sin and death before them results in uncontrollable crying, wailing, sobbing, moaning, lamenting, crying out to their loved one in affection, and that affection only to be met with coldness, death chilling coldness. At times, family members have to be torn away from the casket to which they cling, averse to let go of love and life. Their sobbing is an evocative, haunting, and unnatural cry. It is the cry of death. I know this cry intimately for I have cried it myself.

Can the church ever have this kind of anguish over a wayward brother? The answer is, Yes! Not only can she, but she must if she is to honor God with her obedience in the area of discipline. This is precisely the attitude that Paul called for the Corinthians, and all Christians, to have concerning overt sin within the church. The church is to be brokenhearted over a brother or sister who chooses to walk in sin over walking with the Savior. This is clearly an inestimable distance from where the Corinthian church was and where most churches today are. There is little mourning over sin in an individual's life, the church, the lost testimony of the church, and the lost who become increasingly hardened at the obvious and undeniable hypocrisy and incongruity. I have seen discipline implemented with an attitude of grief on many occasions. I have experienced time after time when the chairman of the deacons or pastor would stand before the flock of God sharing with tears the sin of a wayward brother or sister, and the church's responsibility toward them; then witness that grief spread throughout the congregation. It is as though a death has taken place, and that is not by accident.

The practice of church discipline is not something that is supposed to be uplifting and easy. It is the reminder of death, and the cause of death succeeding once again in hurting the church of the Lord Jesus Christ. It is the death of a walk with God, fellowship, and a testimony for Christ, and it should evoke deep grief. What makes the Corinthians' and the contemporary church's response all the more hideous, scandalous, and unchristian is that they not only fail to mourn but are arrogant about their tolerance. They are more zealous to capture the zeitgeist than they are to be filled with the Holy Spirit, more zealous for worldly acceptance than the winning of a brother. The word arrogant (1 Corinthians 5:2) is from the Greek word *fusiovo,* which means "to puff up, to inflate, to cause someone to be proud, arrogant, or haughty—to make proud, to make arrogant, to make haughty."[125] The image that is vividly portrayed is the unthinkable event of someone laughing during the death and funeral of a loved one. This is also a piercing indictment of the contemporary church who not only fails to mourn, but with humanly-derived humility, she cloaks her infatuation with the zeitgeist, which interprets the toleration of sin as a sign of maturity and grace.

The Corinthians, being Greek, prided themselves in diversity, tolerance, religious ecstasies, and extreme individualism, which quite naturally result in the normalization of sin. When they became Christians, they brought these secular perversions into the church. Rather than being heartbroken and weeping over the sin within the fellowship, they were proud of their accepting attitude and non-prudish behavior. In like manner, the modern church flaunts her libertarianism as an icon of her accepting love. Without a mourner's attitude, discipline cannot be done spiritually and most often will not even be attempted. This is one reason Paul castigated the Corinthians so severely for their lack of grief before giving them instructions to follow.

Jesus' feelings concerning Israel and her unwillingness to repent and how that affected Him demonstrate a true attitude of grief. As Jesus entered Jerusalem as the Messiah, "He saw the city and wept over it, saying, 'If you had known in this day, even you, the things which make for peace! But now they have been hidden from your eyes'" (Luke 19:41–42). He came to bring them peace. Yet, He watched them miss the promises of God because they rejected Him, and now He must reject them. He wept over the city because its people did not understand the significance of what was going on that day. They could have been saved from their sin if they had accepted Him as the Messiah. Matthew 23:37 makes it clear that He desired for them to come to Him so that He could cleanse and protect them. "O Jerusalem, Jerusalem, who kills the prophets and stones those who are sent to her! How often I wanted to gather your children together, the way a hen gathers her chicks under her wings, and you were unwilling." There is intense pathos in these words, deep and profound grief. Jeremiah expressed this grief in response to Judah being exiled to Babylon because of her defiance toward God saying, "My soul will sob in secret for such pride; and my eyes will bitterly weep and flow down with tears" (Jeremiah 13:17).

Brokenness over sin within the body of Christ must first overshadow the undershepherd. The Scripture is lucidly clear; the sinning brother is already lost—not meaning that he lost his salvation, but his way—because Jesus said "And if your brother sins, go and reprove him in private; if he listens to you, *you have won your brother*" (Matthew 18:15, italics added). When someone is visibly walking off from the Lord or His church, internally they have already gone farther than what appears, and thus discipline is the attempt to gain or win a brother or sister who is already lost. Ignoring, tolerating, or minimizing sin in a brother's life seals the loss of a brother, and only grief wins him. Without grief, discipline is lost. There is surely much to rejoice about as a Christian, and laughter is good for the soul; but when churches extol happiness and excitement to the point of excluding mourning over a wayward brother or sister, there is far less to laugh about.

The second essential feature of the biblical attitude required for church discipline is humility. Paul warned the Corinthians against pride saying, "Therefore let him who thinks he stands take heed lest he fall" (1 Corinthians 10:12). Albert Barnes commenting on that caveat says, "Wherefore, as the result of all these admonitions, let this be the effect of all that we learn from the unhappy self-confidence of the Jews, to admonish us:

(1) Not to put reliance on our own strength.
(2) That a confidence in our own security is no evidence that we are safe.
(3) Such a confidence may be one of the strongest evidences that we are in danger. Those are most safe who feel that they are weak and feeble, and who feel their need of divine aid and strength. They will then rely on the true source of strength; and they will be secure.

(4) All professed Christians should be admonished. All are in danger of falling into sin, and of dishonoring their profession; and the exhortation cannot be too often or too urgently pressed, that they should take heed lest they fall into sin. The leading and special idea of the apostle here should not be forgotten or disregarded . . ."[126]

God has recorded the failing of Israel, men and women of God from the greatest to the least, not merely to inform us of their failings, but to serve as warnings of our own debilities and encourage us to walk in humility. While believers are a new creation in Christ, we, in this life, retain our fallen nature. As unpalatable as it is, the reality of that retention is that each and every person possesses the necessaries to, under the right circumstances, commit the most heinous, monstrous, scandalous, and repulsive of deeds. Thus, the ever-present actuality is that one may stand strong for the Lord today, only to succumb to a temptation tomorrow. Statements such as, I am going to live faithful to the Lord for the rest of my life, are prideful, which deserve the scriptural warning "let him who thinks he stands take heed lest he fall" (1 Corinthians 10:12). The only statements concerning the future that avoid pride and reflect loyalty are those that reflect an absolute reliance on grace such as, By the grace of God, I will live for the Lord the rest of my life. The humbling truth of humanity is, no human knows what the future holds or what one will be able to withstand at that time. A worn out soldier is more susceptible than a fresh one to the enemy's attack, and a young soldier is not as aware of the enemy's devices and his own weaknesses. In addition to these humbling realities, we often view temptation as simple—made up of only one component—rather than complex. However, temptations are often complex, involving different temptations, weaknesses, relationships, and a multiplicity of other variables working synergistically, which no one can even understand prior to the fact, much less proclaim victory over. Consequently, everyone should live with the awareness that they can commit the same sin as the one they are being called on to expose and discipline. This is hard for many to imagine, which is a caveat of the pride "crouching at the door" (Genesis 4:7). This awareness never allows for the overlooking of sin in the church, but it does bathe the process in humility.

Galatians 6:1–3 also speaks to the need for humility when dealing with brothers and sisters caught in a trespass, "Brethren, even if a man is caught in any trespass, you who are spiritual, restore such a one in a spirit of gentleness; *each one* looking to yourself, lest you too be tempted. Bear one another's burdens, and thus fulfill the law of Christ. For if anyone thinks he is something when he is nothing, he deceives himself." This passage speaks to both the humility needed in viewing one's own potential to fall and the humility needed for properly viewing one who has already fallen.

This passage also reiterates the believer's spiritual responsibility to help a repentant brother or sister. In addition, this verse has application to anyone caught in sin and particularly to the one who is repentant and desirous of restoration. Even when a wayward brother has confessed and repented of his sin, he may still be tempted by that sin as he seeks to grow stronger in the Lord. It is during this period that Satan often unleashes hellish assaults, and the flesh wars relentlessly against the soul for more of the sin it has become accustomed to feeding on. The cravings of the flesh can never be satiated, but they can be resisted and this is the battle. All of this reinforces the need for spiritual brothers and sisters to bear his burden and help him resist. The word for burden is from the Greek word *baros*, which refers to carrying heavy loads, and includes the ideas of oppressive suffering. The intent is that the humble brother does not look down on a brother who was overtaken by sin, but in response to his repentance, he helps carry the burden of emotional hurt, spiritual warfare, confusion, and is committed to the time consuming struggle of restoration and just being a spiritual friend. This can prove to be exhausting labor for the one who comes alongside to help, but he not only fulfills the law of Christ to love one another; but he also sees, firsthand, the imprisoning nature of sin. This can prove to be a powerful reminder to him of the seriousness of straying from Christ.

The verb *bear* is present tense, plural in number, and imperative. The present tense signifies a continuous or repetitive action, plural in number signifies all the members and not just the leaders, and the imperative means this is a command. The body of Christ is commanded to care for and help those who are weak or are trying to overcome temptation. This is unglamorous and difficult to put on the statistical reports, but it is authentic Christianity. This verse portrays a loveliness of Christianity found most prominently in a church practicing discipline.

Therefore, Christians are continually (present tense) to bear one another's burdens. Bear has the idea of carrying with endurance, and burdens, *baros*, refer to heavy loads that are difficult to lift and carry. When walking with a brother in Christ on the road of restoration, there will be times of much needed counsel, prayer, listening, and being intimately involved. These may prove to be laborious burdens, but they are essential; "Prayer is the most powerful weapon believers have in conquering sin and opposing Satan, and nothing helps a brother carry his burdens as much as prayer for him and with him."[127]

This is all done in a spirit of gentleness. The prescription set forth in Galatians 6:1–3 is unfortunately and regularly presented as an alternative to supposedly legalistic church discipline. However, it is not an alternative, but an indispensable element of it. This explains how a brother or sister, who is overtaken by sin and repents when confronted, is to be handled.

"For if anyone thinks he is something when he is nothing, he deceives himself. But let each one examine his own work, and then he will have *reason for* boasting in regard to himself alone, and not in regard to another. For each one shall bear his own load" (Galatians 6:3–5).

It is easy to become pharisaical; a Christian can look down on those who have been overcome by sin, as though he lives on a higher spiritual plane than the sinning brother does. Thus, he remains aloof from the weaker brother, not wanting to be tainted by the commonness of it all. However, this aloofness discloses his own lack of true spirituality. He apparently has not examined his own heart and been startled by the thoughts, desires, weaknesses, and potential for falling. Before we judge a brother unworthy of us to carry his burden, we should evaluate ourselves to see if we are worthy of boasting. In other words, first take the log out of our own eye (Matthew 7:5).

These verses shatter the superciliousness of the human heart, which if left intact, defaces the tenderness of church discipline. The walk away from embracing these verses is a walk away from humility and working "out your own salvation in fear and trembling" (Philippians 2:12). The person helped here is someone who wants help to be what God desires them to be. This wayward brother or sister is repentant and really is trying to overcome the temptations, but they are also very weak. It could also be a person who is simply struggling with a temptation and has asked someone for counsel, prayer, or some other form of help. This situation may only involve one or two other people, or it could involve more who are seeking in some way to help a struggling spiritual sibling. As long as they admit their sin and seek to deal with their temptation by working with a brother or sister, there is no need to unnecessarily involve others in the process. This is church discipline, but it is a brother going to a brother for help.

Remember, the escalation of church discipline from one on one to higher levels is brought on by the unwillingness of the offender to repent. The sin may fall into one of the categories requiring formal church discipline, but that is only after he has rejected all attempts at restoration. The escalation of the disciplinary process to higher levels of public awareness is merely the church's response to the unrepentant heart of a wayward brother. As long as the offender is seeking to follow Christ and deal with his sin, we are there to bear his burden (Galatians 6:2).

Church discipline encompasses the totality of life in the Christian community. This wonderful passage is at the heart of church discipline where brothers and sisters carry one another's burdens because they love them like Christ loves them. They are willing to pray, counsel, console, walk through the valley of the shadow of death, weep with their hurting brother or sister, and lay down their lives for them. They give their time, wisdom, strength, and soul for their weaker brother. It is the repulsion of that kind of giving, love, and sacrifice that eventuates in more severe discipline. Even if the time of disfellowshipping comes, it is not exercised in anger or frustration but in humility and grief. It is indeed a sad day. What is surpassingly sadder is when a church decides not to follow her Lord's teaching on discipline, and wayward children of God are abandoned to a spiritual skid row.

The third essential aspect of a biblical attitude for exercising church discipline is love. The wayward brother is just that,

251

a brother. "And *yet* do not regard him as an enemy, but admonish him as a brother" (2 Thessalonians 3:15). There may come a time to treat him as a tax gatherer and a heathen (Matthew 18:17), but that is only after all attempts to restore him have been obstinately rejected, which evidences that the wayward brother is determined to act as a heathen, or he is not a true believer and thus he is to be treated like what he appears to be. However, up to that point, he is to be treated as a brother who needs understanding, support, guidance, tender loving nurturing, and compassion. Even at this stage, we love as God loves the lost.

Church discipline has to be immersed in the love of Christ since it is from start to finish a love endeavor. We demonstrate real love for one another when we are willing to give of ourselves in carrying a burden for a weaker brother or remove a potential wolf in sheep's clothing. Jesus made love intrinsic to the Christian life by his life and words; He said, "A new commandment I give to you, that you love one another, even as I have loved you, that you also love one another. By this all men will know that you are My disciples, if you have love for one another" (John 13:34–35). Our love for each other and the body of Christ is to be the same quality as the love of Jesus. His love was sacrificial, giving, and confrontative when it needed to be. Love that is unwilling to confront an erring brother in grief and humility is not the mature love of Christ. Often the love of Christ is portrayed as only smiles, acceptance, and overlooking any and every wrong; real love desires holiness, and it will not overlook a brother who is headed into or living in unholiness.

Jesus also made an inviolable union between loving Him and keeping His commandments. He said, "He who has my commands and keeps them is the one who loves Me" (John 14:21). "He who does not love Me does not keep My words;

and the word which you hear is not Mine, but the Father's who sent Me (John 14:24). These are unambiguous and gripping words indeed. The truth is not difficult to see. Our love for Christ is to be measured by our obedience to His Word. It is simply that simple. He does not measure our love merely by what we say, but by what we do. When we apply this truth to the area of church discipline, we must conclude that the failure to practice discipline is ultimately a failure to love Christ supremely. It is that our love for Him is insufficient to produce obedience in this difficult and lonely place. Our love for Him is only adequate for practicing the more pleasurable of instructions, the things that are more palatable to the modern church. Our love for Christ is not merely measured by how much we do, but by what we are willing to do. Following Christ, especially in the difficult or unpopular areas, testifies to us and to the world of our love for Christ supremely. To fail to follow is the reminder that the tyranny of self-love is alive and well in the heart of Christians and the church.

As stated elsewhere, this is not meant to say that if a person is not perfect, he does not love Christ. We all fail, and at times repeatedly and tragically so. We are all learning. Many of God's shepherds are not even aware of the inextricable relationship between the gospel and discipline. They may know of the teaching, but they do not understand the importance of it. I am not saying that makes it right, but it is categorically different to fail to be obedient because you do not know or fully understand something than to know and choose with intentionality not to obey. Both are sin, but the love for Christ and the heart can be right in the former, but not in the latter. To desire, strive, and fail is to fail. To refuse because of the difficultness or out of willful ignorance is rebellion. Singing songs about loving Jesus will never compensate for or expunge the disobedient life's claim to the contrary.

"This is My commandment, that you love one another, just as I have loved you. Greater love has no one than this, that one lay down his life for his friends." (John 15:12–13) Jesus love for us is evident in that He lay down His life for us. If He did not love us, He would not have given Himself as a sacrifice for us. Conversely, if He said that He loved us, and yet did nothing to show that love, they would be hollow words, undeniably hollow. The same is true with the followers of Christ. If we give only what is beneficial to self or is convenient, then our love is self-love not Christ love and our words are hollow. Thus, the acid test of love is if we do what He says to do, even at great personal cost. That is love.

Anyone who has practiced discipline knows that love has to be the driving force. It is first a love for Christ and His Word, then a love for the community of Christ and what Christ established her to be. Out of that love comes obedience to the Scripture and willingness to do what is right even if it is difficult; you run the almost certain risk of being misunderstood, attacked, and misjudged, but you do it for the wayward Christian because you love them.

Some aspects of church discipline like prayer, counseling, and encouraging are acceptable to every church because they see these things as demonstrating the love of Christ. Rebuking, public disclosure of a brother's sin, disfellowshipping, and treating as a tax gatherer are actions categorized as legalistic and unloving. Thus, they are either ignored or viewed as the remnants of an antiquated Christianity meriting nothing but being scorned as Pharisaism because they cannot be love, for love is gentle. However, the modern definition of love comes from psychologists like Eric Fromm, Abraham Maslow, and Carl Rogers "who intentionally ignored two thousand years of teaching and the expression of Christian love when defining love."[128] The idea of love that permeates the church and excludes discipline clearly did not come from a biblical definition of love.

For example, Jesus' cleansing of the temple is seldom used as an example of the love of Christ. It appears to modern psychologized Christianity that it cannot be love. Jesus enters the temple with a whip, turning over tables, casting money away, running people out of the temple, and using physical force to stop their merchandising. If context tells us anything, Jesus was not speaking in some monotone voice when He said, "Is it not written, 'My house shall be called a house of prayer for all the nations'? But you have made it a robbers' den" (Matthew 21:12–16; Mark 11:15–18; John 2:13–16). In contrast, Jesus' words to the woman caught in adultery, "Neither do I condemn you; go your way. From now on sin no more" (John 8:11) are viewed as pure love while the temple scene is seen as merely wrath. Actually, nothing could be further from the truth, for the actions of the temple cleansing demonstrated a sacrificial and selfless love for all who were being taken advantage of by the robbers and thieves, who were corrupting God's house of prayer into a den of damnation. It is love to rescue those who want to walk with God from those who use His name and possessions for their own ends, thus, making themselves to be a god while holding the church captive to their selfism. It is unloving to know the house of the Lord is to be a place of prayer and not to cleanse it.

God's love never shuns the painful, degrading, or costly. God's love never sees someone in sin and sits idly by. God's love will act for the benefit of the object of His love regardless what the cost is to Him. God's love is inexhaustible. God's love is for all who will accept it. God's love stops at nothing short of transformation of the unholy into the holy. God's love cannot be deterred even by Golgotha's hell. We shall exercise biblical discipline because of God's love and only because of God's love.

The fourth quality necessary for completing the proper attitude for discipline is forgiveness. Forgiveness is a beautiful and godly response to wrongs. Every Christian knows the beauty and wonder of forgiveness because we have all been forgiven a debt we could never pay, which is something to keep in mind when approaching church discipline. King Louis XII of France articulated the feeling of many people when he said, "Nothing smells so sweet as the dead body of your enemy." This is in glaring contrast to Jesus words when He hanged on the cross and said, "Father, forgive them; for they do not know what they are doing" (Luke 23:34).

The attitude of forgiveness must be present from the beginning of the process of discipline through every step or level of the discipline procedure. Understanding the centrality of forgiveness in the discipline process is profoundly important for understanding biblical discipline. Forgiveness is not something that surfaces at a certain point in the process nor something which pre-empts the practice of discipline. The puzzlement concerning the place of forgiveness in discipline arises from confusing the attitude of forgiveness and the act of forgiveness, and when this happens discipline suffers.

First, we will look at the biblical attitude of forgiveness, which is seen clearly in the words of the apostle Paul, "And be kind to one another, tender-hearted, forgiving each other, just as God in Christ also has forgiven you" (Ephesians 4:32). The basis for, the ability to, and the pattern of forgiveness are all established by God. First, the basis for forgiving others is that we have been forgiven. God has already completely forgiven us in Christ of all of the heinous sin we committed against Him. In light of this, how could a Christian not forgive others? Second, the ability to forgive even the most egregious offenses comes from the great Forgiver living within us. Even "while we were enemies" against God in league with the host of hell, He died for us (Romans 5:10). Forgiveness not only honors God and sets the forgiver free, but it most poignantly allows the forgiver to experience, although in an infinitesimal degree, what Christ felt in forgiving us. Third is the pattern of forgiveness, and this is what generally causes the greatest amount of confusion. Notice that the blueprint is to forgive "just as God in Christ has forgiven" (Ephesians 4:32). Thus, the pattern established by God in the plan of creation and redemption is how we are to forgive. There are three steps involved: first, recognition of sin; second, a realization of the need for forgiveness; third, repentance and asking for forgiveness. This is not to say that there is never a time that one might forgive another person without being asked. There are times when the offender may not even be aware of the offense, or it is so small of an infraction that it seldom warrants a thought—like someone who forgets to say hello to you. Surely those incidents do happen. However, this does not change the blueprint for obtaining salvific forgiveness when one becomes a Christian, forgiveness as a Christian in order to maintain intimacy with God, and for obtaining forgiveness from other Christians or the church. The model is the same.

Salvation is given when someone recognizes they have sinned and broken God's law, repents, and asks forgiveness by faith in Jesus Christ (Romans 10:9–10). For a Christian, an intimate walk with God is maintained or restored by recognizing his sin and confessing it to God (1 John 1:9). Technically, the Christian is forgiven of all sin; it all has been paid for by the substitutionary death of our Lord Jesus Christ, but our walk with the Lord each day necessitates that we acknowledge sin by confessing it to God. The word confession means to agree or to say the same thing. Therefore, confession happens when a believer says to God that he agrees with God about his thoughts or actions being sinful, and in that agreement—which is more than a mere recitation of one's sins and mental agreement that they are sinners—there is repentance. Technically, the word for repentance means change of mind. That is a dictionary definition. However, biblically it means far more. Repentance in the Bible is never merely an intellectual decision, but rather it is a change of mind, heart, and being, and a heartfelt sadness over hurting our loving Father, which evokes a plea for forgiveness that is always responded to with forgiveness. This pattern is the same in all three occasions. There is the recognition of the sin, confession and repentance, and then forgiveness.

It is the biblical pattern of forgiveness, which is normally not followed when dealing with brothers and sisters who have sinned. This is because of a failure to understand the biblical pattern and to maintain the distinction between a willingness to forgive, an attitude of forgiveness, and the actual act of forgiveness. When the willingness to forgive is not maintained as distinct from the act of forgiveness, then the biblical pattern is disfigured. The consequences are disobedience, distortion of the real meaning of forgiveness, and inevitable corruption of the church because biblical discipline will be displaced by an unbiblical forgiveness.

In order to maintain this crucial distinction, one must remember that the willingness to forgive resides in the heart of the offended. The willingness to forgive is present because of an intimate relationship between the offended and God. The willingness to forgive is present regardless of what the offender did or does. It is based solely on the grace from God and the desire of the offended to walk with God. This willingness to forgive is all borne out of an understanding of and appreciation for how much we have been forgiven in Christ. Understanding the magnitude of the love and forgiveness of our Lord Jesus Christ toward us causes our heart to overflow with forgiveness. The believer who walks in the willingness to forgive does not hold grudges or allow bitterness, revenge, and resentment to fester in his heart because of the wrong done to him or the course of action taken by the offender. This is what is meant by walking in forgiveness. In a person's heart, between God and himself, there is the same forgiveness for the offender that God demonstrated toward the believer.

It is monumentally important not to confuse the willingness to forgive with the act of forgiveness. If the two are confused, it makes forgiveness of the heart dependent on the repentance of the offender. That is unbiblical, and will surely breed bitterness and resentment in the heart of a believer. Granted, when very personal, vicious, and malicious attacks have been launched against you, this willingness to forgive may not happen overnight. And once you have chosen to walk in this willingness to forgive, you may have to do so for a while before your emotions against such forgiveness subside. This is a spiritual decision and not an emotional decision.

Now concerning the outward act of forgiveness, this takes place between the offended and the offender allowing the forgiveness already in the heart of the offended to be expressed and experienced by the offender. The restoration of relationships is now possible. The critical distinction between the attitude of forgiveness and the actual act of forgiveness is that the latter is dependent upon the appropriate response of the offender, and the former is not. The attitude of forgiveness is dependent upon the offended party's desire to walk with God. In salvation, God made the offer of salvation unconditional, but He made the reception of salvation conditional. That condition is faith in Jesus Christ. Jesus died for the sins of the world, which demonstrates the willingness of God to forgive.

But the reception of the benefit of that death, which results in being restored to right relationship with God, is conditioned upon the recipient exercising faith. Jesus' prayer to the Father from the cross demonstrates this reality; Jesus prayed for his accusers and abusers to be forgiven (Luke 23:34), but they are not forgiven until they repent and put their faith in Him as Lord and Savior. Stephen demonstrated the willingness to forgive when he prayed, "Lord, do not hold this sin against them!" (Acts 7:60). This demonstrates the attitude of forgiveness, the willingness to see them forgiven by God for the wrong against himself; but the act of forgiveness came when, and if, they repented and trusted Christ as Savior. One of the reasons David was a man after God's own heart was his own forgiving and merciful heart. Although King Saul repeatedly tried to kill David with a javelin and pursued him relentlessly in the hills of Judah with his army, David not only refused to harm Saul because he was the Lord's anointed but even refused to harbor any hatred against him (1 Samuel 24:6, 12; 26:11). In another example, although David was at first enraged by Nabal's ungrateful refusal to give food and provisions to David's men who had helped protect Nabal, he was persuaded by Nabal's wife, Abigail, to withhold revenge.

The simple truth is that God has provided forgiveness for all, but he does not apply it to any except those who request it by repentance and faith, which presupposes a recognition of their sin. Thus, God lives in the constant state of being willing to forgive, but the act of forgiveness is not implemented and experienced by the offender until he repents. This understanding helps to explain the paradox of God providing forgiveness for all through the death of Christ, and yet judging some of the ones who make up that *all*. God lives in perfect love and forgiveness. However, the person who does not repent will not experience that forgiveness. It will forever remain in the willingness to forgive status.

This distinction is because mankind was created as a free moral agent in the image of God. As stated previously, God did not create man and then give him a free choice as though man can be man without free choice. Actually, free choice is an essential aspect of what it means to be created in the image of God. Without free choice, it cannot be said that man is created in the image of God. Of course, man's free choice was only truly free until he chose to sin, and from that time on man is not totally free in his choosing. The image of God, free choice, is still there, but it is damaged and corrupted.

Being created in the image of God means that man may choose to do good or evil, and that he is also responsible for his choices and must eventually suffer the just penalty of those choices. This is true in the garden before the fall and after the fall of mankind (Genesis 3:8–4:16). When Adam and Eve sinned, God made them admit their sin and reap the consequences of their choice. After their expulsion from the garden and the corruption of man by his sin, God did not lessen the standard of accountability for the choices of mankind. For example, Cain's heart was wrong when he brought the sacrifice to God and killed his brother Abel. God held Cain accountable for his actions, and God pronounced judgment on him because even though the image of God was corrupted, it was still present and Cain was still culpable. In both the Edenic and post-Edenic eras, God called on mankind to own up to his choices through a series of questions. For example, after Adam had sinned, God came into the garden and said to him, "Where are you" (Genesis 3:9)? God was not in doubt of Adam's location, nor what He had done, but He wanted Adam to admit what he had done. Then he said to Adam, "Who told you that you were naked? Have you eaten from the tree of which I commanded you not to eat?" (Genesis 3:11). God knew the answer to each of these questions, but it was important that Adam admit them and thereby come to grips with his decision and sin.

We find this same scenario after the fall. After Cain killed Abel, God said, "Where is Abel your brother? . . . And He said, "What have you done?" (Genesis 4:9–10). Here again man is approached with his sin and God seeks to get him to own up to what he had done.

God did not forgive without any requirement on man's part, for that would be to degrade the *imago dei*. It would present man as a mere victim and make him not responsible or capable of self-governance. Thus, we see that since the fall, although man cannot make a choice to save himself apart from the convicting work of the Holy Spirit, he can still make many choices. He is not so depraved that God no longer holds him accountable for those choices. After God rejected Cain's offering because of Cain's sinful heart, God said to Cain, "Why are you angry? And why has your countenance fallen? If you do well, will not *your countenance* be lifted up? And if you do not do well, sin is crouching at the door; and its desire is for you, but you must master it" (Genesis 4:6–7). That question and promise are based upon the fact that the image of God is still present, along with the essential free choice. Notice that God gave Cain a clear choice of which direction he could take and told him each choice had a consequence. There is nothing in the text to imply that Cain was somehow unable to choose his direction.

The significance of this dialog is that it happened after the fall and contained the same elements of the first sin which was committed out of a totally free will. God offered man a choice, and man still had a real choice to do right or wrong. God held Cain equally responsible for his actions as God did his parents. It is lucidly clear that man was capable of choosing the good or the bad. Again, God would not bestow forgiveness upon Cain until he sought it. God brought the sin to the surface, ready to forgive, but God would not grant the forgiveness until Cain sought it. It is mercy and mercy alone which allowed Cain to live one second after the sin. The same is true with Adam, Eve, and every human being since. Peter says, He "is patient toward you, not wishing for any to perish but for all to come to repentance" (2 Peter 3:9). However, forgiveness is not bestowed until there is repentance, even though God has forgiveness in His heart. Forcing forgiveness upon man when man does not want it is to treat one created in the image of God as one who was not.

The two sides of forgiveness, being willing to forgive and withholding that forgiveness until the person repents, is also seen in some well known New Testament passages that deal with salvation. For example, "For God so loved the world, that He gave His only begotten Son, that whoever believes in Him should not perish, but have eternal life. . . . He who believes in Him is not judged; he who does not believe has been judged already, because he has not believed in the name of the only begotten Son of God (John 3:16,18). These wonderful verses demonstrate the willingness of God to forgive and the requirement of faith, an act of the will, to receive that forgiveness. Man is not so free that he can come to God entirely on his own, nor is man so depraved that he cannot make a choice when convicted by the Holy Spirit; nor is man forced against his will to believe any more than were Adam, Eve, and Cain.

The Scripture is clear; God does not desire that man perish—live in his sin forever, but He will permit it if man so chooses. God "desires all men to be saved and to come to the knowledge of the truth" (1 Tim. 2:4). Therefore, God is willing to forgive every sinner, but the actual bestowing of that forgiveness is granted only when man repents. This is because man is a free moral agent who must admit his wrongs and ask for forgiveness before experiencing the forgiveness that God has provided.

This discussion is not to imply in any way that I accept that the Bible supports the notion that man can be saved any time that he wants to merely by an act of his will. The Bible is clear that man cannot come to God anytime he wants. Since the fall, man no longer has that capacity within him. Adam and Eve had that ability. They could choose God at any time or choose to walk away. They had no internal influences to choose evil only the temptation that came from without. In contrast, man's present situation as being fallen and yet retaining the *imago dei* does not mean that man can come to God on his own, but neither does it mean that man is saved only by being predetermined to do so. Jesus' promise concerning the coming of the Holy Spirit and the role of the Holy Spirit to the world clears up how this process works. He said speaking of the Holy Spirit, "And He, when He comes, will convict the world concerning sin, and righteousness, and judgment" (John 16:8).

The Holy Spirit has come to "convict the world concerning sin" (John 16:8). The key to understanding this passage hinges on the word for convict, *elencho*. The King James Version translates this word *reprove*, which fails to capture the full strength of the word. It is a much more penetrating term. In the New Testament, the word means "to show people their sins and summon them to repentance."[129] Strong's Lexicon says this word means, "conviction, to bring to the light, to expose . . . to call to account, show one his fault, demand an explanation."[130] Thus, the word includes the idea of making a person aware of his sin and then calling him to turn from it to God for forgiveness. Man is incapable of fully grasping his sin

264

or the sinfulness of sin without the conviction of the Holy Spirit because his original concept of righteousness and sin has been severely skewed as a result of original sin. *The Expositors Commentary* captures the full idea when it says, "the word is a legal term that means to pronounce a judicial verdict by which the guilt of the culprit at the bar of justice is defined and fixed" (John 16:8 in loc.) The Spirit does not merely accuse men of sin; He brings to them an inescapable sense of guilt so that they realize their shame and helplessness before God. This conviction applies to three particular areas: sin, righteousness, and judgment. The Spirit is the prosecuting attorney who presents God's case against humanity. He creates an inescapable awareness of sin so that it cannot be dismissed with an excuse or evaded by taking refuge in the fact that *everybody is doing it*. The Spirit's function is like that of Nathan the prophet who said to David, "You are the man" (2 Samuel 12:7), and compelled him to acknowledge his misdeeds. David was so convicted that he was reduced to a state of complete penitence: "Against you, you only, have I sinned and done what is evil in your sight" (Psalm 51:4).[131]

As Adam, Eve, and Cain were summoned into the presence of God, their sins exposed and the consequences of those sins pronounced, so man is still summoned into the presence of God, and his sins and the consequences of his sins exposed. Once man is brought to a place of being able to understand his sin and the impending judgment based on the righteousness of God, he is given the opportunity to repent and be forgiven, and that is all a part of the convicting work of the Holy Spirit. When the Holy Spirit convicts man, he exposes his sin, God's righteous standard, and the judgment that shall come. This is what He did with Cain. The idea of convicting is to fully expose man's sins and call him to repentance. This implies that man has, at the time of conviction, the ability to repent. In other words, the convicting work of the Holy Spirit places man, at the time he is convicted, on pre-fall ground, so to speak, affording him the ability to either make a choice to turn back to God or continue on his path of sin.

This helps to explain many things. First, there are verses that call men to repent and believe, which implies that they can do so. They can because this call is based primarily on the love of God and not His holiness since His holiness would be intact even if He never called anyone. It is incongruent with the nature and love of God to say that He calls people to salvation, but never intends to give them a chance to receive it (Matthew 23:37). That is neither holy nor loving. Conversely, there are verses that make it clear that man cannot come to God on his own no matter how long God called because man is in bondage to sin (Romans 3:11). Because of verses like these, godly interpreters have wrongly concluded that a man must be born again before he can ever believe—this belief is associated with forms of Calvinism. However, John 16:8 gives us another answer. The convicting work of the Holy Spirit can expose a man's sin and then enlighten him so that he experiences a real understanding of his sin, but it does not involve automatic or forced salvation. He is, by the work of the Holy Spirit, placed in a position to fully understand the sinfulness of his sin and the standard of God's holiness, and has a real choice, like Adam and Eve, to accept or reject. Thus, both the depravity and free choice of man and the holiness and love of God are maintained; this means that man will not only suffer God's righteous judgment because of what he inherited from Adam, but because he is given the same choice as Adam, and he also chose to reject the goodness of God. Thus, he will account for his sin in eternal hell. That is the just price for being created in the image of God and choosing to rebel and corrupt the image of God in seeking to usurp the position of

God. The sin in the garden was disbelief in what God had done and said, and the ultimate sin today is to disbelieve what God has said and done in Jesus Christ. The convicting work of the Holy Spirit affords sinful man a real opportunity to receive or reject God's forgiveness.

After the Holy Spirit has convicted a person of his sin, of God's righteous and inflexible standard, and the impending judgment against his sin if he ultimately fails to receive God's forgiveness by faith, he will spend eternity in hell. This offer of salvation is totally an act of God's grace; otherwise man would not have a real choice. The fruit of that choice, which only comes with full conviction of the Holy Spirit, is either salvation as man recognizes his sin and accepts God's forgiveness, or ultimately the unpardonable sin, where man recognizes his sin and chooses to walk away from God's love (Matthew 12:30–32, 21:33–45; Hebrews 6:1–6).

Therefore, the church must have an attitude of forgiveness for the offender, which includes the willingness to forgive and the prayer for the opportunity to be able to express that forgiveness. Then, when the offender repents and asks for forgiveness, and only then, is the church to transfer the forgiveness in her heart to the experience of the repentant. If forgiveness is granted without repentance, then the biblical meaning of forgiveness is corrupted. No one should miss the distortion of the gospel that results from forgiveness being granted apart from repentance and asking for forgiveness. It is another gospel. But as we know, there is no other gospel; thus, the true gospel remains obscured and undesirable because of a distorted concept of forgiveness.

Jay Adams says concerning forgiveness, "Jesus does not say that the sinning brother is to apologize; apologizing and forgiving are two different things. Saying 'I am sorry' only tells another how you feel; it asks him to do nothing about the offense. When you say, 'I sinned against God and He has for-given me; now I want to confess that I have also sinned against you; will you forgive me too?' You ask for a decision on his part. "When apologizing, you keep the ball in your own court; when you seek forgiveness, you toss the ball to the other party. He must now do something with it.

"When he says 'I forgive you,' he makes a promise (which is what forgiveness is) never to raise the matter again. He prom-ises not to bring it up to you, nor to anyone else, and not to sit and brood on it. The matter, he assures you, is closed. A prom-ise can be made whether one feels like it or not; and it can be kept whether one feels like it or not."[132]

When a wayward brother is disciplined, there must be an attitude on the part of the church of grief, humility, and for-giveness every step of the way. Then, when the brother dem-onstrates repentance and asks for forgiveness from the Lord and the church, the forgiveness is gladly bestowed upon him. Many believe that by the time Paul wrote 2 Corinthians, the brother who was disciplined in 1 Corinthians 5 had repented; and Paul calls for the Corinthians to forgive him. "Sufficient for such a one is this punishment which was *inflicted by* the majority, so that on the contrary you should rather forgive and comfort *him*, lest somehow such a one be overwhelmed by excessive sorrow. Wherefore I urge you to reaffirm *your* love for him" (2 Corinthians 2:6–8).

Therefore, forgiving as Christ forgives includes a constant willingness to forgive; with the extending of that forgiveness being contingent upon repentance, and this is to be as often as Christ forgives us. This was precisely the context of our Lord's discussion with Peter in Matthew 18:21–22, "Then Pe-ter came and said to Him, 'Lord, how often shall my brother sin against me and I forgive him? Up to seven times?' Jesus said to him, 'I do not say to you, up to seven times, but up to seventy times seven.'" Peter offered to forgive seven times, which was then, and by most standards today, overly generous. By human standards and power, to forgive someone for the same offense seven times is at best difficult. Nevertheless, Jesus' response to forgive "seventy times seven" is nothing short of supernatural.

The point is not that you keep a record of wrongs, and then at four hundred and ninety, you do not forgive anymore. The number defies that very explanation for two reasons. First, it is too high for any practicality of keeping records. Dealing with all the people that a person interacts with daily would require a sizable computer to keep all of the data in, not to mention all of the time. Second, and more importantly, Christians are to walk in love, and love "does not does not take into account a wrong *suffered*" (1 Corinthians 13:5). To keep up with the wrongs is both unbiblical and impractical, and that is precisely the point. We are to forgive just as Christ forgives. Here again is the command to walk in forgiveness: you forgive the offender in your heart, between God and you, regardless of his response, but the act of forgiveness is not carried out until he repents. It is important to note that the context of this wonderful call to forgiveness is in the context of church discipline. It is the teaching on church discipline that prompted Peter's question. In other words, Peter was saying what we all think—Peter who never thought something without saying it— okay Lord, what if a brother or sister sins, we confront him and he repents, and we forgive him; and then he does it again and again? How many times do we go through that process? Seven times is surely enough and more than anyone deserves. Then Jesus said no, for forgiving as Jesus forgives us means as often as he sins and repents, he is to be forgiven. This forgiveness is only granted if the offender responds appropriately, as Jesus had just stated, "And if your brother sins, go and reprove him in private; *if he listens to you, you have won your brother*" (Matthew 18:15, italics added). A brother is not won unless he listens, which means that he receives the conviction and repents. Every time he repents, he is to be forgiven. Any understanding of forgiveness that abrogates church discipline cannot even be considered an interpretation but only a travesty.

Another word from Adams concerning forgiving and forgetting is helpful, "Forgiving is not the same as forgetting. Nor does the Bible command us to 'forgive and forget.' What it tells us is that our model of forgiveness is God's forgiveness of us (Ephesians 4:32). How does God forgive? He promises us, 'your sins and iniquities will I remember against you no more' (Jeremiah 31:34c).

"'To remember no more' is not the same as forgetting. It is to work actively at not raising a matter; to forget is to have a matter passively fade from memory. The first is forgiveness; the latter is the result of forgiveness. One can promise not to raise a matter again and he can keep that promise, whether he feels like it or not. He cannot promise to forget. Forgiving leads to forgetting, because if a matter is never raised to anyone else and if it is not brooded upon by the one who granted forgiveness, it will soon fade from memory . . . forgiveness is granted upon repentance."[133]

It might be well to note, that just as the attitude of forgiveness does not result in the act of forgiveness until there is repentance, the reception of forgiveness does not mean that a person is automatically qualified to serve in certain positions or immediately enjoy their previous place of trust. Positions of trust are just that, and forgiveness does not mean that the person is all of sudden trustworthy. Jesus said to forgive, but He did not say to keep placing him in a position that requires considerable trust or potentiates great harm to others if he sins. If a marriage partner commits adultery, and there is any real chance of rebuilding the marriage, the sinning partner needs to work on rebuilding the trust that they have scandalized. An individual may be a great lay leader in the church, but if they sin, it severely damages their credibility. To place them immediately back into their place of leadership harms the body of Christ and potentiates a relapse. Some places of trust like elders and deacons have specific qualifications that are required to be able to serve in those positions. One of those is to be "above reproach" (1 Timothy 3:2). If a person fails to meet this qualification, they are precluded from serving in either of these two positions, which are built upon trustworthiness and holiness. However, if a person was serving in one of these positions and committed sins that precluded him from serving any longer, he should still be forgiven upon his repentance.

I believe the Scripture is clear that when a man has been divorced, he is disqualified from holding the office of elder or deacon. This does not mean he cannot be forgiven when he repents. It does mean that he no longer meets the qualification of being a "the husband of one wife" (1 Timothy 3:2). The tendency to interpret that phrase as allowing divorced men to serve as pastors or deacons is flawed and will perpetuate the erosion of the church and her leadership. Interpreting that verse as allowing divorce makes it mean *the husband of one wife at a time.* For those who argue that divorce is not being considered here, I would say two things. First, if divorce is not being considered here, then, one may rightly ask, does it matter if a man has been divorced multiple times—say five or even ten? Are there a number of divorces that even the most ardent proponent of the non-relevant divorce position would consider making a man unqualified to be an elder? If there are a number of divorces that seem to preclude a man from this position, then the question of whether or not divorce is a part of the consideration has been answered affirmatively. The question then becomes how many are acceptable. Secondly, while the verse obviously means "more than" not divorced, it does not mean "less than." Not divorced is the negative side while totally devoted to loving his wife is the positive side of the consideration. It seems patently wrong to merely reduce it to never having been divorced. Conversely, it seems dangerous to say that divorce is not a part of the consideration. Therefore, in light of this and other salient biblical considerations, I believe the qualification is not merely being devoted to one's *present* wife, but rather it is being devoted to one's *only* wife. It is hard to see how this sets a moral example for the people of God to look up to and follow.

In addition, merely excluding polygamists from serving as the spiritual leaders of our Lord's church seems difficult to reconcile with the requirement to be an example for the people of God (1 Timothy 4:12; Titus 2:7; 1 Peter 5:3). Even the pagans have higher standards than that. Remember, if you lower the standard for deacons, you must also lower it for the elders since the same phrase applies to both, not to mention other problems associated with interpreting the phrase to mean *one wife at a time*. When forgiven and qualified are made synonymous, it will either make forgiveness highly improbable, or it will minimize the need for trust and holiness in leadership.

Imagine a baby-sitter who sexually abused your child. After you found out about it and confronted her, she repented and asked for forgiveness, and so you forgave her. Are you then going to immediately ask her to be your baby-sitter and recommend her to your friends? Moreover, if you did give the sitter another chance, and the sitter did it again, would you continue to expose your child to that unnecessary risk? To do so would be unloving and irresponsible to your child, and such

foolishness would come from confusing forgiveness with being qualified. What about allowing a person with serious offenses on his driving record to drive the bus for the youth of
your church or a convicted embezzler to be the church treasurer? Some acts make you permanently unqualified for some
levels of trust, but never permanently unqualified for forgiveness. Other acts make you unqualified for certain levels of
trust, but over time the offender can rebuild his trustworthiness and be restored.

Several years ago, the worship leader of the church I
pastored was accused of committing adultery with a young
lady in our church. The accusations were such that I felt compelled to investigate the situation. I do not investigate some
accusations because of 1 Timothy 5:19. However, others had
been brought into this situation, and so it seemed prudent to
investigate. As I sought to determine the validity of the accusation, she could not produce any undeniable evidence, and
he continually and adamantly denied her accusations. Finally,
I told the lady that unless she had undeniable proof, I would
not continue to listen to her accusations.

Later, I asked the worship leader to please tell me if there
was any truth to the accusations. He unequivocally assured
me that the accusations were in no shape or form true, and
that he loved his wife, the church, and me; and that he would
never do anything to hurt us, especially something like this.
From that point on, I did not bring it up again.

Only the two other people that she had told at that time
were aware of the charges. He continued to lead worship,
and I continued to support him. I never mentioned it to anyone except my wife, but at times I would feel so strongly that
he had actually done what the woman accused him of that I
would get physically sick before I preached. However, I believed more strongly that I was subject to the Scripture (1

Timothy 5:19), not my feelings, and so I remained quiet. I had confidence that God would eventually manifest it if it was true, and I would not have to resort to going by my feelings and disobeying the Scripture.

Approximately one year later, the woman called me and said he was seeking to rekindle the relationship. I told her to record their next conversation on her answering machine, and then take the tape and place it under her mattress until she could give it to me. Then, if he said he wanted to come over and see her, let me know the time. He did set up a time to see her. I asked that she keep the door unlocked and a window raised, and I called one of the other pastors to go to her home with me. We arrived shortly after he did, and we sat by the window and listened until we were convinced of what was going on. After we had heard enough from outside, I opened the door and walked in. I said to him, "You really think that character does not matter, but you are dead wrong." I fired him on the spot. The evidence was irrefutable.

The church was crushed to hear the news. I was devastated because he was not only a staff member, but also someone I counted as a friend. His wife's hurt and humiliation were beyond words. We removed him from his position as worship leader and disfellowshipped him as a church member.

I took two steps in this situation that I had never taken before. First, I refused to be the one who counseled him. My wife and I did counsel and work with his wife for about a year, but I refused to counsel him. Second, I refused to accept his repentance until I was convinced his repentance was real. This simply meant that unlike other discipline cases I had been involved with where a person was immediately restored to the fellowship at the time of his repentance, he could not.

These two decisions were based on the level of deception he demonstrated and the position of trust he violated. It

seemed so arrogant to assume that I could effectively counsel him, which means being able to tell when he might be
deceiving; I had not done well at seeing his deception before, coupled with the fact that he had actually deceived the
entire church during the year of the actual sin and the year
of hiding it. How would I know he was telling the truth? At
that point there was no trust, not to mention that he was par
excellent in the art of deception; and his willingness to deceive seemed to know no bounds. I did not know if I could be
objective enough to help him.

I also found it impossible to imagine how we as a congregation could know that he was truly repentant since he had
masterfully deceived us for over a year. This may seem to be
an unwarranted presumption. However, one of the issues,
which is not considered in many of the discussions concerning restoration, is the level of deception required for the sin.
His sin was adultery, and with adultery there is a serious level
of deception; but with multiple occasions of adultery, denial
for a long period of time, denying it to my face, continuing to
lead people in the worship of God, while all the time sharing
words with the congregation about walking with God, holiness, fidelity, etc., he demonstrated a deception that was profoundly and incalculably deep.

Thus, to assume that someone, who can appear to walk so
uprightly while living for an extended period of time involved
in gross sin and deception, can be trusted the next day to tell
the whole truth and nothing but the truth; and that we whom
he had so successfully deceived would know it, requires infinite credulity. Further, the position of trust given to him by
the church makes his sin and deception all the more heinous.
"And that slave who knew his master's will and did not get
ready or act in accord with his will, shall receive many lashes,
but the one who did not know *it,* and committed deeds wor-

thy of a flogging, will receive but few. And from everyone who has been given much shall much be required; and to whom they entrusted much, of him they will ask all the more" (Luke 12:47–48).

He led people to worship God, and worship of God is the highest thing we can do; the people of God entrusted their selves, their children and the leadership of the church to him. When he fell, he violated everything that is good and holy and also the enormous trust that had been given him. In addition, one must consider the incalculable, negative impact his sin had on some who were close to being saved, young Christians, and the reputation of the church in the city because the story of this sin will not be forgotten for a generation.

The consequences of sin in places of visible trust have an unsettling lifetime legacy. The person's name may be forgotten, but Satan uses the sin and deception for years, and for some eternally. When someone assumes a place of leadership among the people of God, the standard of behavior is raised, and the responsibility is eternally greater. This is a clear biblical mandate, whether one looks at the Old Testament priest and prophets or the New Testament elders and deacons.

Fortunately, the man went to another church that did not just accept him by statement, but took him in under the watch care of the church and assigned a staff member to work with him and hold him accountable. As I recall, about two years passed before the pastor of the church told us that they believed he was truly repentant and that he desired to ask for forgiveness from our church. Based upon their assessment of him, we allowed his wonderful wife and him to come to the church one Sunday night, where he shared how God had saved him since he had been disfellowshipped by our church; how he had always been able to get away with anything he tried until the incident at our church. He humbled himself, apologized, repented, and asked for the church's forgiveness for all that he had done. He owned up to everything, and the church then voted unanimously to grant him forgiveness and welcome him back into the fellowship of the church. Then the church stood in a very long line, weeping tears of joy, to hug him and individually assure him of our love and forgiveness. What a beautiful time. He chose to remain at the church where they were attending, but he knew he was welcome at our church.

CHAPTER 8

What Did Jesus Say?

God desires that His people be holy. This is true in the Old Testament and New Testament as well as this present hour. Salvation is the work of God to restore people to holiness by faith in Jesus Christ so that they might know and enjoy God and His works forever. The cross demonstrates the unyielding requirement of holiness for those who will walk with God. Had God been able to relate to mankind, or save us apart from making us holy, the cross could have, and should have, been avoided. Through the death of Christ, God furnished the necessary provision required to make people ontologically holy in response to their exercising child-like faith in Jesus Christ. Thus, when a person is saved, he is not just forgiven, as wonderful as that is, but he is created a new person in holiness and righteousness (Ephesians 4:24; 2 Corinthians 5:17; John 3:3). God's plan and will has always been to save people by faith in Jesus Christ and restore them to holiness; once saved, He commands them to walk in holiness. The former is positional holiness, what we are; the latter is practical holiness, how we behave. God commands His people to act holy because He has made them holy.

This is true under the law where God commanded Israel, "For I am the LORD your God. Consecrate yourselves therefore, and be holy; for I am holy" (Leviticus 11:44). The whole of the law could be summed up in the phrase, if you obey, I will bless and if you disobey, I will curse (Deuteronomy 27–30). God desired for them to be different from the rest of the world, to remind us of the seriousness of sin, and emphasized that He would not tolerate it even among His own people, consequently they suffered many calamities because of their sin.

Some think that the Old Testament emphasizes holiness and the New Covenant emphasizes only love. Of course, this is contrary to the very words of Jesus, "For I say to you, that unless your righteousness surpasses *that* of the scribes and Pharisees, you shall not enter the kingdom of heaven" (Matthew 5:20). He also promised blessings upon those who desire righteousness. "Blessed are those who hunger and thirst for righteousness, for they shall be satisfied" (Matthew 5:6). Jesus is called the holy one (Acts 2:27). We as His followers are called Christians. Even though that name was first used by the enemies of Christ, it is a fitting title for His followers. It means little Christ or followers of Christ. The very name we bear is the title of the one that the Scripture calls the holy one. What an ever-present reminder of our call to holiness. Every Christian has the responsibility to honor our privileged status of being called by the name of our Lord Jesus Christ. It will not surprise anyone that God commanded Israel, "Speak to all the congregation of the sons of Israel and say to them, *'You shall be holy, for I the Lord your God am holy"* (Leviticus 19:2, italics added). However, it may surprise some to see that very verse is quoted in 1 Peter 1:16 for the church. God's call to holiness transcends time and covenants. The work of God and the call of God are always for His people to be holy and live holy.

The number one plague in the modern church is a lack of holiness. On the surface, it may seem to be a lack of evangelism, prayer, love, or countless other disciplines, but ultimately it is holiness. If the church is striving for holiness as she should, the rest will follow. The loss of holiness in much of the modern church has undermined her authority and credibility to speak against sin. The virtual absence of church discipline is undeniable proof of this loss. The only other conclusion is that people do not sin as much as they did in the early church and every other era of church history; therefore, there is no need for church discipline. I seriously doubt that anyone would be willing to use the sinlessness of the church to defend the lack of discipline. Today the message is often more of a call to happiness than holiness, and comfort rather than consecration unto God.

While the overwhelming majority of Christians and churches are against sin in their doctrine and teaching, for many there is a chasm between their belief and their practice. They preach that the church is to be a holy community unto God, but they do not follow the steps laid out by God to make that a practical reality. Thus, the call to holiness in much of contemporary preaching does more to promote hypocrisy than holiness.

The church's sin is in many cases equal to that of the world. The sin in the membership goes unchecked and then creeps into leadership, which eventuates in its normalization. Far too often, a pastor or staff member who descends into sin is quietly ushered off to another church without a word of his sin spoken publicly. This silence is ostensibly for protection of the church. Of course, all of this is done under the guise of compassion. The reality is that it is another manifestation of spiritualized narcissism, which calls not following the teaching of Scripture, failing to lovingly deal with a brother and his sin and sending a brother in sin to another church just to save face, acts of compassion. People actually argue that helping to stealth a sinner away is more compassionate than exercising church discipline. God help us! Tommy South comments, "It's not unusual, when someone begins to raise the subject of discipline, or when some disciplinary action is taken, to hear someone lament that this will surely cause trouble. Doesn't it say something about our lack of understanding of holiness that we label godly discipline as 'trouble'? When there is unrepented sin in our midst, we already have trouble, and it will only get worse unless something is done to preserve or reinstate our holiness."[134]

God disciplines out of love in order to bring His people to holiness, "For those whom the Lord loves He disciplines . . . .He disciplines us for our good, *that we may share His holiness*" (Hebrews 12:6,10, italics added). God's whole desire is that we might share His holiness, and God uses all five types of discipline to fulfill that desire. The exercising of church discipline is a vital feature of this. "It is no more 'unloving' for us to discipline one another in the interest of holiness than it is for God to discipline us for the same purpose. In fact, the lack of discipline is a distinctly un-God-like characteristic."[135] The church's ability to relegate church discipline to being a cause of trouble is symptomatic of the church's permissive regard for sin, which has resulted in her being in the appalling position of calling right wrong and wrong right.

The unwillingness of the church to discipline herself has not diminished God's commitment to discipline her, and it never will. In the Old Testament, when Israel would not discipline herself, God used Babylon to do what Israel was unwilling to do. In like manner, He has used the world to expose the hypocrisy of the church and humble her because she has been unwilling to discipline herself. Repeatedly, the sin of the church has been exposed by the media and then replayed ad-infinitum. Consequently, the church has had her sin, which she refused to deal with, aired internationally in a multiplicity of ways and none of them kind to the church. The world has every right to expose such blatant hypocrisy, although any concomitant distortions are inexcusable; not only does the world expose the hypocrisy, but she also makes specials out of it and runs them over and over, infecting a new generation with cynicism and distrust of the church. The untold harm that has been done to Christ is only surpassed by the grief of the Father over His church that will not do as she is told. But He is still determined that we "share in His holiness" (Hebrews 12:10). The church is drowning in the self-imposed deception that holiness can thrive without discipline, evangelism can flourish without holiness, and God can be pleased with a lack of obedience. These are spiritually lethal self-deceptions.

Commenting on the contemporary church, Richard Lovelace writes: "The whole church was avoiding the biblical portrait of the sovereign and holy God who was angry with the wicked every day and whose anger remains upon those who will not receive His Son. Walling off this image into an unvisited corner of its consciousness, the church substituted a new god who was the projection of grandmotherly kindness mixed with the gentleness and winsomeness of a Jesus who hardly needed to die for our sins. Many American congregations were, in effect, paying their ministers to protect them from the real God. It is partially responsible not only for the general spiritual collapse of the church in this century but also for a great deal of [evangelistic] weakness; for in a world in which the sovereign and holy God regularly employs plagues, famines, wars, disease, and death as instruments to punish sin and bring mankind to repentance, the idolatrous image of

God as pure benevolence cannot really be believed, let alone feared and worshiped in the manner prescribed by both the Old Testament and New Testament."[136]

John MacArthur says, "It is not surprising, therefore, that public discipline for sin is rare in the church today. Where there is little genuine desire for purity there will also be little desire to deal with impurity. The misinterpreted and misapplied statement of Jesus that we should not judge lest we be judged (Matthew 7:1) has been used to justify the tolerance of every sort of sin and false teaching. The ideas that every person's privacy is essentially to be protected and that each is responsible only to himself have engulfed much of the church. Under the guise of false love and spurious humility that refuse to hold others to account, many Christians are as dedicated as some unbelievers to the unbiblical notion of 'live and let live'. The church, however, is not nearly so careful not to gossip about someone's sinning as it is not to confront it and call for it to stop."[137]

Now, we will look at the definitive passage on church discipline. Also, it is important to be reminded that Jesus only mentioned the word church twice. The first time He did so in reference to the universal church and the second to the local church. This is the only time that Jesus referred to the local church. It should at least catch our attention that in this one instance He chose to speak on church discipline.

Matthew 18:15–20 says, "And if your brother sins, go and reprove him in private; if he listens to you, you have won your brother. But if he does not listen *to you,* take one or two more with you, so that by the mouth of two or three witnesses every fact may be confirmed. And if he refuses to listen to them, tell it to the church; and if he refuses to listen even to the church, let him be to you as a Gentile and a tax-gatherer. Truly I say to you, whatever you shall bind on earth shall be bound in heaven; and whatever you loose on earth shall be loosed in heaven. Again I say to you, that if two of you agree on earth about anything that they may ask, it shall be done for them by My Father who is in heaven. For where two or three have gathered together in My name, there I am in their midst."

Here Jesus lays out the process for dealing with a wayward brother or sister in need of repentance. Chapter 18 is about how believers are to relate to each other. We are compared to children in the first six verses, which demonstrates our weaknesses, needs, and dependence on God. The flow of the chapter is as follows: everyone enters the kingdom as a child (verses 1–4); those within the kingdom must treat each other as children (verses 5–9). We are to be cared for as children (verses 10–14), disciplined as children (verses 15–20), and forgiven as children (verses 21–35). Jesus prescribes four steps for the discipline process; the steps are: private reproof, semiprivate reproof, public reproof, and public removal; there is also a promise of God's approval and presence.

The first step is that of private reproof, verse 15 "And if your brother sins, go and reprove him in private; if he listens to you, you have won your brother." Before looking at the meaning and application of this verse, consideration needs to be given to a variant within this verse. The New International Version reads, "If your brother sins against you" and the King James Version reads "moreover if thy brother shall trespass against thee." The difference between these two translations and the New American Standard is that they include "against you (thee)" at the end of the statement. The reason for the difference in translations is that there are some good manuscripts that include "against you," indicating that it is a part of the original, and some exclude it, believing that it is a later addition by a copyist. The Nestle-Aland Greek New Testament rates the variant with a C, which signifies "that there is a considerable degree of doubt whether the text contains the superior reading."[138] This means that the more likely reading excludes the words "against you." In light of this, we cannot be sure which way it should read. However, with regard to interpretation, it does not make a great deal of difference. If "against you" is included, then it clearly is prescribing how an individual who has been offended has the responsibility to approach the offender and reprove him. This fits well with Peter's question, "Then Peter came and said to Him, 'Lord, how often shall my brother sin against me and I forgive him? Up to seven times?'" (verse 21).

If the "against you" is not authentic, then it is a general prescription for the church on how to handle a sinning brother; and even if the "against you" is there, it still is prescriptive for the church about how to deal with a sinning brother because the sin of a brother in community affects everyone. It may affect others directly, like someone stealing from an individual, or it may affect others indirectly, like someone living a life that reproaches a local church; thus any individual's sin may affect someone within the body directly and everyone indirectly (1 Corinthians 5). Therefore, either rendering of this verse results in basically the same teaching. That is, how does a church handle a sinning brother? Clearly, if the sin is against someone personally, then that person is the one who needs to go first to the sinning brother. If it is not against him personally, but he is the only one privy to the situation, he should also go first because resolving the issue at the lowest level of numerical involvement is of immeasurable importance. The clear teaching of the passage is that the goal is to win the brother rather than to unnecessarily expose and embarrass him. Consequently, a private meeting is the place to begin.

It is quite common for someone to refuse to go to a particular church that allows a person to remain a member who lives an immoral life and practices shady business dealings and undeniable hypocrisy. Of course, any such charges must be corroborated and not simply taken at face value. Nevertheless, the numbers of irrefutable situations of this sort are abysmal. Concerning the seriousness of the harm that comes to all Christians and the church because of hypocrisy, James S. Spiegel states, "next to the problem of evil, this is the most commonly cited reason for rejecting the Christian faith."[139] The word sin means "to miss the mark, to err, be mistaken, to miss or wander from the path of uprightness and honor, to do or go wrong, to wander from the law of God, violate God's law, sin."[140] Reprove, *Eleycho,* means "to show people their sins and summon them to repentance, either privately (Matthew 18:15) or congregationally (1 Timothy 5:20)."[141] When the meanings of these words are considered, the sense of the verse is obvious. In true community, there is to be great concern about a brother or sister who is walking in sin, and the implication is that the sin is unconfessed. The words *go* and *reprove* are both commands in the original. Thus, this is not an option, and it is not a command to just leaders or certain ones in the body of Christ. To fail to do this is nothing less than disobedience to the Lord. Jesus says, "if he listens," meaning responds appropriately, "you have won your brother" (verse 15). In other words, you have helped him come back to walking in fellowship with the Father. Many are afraid to approach a brother in sin because they are afraid of pushing him away or losing him. Jesus' words make it apparent that He is already lost and going to him only potentiates winning him, and not going leaves him lost to the work of God. Another, probably a more prevalent, reason why Christians find it difficult to approach a sinning brother, is that we are afraid of what he or others will think of us; when this is the case, it is confirmation that a person loves himself more than his wayward brother. While all of us would agree that approaching a brother who is in sin is difficult, it is indeed serious when we find it more difficult than walking in disobedience to the Lord Jesus Christ.

A church of new beginnings is unattainable until the church is willing to obey the command to go. Who is to go? Most naturally it would be the one directly offended by the offending brother. If no one has been directly offended, but indirectly as a fellow believer, then the one who is privy to the situation would be the appropriate one to go. If more than one is privy to the situation, then wisdom would dictate who should go. This might be a friend, someone the brother respects, or a leader of the church. All consideration should be given to who would have the best chance of winning the brother. The others can pray for the meeting. More often than not, more than one will probably know about the problem before the private meeting. At least, this has been my experience. This is due in part to several things: first, the nature of hypocrisy is to conceal until it is unconcealable. Second, people sometimes talk to others before they talk to the appropriate person. These first two reasons are not defended as being right, but merely noted as what seems to happen. Naturally, the church should work to correct these types of situations. Third is the nature of community. Living in close community means that it is common for more than one to detect a problem at the same time. Fourth, the wayward brother often does an adequate job of concealing his sin until it becomes public knowledge. Consequently, not only do several in the church learn of it at the same time, but the secular community at large learns of it also. Fifth, the human tendency is not to ask for help until the problem is out of control. Sixth, the human inclination is to hope that things will get better on their own, and thus prayer is offered for the wayward brother, but confrontation is put off as long as possible. By the time it is no longer plausible to postpone a personal encounter, the issue will likely have already become public. While prayer and hoping the situation will correct itself without a personal encounter does create the problem of waiting too long, the other danger is to create a church full of "Mr. Cleans" who live to pounce on the spots of impurity in their brothers and sisters lives. Some waiting is often wise since many temporary spiritual weaknesses are taken care of through the ministering of other disciplines. As long as the waiting is bathed in prayer, immersed in love, and involves a willingness to approach if necessary, it may be wise to wait. I would rather see a church be a little cautious than to spiral into legalism. This is not meant to afford an excuse to churches that are simply unwilling to reprove a brother all under the guise of "praying for him." For that is nothing but disobedience and self-love.

When the person goes, it is to reprove the brother. He must tell him of his sin, and warn of the potential damage to the person, others, and the body of Christ. He must also call for repentance. All of which must be bathed in love for the brother. One thing that the erring brother must be assured of is that this meeting is done out of love, and forgiveness and restoration are waiting at the door of repentance. Scores of times, church discipline is viewed as unloving by the world and immature or carnal Christians. What is really unloving is to leave one of God's children in sin. God's love always seeks to make the object of His love holy (1 Peter 1:15).

There are several things of importance to note here. First, discipline is not the responsibility of the leaders alone. It is the responsibility of every believer in the community. More often than not, these private meetings would not involve the pastor or a leader of the church if they were done soon enough.

Second, a prerequisite for this type of meeting is that the one going to reprove is set apart unto God, though he does not have to be perfect. If not, he will have little desire to do such a difficult thing as approach a fellow believer about his sin, and if he did, it would merely add hypocrisy to hypocrisy. Third, the term brother is used of Christians denoting our familial relationship, consequently, it includes female believers in everything that is being said—sorry ladies this is equally your responsibility. Fourth, the term brother is a term of affection. It bespeaks of a family member and a deep love for the people of God. This is not an enemy, but a sibling.

Having practiced discipline for several years now, some things have become apparent which need to be understood and addressed. First, there are usually some in most churches who have such a high view of their own spirituality, along with a total lack of compassion, that they believe they are God's messengers of reproof. As Gabriel is the angelic messenger of the coming Messiah, they are the not so angelic couriers of castigation. They love reproving others. Care must be taken that these do not become the church's celestial censures just because it does not bother them to go to a sinning brother. That is in fact a valuable caveat. If it does not bother someone to go and confront a sinning brother, something is dangerously wrong. It is true that the church needs people who are willing to go, but willing to go and supercharged at the idea of going are two entirely different spirits. Just because they are willing does not mean that they are the best ones to go unless they are the only one who knows about the situation. We must guard against creating a situation where everyone is going to everyone over every petty thing. Some people seem to thrive on finding fault with others especially when it comes to how they were treated or mistreated by them. These are the ones who are still personally unconvinced that Copernicus was right;

they believe all of the evidence, at least the important corroboration, still demonstrates that the world revolves around them. It will not take long to figure out who they are because they have an uncanny ability of sharing with you about their incalculable importance to the kingdom, albeit in an ostensibly humble way.

A second issue, which arises in the practical application of church discipline, concerns what kind of offense constitutes going to a brother and not going to a brother. When I am asked, I normally counsel people to handle personal hurts in one of two ways. If the hurt is minor and will not affect either the offender or the offended's life, then handle it with prayer. Give it to the Lord and move on. There are so many things that happen in the course of serving Christ that this must be become an everyday part of our Christian lives. If not, many very active Christians will spend countless hours daily dealing with minor infractions. This is not intended to be contrary to the teaching of the Lord, but in the spirit of that teaching (1 Corinthians 13:6; 1 Peter 4:8; Proverbs 10:12). I believe the Lord clearly intended bigger things than a failure to smile or say hello, unless of course that would cause a Christian to stumble. If the offense cannot be handled sufficiently by prayer, then the brother must be approached. If the person who was offended feels a need to talk to anyone about the offense then that person needs to go to the offender. Gossip has no place in the life of a believer. I would make an exception for those who come to their pastor or another spiritual leader seeking biblical guidance concerning how to handle the situation. This is entirely different. We must allow for this because we know that not every Christian knows how to deal with everything in a biblical manner. That is the whole idea of discipleship.

A third concern, which arises in the real life of church discipline, is whether it is ever appropriate for more than one person to go to the sinning brother on the first visit. Many times, if not most of the situations that I have been involved in, the situation of the person who needs to be approached about his sin is already known by many, if not the entire church and community. Maybe this should not be, and they should be dealt with sooner; but this is what happens. When this is the case, it would still be preferable to send one person, but since the one-on-one level of privacy has already been violated by the individual or the rumor mill, it seems that the one-on-one prescription is not obligatory although it would still be preferred. This is based on the fact that the one-on-one and the two or three is primarily related to winning a brother or sister with as little publicity as possible. Therefore, while it still is best to send one, there are circumstances that seem to make one-on-one meetings, once confidentiality has been broken, unwise.

For example, I remember a young lady who, to the best that we could ascertain, was taking drugs and dealing in them. Her lifestyle had become known to many—she had not attended church for a considerable period of time. We also knew that many others stayed in the same residence that she did, and purportedly some of these were men who were of an unsavory type. When we sought to fulfill what Jesus said about going to her, it did not seem wise to send one person. As a matter of fact, the ones who knew most about the situation said it would in fact be a dangerous situation for one person to go. Consequently, we sent the two biggest deacons we had, and yes you are right, that was not by accident. Another situation that could require two is where there is a high probability of the wayward brother vilifying or making false accusations about the one who comes. Also, if it is a woman, I recommend sending one or two women, or two men if it is not appropriate for a woman to enter that particular circumstance. Again, sending more than one on the first visit is not intended to abrogate Jesus' words, but this is done only if the lowest level of privacy has already been violated and other circumstances such as have been mentioned seem to make it the wisest. Seldom is a case of discipline a textbook case. Further, it is prudent to remember that it is safe to assume that not all of the wayward who we will deal with are actually brothers or sisters. This is especially true since the modern degrading of membership.

A fourth situation is when distance or law precludes you from going personally. This can happen when a member has been sent to prison in another state or is in a state institution where visitors are not allowed. In such cases, we have sent a letter and/or sought to talk with him by phone. Letters and phone calls are not appropriate unless a face-to-face meeting is virtually impossible. When letters are used, they must be of a nature that is commensurate with seeking repentance. This includes clear confirmation of the church's willingness to work with the wayward brother, regardless of what they have done. It cannot be the kind of letter that pastors often receive, which are intended to take him to task rather than to resolve a conflict or receive feedback from a brother. This is obvious before the letter is even read since they live in the same city and could have come and met face to face; instead, they opt for a letter that is not normally signed, a sure sign of the desire to give a good talking to rather than resolve an issue. I have made it a policy not to even read unsigned letters. They simply want to emit their verbal smog, with no feedback, leaving the recipient to deal with the criticism alone. There is no biblical reason to read unsigned letters that violate the letter and spirit of the New Testament. The same can be said of letters written to the church by a disgruntled church member, to be read by the pastor after the authors have departed. They want no feedback or reconciliation between brothers, but merely to speak their mind. Thus, I refuse to read them because these kinds of letters do not allow for the first goal of discipline, to gain a brother, reconciliation, and redemption. I am still looking for the verse that says, "If you have something against your brother write him an unsigned letter." Go is a command, and it is intended to be obeyed.

The difference in the letter being used with a brother in prison is that the goal is redemption and to follow Christ, but because of distance, unusual measures must be taken. In these cases, without the use of letters, discipline will probably be circumnavigated. Also, there may be times that the prisoner is either not allowed to have visitors or simply refuses to. Neither scenario excuses us from seeking to obey Jesus. I am not proposing letters in order to create an easy way out; I have made visits where I had to drive for over three hours, and in one instance along with two other men I flew to another state in order to make the visit face to face.

The semi-private meeting follows only if the private meeting fails to bring about restoration. Whether or not the process escalates to this next level, or the next, is determined by the choice of the wayward brother. He can stop the process at any time by repenting. "But if he does not listen *to you,* take one or two more with you, so that by the mouth of two or three witnesses every fact may be confirmed" (verse 16). Only if he does not listen to you the first time is it necessary to involve more people. The word *take* is the third of five commands found in verses 15–17. The first two were, *go* and *reprove.* This is demonstrative of the love of the Lord for His people and church. God is so concerned about His people that

What Did Jesus Say?

He does not give up after one try nor does He want His church to give up after one try.

He does not give up after one try nor does He want His church to give up after one try.

God is serious about the church seeking to restore the wayward brother. This is a continuation of the procedure laid down by Moses, "A single witness shall not rise up against a man on account of any iniquity or any sin which he has committed; on the evidence of two or three witnesses a matter shall be confirmed (Deuteronomy 19:15). Jesus said the purpose of this second meeting with two or three is "so that by the mouth of two or three witnesses every fact may be confirmed" (verse 16). The need to confirm every fact is in regard to several things. First, another witness would confirm that the brother had been rebuked clearly and properly. This is necessary for two reasons. The wayward brother may not have understood the first time. Sometimes people either have a difficult time understanding others or have a struggle communicating clearly. Also, remember these are very difficult situations in which the lack of complete candor is not uncommon. Therefore, this serves as a protective for the rebuked in that if it was not communicated clearly, it can now be elucidated. It also serves as a protector for the rebuking brother. Surely, his goal is to redeem, and thus he will be thankful for any help that might assist in achieving the goal even if it means being corrected. In addition, he knows that if the wayward brother refuses to repent, the next step is to take it to the church. Thus, it would benefit the first individual who approached the wayward to have confirmation that what he did was done correctly.

Secondly, this second step would make sure that the wayward brother was not only reproved properly, but that he also is adequately informed of the full scope of what is going on. This is not just a brother who has come to him, but if the wayward does not repent, this heretofore private issue will become very public. This could have a strong impact upon the wayward. The private meeting can produce repentance at times based on the desire to keep it private, but the semiprivate meeting can produce repentance because of the increased formality of the meeting. If there was any doubt that the reproving brother would take it all the way to the church, that bit of hope is dashed by the semiprivate meeting.

The importance of the selection of these second and third witnesses cannot be overstated. Apparently, at this step there is some discretion as to who the other two witnesses can be. For example, if it is a private issue, the initial accuser can now choose the two whom he wants to go with him. Serious consideration should be given to choose individuals who will not be unnecessarily offensive to the wayward. Also, choosing men or women of recognized integrity and esteem in the church will prove invaluable in dealing with the wayward and also the church if the case has to come before them. These two or three will be the ones bringing the charge to the church provided the brother does not repent. It is important to give due consideration to making them people that the wayward respects and would be most inclined to listen to. It is imperative that these will be people who will handle the situation in a Christian manner regardless of the wayward's response. He needs to be someone who can keep his temper under control; he also needs to be able to keep quiet about the situation if the person repents or until the time it needs to come before the church; further, he needs to be someone who can be strong enough to confront, and humble enough to forgive and live with the facts of the sin. This will take substantial consideration since regrettably, not every Christian has these qualifications.

Regardless whether it is a situation like the one just described, or one where others, like deacons or elders, are making the decision about who should go, it is important to select people who can cope with the pressure of discipline. If the discipline process is at level one and only one person knows about it, then the person to go is already chosen; but if the sin is already known beyond the private one-on-one level prior to the first encounter, or if it is at the second level where two or three go, I would strongly advise choosing men or women who are not only respected by the church but strong enough to endure the potential fallout. It is to a pastor's peril if he ever forgets that temple cleansing is tough business.

If deacons are what they are supposed to be in the church, they make excellent people to send. They are servants that have been set apart by the church to help the pastors care for the church. However, not all deacons are qualified for this task. Yes, they should be, but that does not mean that everyone serving as a deacon is. Even among deacons who are truly serving as deacons, there will be some who are better suited to this challenge. When I have had the chance to send a deacon, there are always some I prefer not to send since they can hardly make a decision about any difficult issue or express themselves in no uncertain terms on any subject. They may be valuable in other areas, but in the area of discipline they can cause enormous harm and confusion. The ones that go may be criticized, lied about, turned on by friends, and have their families hurt. If they crack under the pressure at any place in the process, the church, and the pastor and his family, will suffer profoundly. This is another one of those points that cannot be overemphasized. A pastor should find someone he thinks would endure to the finish. Whether elders, deacons, or laymen are used, remember that there are some who are better suited for hospital visits and some for discipline. This is not intended to absolve some from their responsibility of participating in church discipline. However, it is wise to send the best suited when opportunity allows. We would do the same in any other area of church life. The main point of this step is to offer another chance for repentance and confirm the facts.

The third step is public reproof. "And if he refuses to listen to them, tell it to the church" (verse 17). This step is often erroneously combined with the fourth step, but it is actually a third step; a third attempt to bring the brother to repentance. This step involves the church being informed of the situation and being brought into the disciplinary process. By the time it reaches this level, it is important to have the pastors and deacons aware of the situation and giving leadership to the body. This is a pivotal point in the process. If it is handled properly, it can increase the chances of reclamation of the wayward, or bringing unity to the church body in the event that disfellowshipping becomes necessary. The communication in this situation needs to come from the pastor or at least in a way that clearly signifies to the church that he and the other leaders support the action.

Telling the church requires a delicate balance of telling enough but not too much. Considerable attention should be given to what will be told to the church body. Enough must be told to make it clear what the charge is, and yet no more than necessary needs to be told. While the goal is not to hide essentials, it is also not intended to produce fodder for the gossips or to seek recognition by the tabloids. One example is the staff member mentioned earlier who had been involved in repeated adulterous affairs over an extended period of time, habitual lying, and profound deception. When the church was informed, it was done without going into every dreadful detail. They were told that he had been involved in an affair and cover-up for over a year. This was absolutely true, but it was not every lurid detail. On the other hand, if you use

298

something as vague as "caught in immorality," then that leaves people speculating what kind of immorality, which can make the situation worse. Consequently, make it clear but not titillating.

The obvious purpose in telling the church is to increase the number of people going to the wayward brother or sister to the maximum. There is no higher court of appeal than the local church. At this point, depending on the size of the church, there may be hundreds of people aggressively pursuing this brother and asking him to repent. It may be easy for some who name the name of Christ to ignore the pleas of one or two, but ignoring the whole church is quite another matter. Church discipline is not merely a pastoral or deacon issue, but it is a church issue. This step is important for several reasons: First, because it is biblical. Second, numerous people aggressively reproving and confronting may produce repentance where other attempts have failed. I have seen this in operation, and it is powerful for the wayward to know that the church will, over the next week or so, be standing on his doorstep; that they care enough to be involved in his life cannot be ignored or written off as a personal vendetta. Third, it also teaches the entire congregation about their responsibility to care for their brothers and sisters. Fourth, if disfellowshipping becomes necessary, this step provides an enormous safeguard against trouble at the time of the vote to disfellowship. If the people go and plead for him to repent, and he has refused their pleas, they will be less inclined to oppose the fourth step to disfellowship because they have seen firsthand his unwillingness to repent. His recalcitrance is undeniable. They know first hand that everything that could be done was done.

If, after the third step is followed, someone ends up opposing disfellowshipping the wayward brother at the time of the vote, then the first question to ask the person is whether he went to the wayward brother. If he did not go, and many others did, then the question is why did he not do what the Bible says to do, and how could he know how to vote if he has not been? If he did go, then he should be asked to share what happened when he met with him that has influenced his vote against disfellowshipping. In other words, if he repented, then the church needs to know about it and pursue that course of action. If the wayward did not repent, how can he biblically vote against discipline? Further, he can be asked during the meeting, "If you did not go to him, how can you oppose the conclusion of the hundred who loved him enough to go to him?" Although there may be someone who opposes the discipline—probably someone who has not followed the biblical instruction thus far—when the entire church has had the opportunity to see his resistance firsthand, it makes the church more unified and the vote much more decisive. It is highly unlikely that anyone will have the nerve to oppose at this point, although it is possible. This step also helps the church to deal with the issue of sin in their own lives and in the body as seriously as Jesus intended.

I am often amazed at the cruel caricatures that are made by other churches of churches that practice church discipline. A popular one is that little time or concern is invested by churches that practice "kicking people out." I mean how long could it take to kick someone out of church? Maybe a few hours, or at the most a week, and then just kick the person out. The reality is, most discipline cases actually take around six months from the time that the sin becomes known to the time of disfellowshipping. I have spent as long as a year. Part of the reason for the need for this length of time is to confirm the facts before approaching a brother, report back on the situation in order to fully inform the principals, and prayer. We normally spend three to four weeks between each step praying that God will grant us wisdom and will change the wayward brother's heart. Arranging for a suitable time to go to the person's house can also require a significant amount of time. All things considered, six months can expire before you know it. If it is done right, and that is the only way it should be done, discipline requires quite an investment of time and energy, in spite of the plethora of caricatures.

The fourth and final step of discipline is removing the rebellious brother from the fellowship, encouragement, and blessings of church life. "And if he refuses to listen even to the church, let him be to you as a Gentile and a tax-gatherer" (verse 17); *Let him be* serves as the fifth command in this passage. The previous four are: go, reprove, (verse 15) take (verse 16) and tell (verse 17). He is to be viewed as a "Gentile" and a "tax-gatherer." The Gentile was a heathen who had no part in the Jewish covenant. The tax-gatherer was even worse because he was born a Jew and became a traitor to Rome. He was regarded as a thief. Both of these ideas communicate the intention that they are to be treated as someone who is outside the Christian community or Covenant. It is similar to the Old Testament practice of "cutting" someone "off" from the assembly of Israel (e.g., Genesis 17:14; Exodus 12:15, 19; 30:33,38). The "you" in "let him be to you" is plural in number meaning this is a command that everyone is responsible to obey.

Simply put, the wayward wants to live like an unbeliever and discipline affords him that opportunity. As an unbeliever, he is not allowed into the fellowship of the church. This reiterates the New Testament teaching and importance of a regenerate church membership; and the appellation "tax-gatherer" emphasizes the wayward brother's potential and willingness to do harm to the church. The same idea of separation is clearly communicated by the apostle Paul when he said, "*I have decided* to deliver such a one to Satan for the destruction of his flesh, that his spirit may be saved in the day of the Lord Jesus. . . . Clean out the old leaven . . . I wrote you in my letter not to associate with immoral people; I *did* not at all *mean* with the immoral people of this world, or with the covetous and swindlers, or with idolaters; for then you would have to go out of the world. But actually, I wrote to you not to associate with any so-called brother if he should be an immoral person, or covetous, or an idolater, or a reviler, or a drunkard, or a swindler—not even to eat with such a one. . . . Remove the wicked man from among yourselves" (1 Corinthians 5:5,7a, 9–11, and 13). The message is clear. The person is to be treated as an unbeliever who potentiates harm to himself and the church.

Because he does not demonstrate characteristics commensurate with possessing the new life, he must be separated from the body of Christ. Paul said, "But actually, I wrote to you not to associate with any *so-called brother* if he should be an immoral person, or covetous, or an idolater, or a reviler, or a drunkard, or a swindler—not even to eat with such a one" (1 Corinthians 5:11, italics added). Interpreters debate whether that means he is to be excluded from the Lord's Supper or from sharing a regular meal. It seems like both are in view. If he is to be removed from the fellowship and treated as an unbeliever, then there could not be Christian fellowship with him at a common meal, and removing him from the fellowship of the church automatically precludes him from partaking of the Lord's Supper. If you factor in the ideas of "Gentile" and "tax-gatherer" the meaning is clear. No Jew would have considered spiritual fellowship with a Gentile or tax-gatherer in or outside of the assembly. Logically, he must be treated differently, as an immoral person, than when he was a moral believer, or else all of the New Testament distinctions between lost and saved, brother and Gentile, in and out, evaporate. Thus, it appears that both are in view. I have practiced mentioning the most recently disciplined person by name when the church gathers to partake of the Lord's Supper. This is done to remind us of our ongoing responsibility and the seriousness of sin, and to help the fellowship not to forget to pray for our estranged brother or sister. When they repent and are welcomed back in the fellowship and the Lord's table, I mention their restoration to the fellowship at the beginning of the Lord's Supper. The former mention is a time of prayer and the latter is for celebration.

Paul also gives a much-needed reminder that this "so called brother" is not an enemy. "And if anyone does not obey our instruction in this letter, take special note of that man and do not associate with him, so that he may be put to shame. And *yet* do not regard him as an enemy, but admonish him as a brother" (2 Thessalonians 3:14–15). We are not to hate him, but grieve for him. There is a time to associate with someone who has been disfellowshipped, and that is when there is opportunity to "admonish him as a brother." God never tires of calling His people to repentance and neither should we. On the other hand, to begin to accept him without repentance is to minimize his sin and facilitate his continued walk of deception.

After the instruction of verses 15–17 comes the wonderful promises of verses 18–20, "Truly I say to you, whatever you shall bind on earth shall be bound in heaven; and whatever you loose on earth shall be loosed in heaven. Again I say to you, that if two of you agree on earth about anything that they may ask, it shall be done for them by My Father who is in heaven. For where two or three have gathered together in My name, there I am in their midst."

This passage has been abused so often and for so long that the misinterpretation has become the accepted popular interpretation. One reason for the widespread acceptance of the misinterpretation is that the desire to maintain the power of God and the promise of self-fulfillment is strong even if the desire for holiness has perished. Unfortunately, this trendy misinterpretation consigns these wonderful verses to the cliché status of many other Scriptures that have been extricated from their context at the expense of their original beauty and richness. These verses have been used by the Church of Rome to support the doctrine that the church has the authority to forgive sin. This has facilitated the perpetuation of their colossal perversions concerning their teachings on sacraments, salvation, and forgiveness.

The charismatics are well known for claiming these three verses as a carte blanche for whatever they want. Thus, it is common to hear expressions like binding Satan or binding demons, sickness, poverty, nicotine, and a galaxy of other unwanteds. Of course, there is also the positive side of the loosing of health and prosperity, ad nauseam. Little thought is given to the real meaning indicated by the context, which limits it to church discipline; not to mention other Scriptures such as 1 John 5:14, and the experience of every believer who has sought to make it to mean anything. How many believers will be honest enough to admit that they do not get everything they pray for when quoting (misquoting) these verses as a guarantee. The term "whatever" is limited by the context. It means "whatever" in relation to following Jesus' commands concerning church discipline. We use terms like whatever, all, and everything regularly, and would be appalled if someone took it for an absolute limitless word like is done so often with the Word of God.

For example, if someone comes to your office and asks to borrow some things, and you respond, "sure get whatever you need." It would probably not sit well with you if they took all of the furniture, supplies, computer, etc. Your "whatever" was limited by the context. In like manner, this is a wonderful promise that is limited by the context of what Jesus is talking about. For those who practice church discipline, the real blessings of these promises are of incalculable comfort.

"In light of the context of what Jesus had just said, in the light of common rabbinical expressions of that day, and in light of the grammatical construction of the text, it is clear that He was not teaching that God's power can be bent to men's will. He was not saying that men could force heaven to do things. Quite to the contrary, His promise was that when His people bend their wills to His, He would endorse and empower their act of obedience.

"Jesus was here continuing His instruction about church discipline. He was not speaking about petitioning God for special blessings or privileges, and even less was He teaching that the church or any of its leaders has power to absolve the sins of its members. He was declaring that the church has a divine mandate to discipline its members when they refuse to repent."[142] Another commentator says the words, "about anything are restricted by the context and by the phrase *peri pantos pragmatos,* which should here be rendered "about any judicial matter": the word *pragma* often has that sense."[143]

Equally lamentable is the fashionable distortion of verse 20, which has also been extricated from its context. This verse is quoted almost every time people gather for prayer, worship, or a conference; when in reality, it actually has nothing to do with any of those situations. Those who seem to gain such wonderful comfort from verse 20 promise that Jesus is with us when two or more gather together to pray or worship; however, they must at some point think about the implications of what that means when they are alone. Whatever comfort is gained by the blanket understanding of Jesus' presence when two or more are gathered together is overshadowed by the emptiness that must follow when people leave and go their individual ways. Unless this verse is misinterpreted, because really we know He is present when we are alone because He said, "I will never desert you, nor will I ever forsake you" (Hebrews 13:5). Hence, if He is with us when we are alone, He is most assuredly with us when we are together for prayer, study, worship, etc. The Bible has many verses that address the issue of general prayer and worship, but this is simply not one of them.

Now that some of the prevalent misinterpretations have been dispelled, we are in a better position to see what these verses actually teach. When Jesus says, "Truly I say to you," the "you" is plural. Then it referred to all of the disciples, now it applies to the local church, which verses 15–17 demonstrate is the highest court of appeals. It can also be the "you" of the two or three that have pursued the discipline case. Binding and loosing (verse 18) were common rabbinical expressions, which meant forbidden or permitted according to the revealed will of God in His Word. "In heaven" was another way to refer to Jehovah God.

Another important grammatical note on these verses is that "shall be bound" and "shall be loosed" are periphrastic, future, perfect, passive participles, which are better rendered "shall have already been bound" or "shall have already been loosed." For a more detailed study of this topic, see *The Expositors Bible Commentary*, Matthew 18:18. Thus, this verse does not teach that God is waiting to conform to what the church does, but rather God has already decreed; and when the church obeys, in this case with regard to church discipline, she does so with full blessing and authority of God. In other words, the church clarifies and carries out heaven's business rather than heaven waiting to ratify the church's decisions. Even though many may scorn those who exercise discipline, the church that follows God's commands has heaven's approval, which in the final analysis is all that matters. John 20:23 also uses perfect passives concerning forgiving, which is not granting to the church the power to absolve sins, but means if someone does what the Bible says, either as an unbeliever repenting and trusting Jesus Christ as Lord and Savior, or as a believer, who confesses his sin, we can assure them of God's forgiveness because He has already established that in heaven, and recorded it in His Word.

Verse 20 is a reference to verse 17. After two or three went to the wayward brother, and he refused to listen, those same two or three must take it to the church. This can be a daunting experience. The fear of how it will be received, and what you might be accused of can be sufficiently intimidating to cause even the boldest to have second thoughts. Thus, our all-knowing Lord Jesus gives the absolute assurance of His presence in this very difficult endeavor. For we do not know what will come, but we do know that He is with us and confirms the actions and decisions of the ones who follow His will in the area of church discipline. That the Lord saw the need to supply this promise does remind us of the difficulty of church discipline. Even our Lord knows that discipline is extremely difficult; therefore He gives a blessed special promise of His presence. It is during these times that your feelings, and some people's responses, will communicate that you are all alone, but Jesus promises that you are not. I can tell you that this blessed promise can bring comfort to your soul beyond measure. It is indeed sad that this verse can be so oft quoted and yet misunderstood. Even many commentators see it as a general promise, but those who have actually practiced church discipline see it for the blessed promise that it is. The blessedness of this verse is lost to the church because the church fails to walk the corridors of church discipline. When we do what God wants in the way He wants, He acts, empowers, and confirms those decisions. This promise is also a reminder to those who criticize people who practice discipline that the Lord is on the side of those who follow Him in church discipline.

"This was in keeping with Old Testament precedents, as in Deuteronomy 19:15. The apostles would have been familiar with these words. Albert Barnes notes, 'The witnesses in the Old Testament were to be the first to execute the judgment of the court (Deuteronomy 17:7); here they are the first to pray.'" [144]

The significance of the words "in My name" is pointed out by Adam Clark when he says, "In my name—That is, By my authority, acting for me in my church. See John 10:25; 16:23 . . . assembled in obedience to my command, and with a desire to promote my glory."[145] Gathering in His name is to not merely to speak His name but to do His will. The desire to promote God's glory outweighs the desire for self-preservation. These words also speak of the deity of Jesus Christ. "There am I in the midst—None but God could say these words, to say them with truth, because God alone is every where present, and these words refer to his omnipresence. Wherever—suppose tens of thousands of assemblies were collected in the same moment, in different places of the creation, (which is a very probable case), this promise states that Jesus is in each of them. Can any say these words, except that God who fills both heaven and earth? But Jesus says these words: ergo—Jesus is God . . ."[146] Dietrich Bonhoeffer who lived in Germany during the time of the third Reich, spent time in the concentration camps for his faith and was eventually "executed by special order of Himmler at the concentration camp at Flossenburg on April 9th 1945, just a few days before it was liberated by the Allies."[147] Although he was liberal in his theology, he understood the cost of discipleship and believed in the necessity of church discipline.

"Sin demands to have a man by himself. It withdraws him from the community. The more isolated a person is, the more destructive will be the power of sin over him, and the more deeply he becomes involved in it, the more disastrous is his isolation. Sin wants to remain unknown. It shuns the light. In the darkness of the unexpressed it poisons the whole being of a person. This can happen even in the midst of a pious community. In confession, the light of the gospel breaks into the darkness and seclusion of the heart. The sin must be brought into the light. The unexpressed must be openly spoken and acknowledged. All that is secret and hidden is made manifest. It is a hard struggle until the sin is openly admitted, but God breaks gates of brass and bars of iron (Psalm 107:16).

"Since the confession of sin is made in the presence of a Christian brother, the last stronghold of self-justification is abandoned. The sinner surrenders; he gives up all his evil. He gives his heart to God, and he finds the forgiveness of all his sin in the fellowship of Jesus Christ and his brother. The expressed, acknowledged sin has lost all its power. It has been revealed and judged as sin. It can no longer tear the fellowship asunder. Now the fellowship bears the sin of the brother. He is no longer alone with his evil for he has cast off his sin from him. Now he stands in the fellowship of sinners who live by the grace of God and the cross of Jesus

Christ. The sin concealed separated him from the fellowship, made all his apparent fellowship a sham; the sin confessed has helped him define true fellowship with the brethren in Jesus Christ."[148]

CHAPTER 9

Will the Church Discipline Candidates Please Stand?

Whom shall we discipline? Where shall we start, and with whom shall we stop? These are the questions. It is evident that there must be some appropriate candidates for church discipline or Jesus would not have commanded the church to practice discipline. It is equally apparent that the church should not discipline everyone who sins. For that would result in the demise of the church since all who are a part of the church have sinned and still do.

The concern noted earlier about past ill use of church discipline is a valid concern. It does appear to have been misused in the past at times, and it is safe to say that it can be abused in the present as well. Wherever you have humans doing anything, there is the potential for abuse. However, this need not be more than a healthy concern and caveat, and it need not ever become a reality any more than parental discipline must become child abuse.

All that is needed to protect against misuse of church discipline are clear parameters for determining who is and who is not an appropriate candidate for discipline. The Scripture adequately supplies that need. There are four categories of behavior that make someone a candidate for church discipline. In this chapter, we will establish which behaviors merit the beginning of church discipline, and if continued unabated, should result in formal church discipline.

Therefore, we are referring specifically to the process of discipline that results in formal church discipline rather than the many facets of church discipline that encompass all of church life that everyone experiences. Some people exhibit behavior that is annoying, draining, embarrassing, and mildly disruptive, but not worthy of discipline. Rather, they require patience, love, endurance, and discipleship. These individual's sins, in and of themselves, could be serious enough to warrant disfellowshipping, but their response makes it unnecessary. They are repentant, willing to seek counsel, and sincerely believe what they profess about Jesus; but they are weak.

People who are candidates for discipline are the ones who persist in their sin, refusing counsel and admonishment. The Bible determines what sin is and which sins are worthy of church discipline, and the church is to carry out the commands of her Lord; but every individual will determine how he responds to discipline. In other words, it is not always the sin that is determinate, but rather the person's response to the counsel or reality of his sin.

There is an important difference between human rebellion or hypocrisy and moral weakness. Hypocrisy means "to give an impression of having certain purposes or motivations, while in reality having quite different ones—'to pretend, to act hypocritically, pretense, hypocrisy . . . one who pretends to be other than he really is . . .'"[149]

Hypocrites are the prime candidates for discipline. They are in sin, but their only concern is to conceal, deny, excuse, or explain away their sin. James Spiegel says, "Hypocrisy is a

kind of inconsistency in human life which always involves behavior of some sort. Specifically, a hypocrite is one who acts
inconsistently with her beliefs, words, or other actions, due to
either self-deception or lack of moral seriousness."[150] Self deception "is kind of 'make believe' in which one pretends to
believe what she knows is not the case."[151] Hypocrites rationalize their behavior to justify it, but they know that their
rationalization is not actually true. For example, someone who
does not give to the church according to the Scripture excuses their sinfulness because they teach a Sunday school
class even though they know the Scripture says to give—apart
from whether a person does something else.

Another example of self-deception could be when individuals who are angry all the time seek to justify their anger by
telling themselves that they are not really angry but merely
upset, and this is in spite of what they know to be true, both
emotionally and psychologically.

An important distinction that needs to be maintained is
the difference between being self-deceived and being delusional. "The delusional person experiences no conflict in her
belief of a lie, for she is completely convinced. The self-deceived, on the other hand, does experience conflict because
her belief contradicts her knowledge . . . the self-deceived lack
'moral seriousness.'"[152] They do not really believe what they
purport to believe, or they are not as serious as they claim to
be. They outwardly claim to believe one thing and really believe, or value, another. They are hypocrites.

The Pharisees are the clearest example of hypocrisy in
Scripture. Jesus said of them, "You hypocrites! Isaiah was right
when he prophesied about you: 'These people honor me with
their lips, but their hearts are far from me'" (Matthew 15:7–
8). Their speech portrayed them as being dedicated to God,
but that was not their true heart. It is like people who say

313

they want to work out some differences with another person, but their heart is merely to defend their actions or to prove the other person wrong.

Matthew 23:27 affords a lucid picture of what a hypocrite is. "Woe to you, teachers of the law and Pharisees, you hypocrites! You are like whitewashed tombs, which look beautiful on the outside but on the inside are full of dead men's bones and everything unclean." Consequently, hypocrites present themselves in word or action as something that they really are not. Jesus' condemnation of hypocrisy was unflinchingly severe and deservedly so (Matthew 23:13,15,23,25,27,29). Simply put, a hypocrite is a person who acts inconsistently with his beliefs, words, or other actions because of self-deception or moral insincerity.

However, it must be remembered that not everyone who acts contrary to what they claim to believe is a hypocrite or worthy of discipline. In other words, not every failure to live up to one's moral ideals can be classified as hypocrisy or else all moralists (people who believe in some moral standards) would necessarily be classified as hypocrites since everyone fails to live up to their moral ideals at some time. Further, we know that all moralists are not hypocrites or else hypocrites would not be singled out as a separate breed of sinners.

There are actually two other kinds of individuals who do not act consistently with what they say or espouse who cannot be considered hypocrites. First are the individuals of poor moral insight, and second are the morally weak people known by the Greek term akrates. The person with poor moral insight has a genuine desire to do what is right but acts inconsistently with what he believes because of a lack of reasoning skills; he desires to follow Christ and do what is right, but fails to discern or know what is right. The akrates is morally weak.

These three—hypocrites, those with poor moral insight, and the akrates—are prima facie identical, but they are essentially different. "Hypocrites are generally regarded as insincere in their professed adherence to their principles, whereas the faults of the other two are quite different. The sufferer of akrasia is not insincere but weak, and the other character has a genuine desire to do what is right but lacks the necessary inferential powers to see what is right."[153]

The akrates and the person with poor moral insight will desire to bring their behavior into line with their words when they become aware of the inconsistency, while the hypocrite will not. Therefore, while these three are virtually indistinguishable prima facie, Spiegel says there are normally "enough contextual clues in a given situation to provide sufficient evidence to conclude one way or the other."[154] In addition, they are ontologically different.

Two things distinguish the hypocrite from the other two. Unlike the hypocrite, the latter two are sincerely committed to their beliefs. They also experience remorse and are repentant when they become aware that their actions are inconsistent with their words or beliefs. Examples of the three may help to clarify the distinction.

Judas Iscariot was a hypocrite. He acted contrary to what he claimed to believe, and when he was confronted with it, he did not repent (Matthew 26:25, 47). He did finally feel remorse, but he did not repent, which would have signified godly sorrow (2 Corinthians 7:9–11). There is a vast difference between being truly remorseful unto repentance and just being sad that you got caught or things did not go as you expected. Judas did not feel true remorse over the wrongness of his actions and his duplicity, or he would have simply repented and been forgiven, which he did not do (Matthew 27:3).

The apostles' actions, in regard to going into hiding when Jesus was crucified, are an example of poor moral insight—and I suppose moral weakness also. Yes, they were afraid. Yes they acted contrary to their profession of Jesus being the Christ (Matthew 16:16) and their profession of Jesus' deity by their worship of Him (Matthew 14:33). However, the disciples were not hypocrites because they truly desired to follow Christ, they simply did not fully understand the gospel. When they did come to a fuller understanding, they served Christ and gave their lives for Him.

Peter's denial of Christ is a wonderful example of akrasia. Jesus told Peter that he would deny Him three times, and Peter adamantly denied that he would do such a thing (Matthew 26:34–35). However, in spite of Peter's resolve and belief, he denied Christ three times just as Jesus said he would (Matthew 26:70–75). Peter's actions directly contradicted what he said and believed, but he was not a hypocrite; he was simply weaker than he thought. Peter sincerely desired to follow Christ, but under certain circumstances and because of moral weakness, he failed. Before he was even confronted by anyone he "wept bitterly" over his moral and spiritual failure.

Theologically, this phenomenon is regarded as the consequence of man being fallen (Matthew 14:38; Romans 7:18; Galatians 5:19). Man, even as a Christian, may desire to do good but fail to act consistently with that desire because the flesh wars against that desire; consequently, we, at times, succumb to temptations. Peter not only sinned once, but three times in this same scenario.

What Peter failed to sufficiently consider in his oath of fidelity was the weakness of the flesh, the seriousness of the temptation, and its complexity. Peter apparently thought he could withstand someone asking if he followed Christ, and he may very well could have. What he failed to consider was that at the time he would be asked that question, he would be suffering from fatigue, deep sadness, loss, and fear. He also failed to realize that the temptation would happen when Jesus was not beside him, and by all appearances, He would never be there again. In addition, Jewish leaders were going to kill Jesus, and they would surely kill him if he said he followed Christ. When the temptation came, he failed and failed repeatedly; however, he was not a hypocrite, but he was too weak to act consistently with what he believed.

While hypocrites and akrates are at times difficult to distinguish, and someone could seek to use the excuse of akrasia to hide their hypocrisy, the distinction is a biblically valid one and worth the effort to maintain. As stated before, there normally are enough contextual indicators to determine which is present. We should make it clear that akrasia does not remove culpability because it is not synonymous with psychological or biological determinism; nor does it provide an excuse for a life of habitual or accepted moral failures because of unwillingness to grow spiritually, which could lead to discipline. It simply means that because mankind is fallen, man will sin at times regardless of his desires, contrary to the Socratic dictum "To know the good is to do it."[155] Socrates' idea contradicts Scripture and human experience.

The decisions about whether to have church membership or not and whether communion should be closed or open becomes more clear when a church begins to practice church discipline. This is because formal discipline results in the disciplined person no longer being an identifiable part of the assembly. That being the case, some form of membership becomes essential unless one chooses the other option of forbidding the disciplined to come to the public services.

It seems that public worship by definition should be open to the public, as it is now and has been historically, unless the assembling of Christians was illegal; hence, discipline resulting in membership being withdrawn makes more sense. In addition, if public worship is, in some way, not open to the public but only to certain persons, then whether it is called membership or not, it is a form of membership.

Furthermore, if communion is open to all, then Paul's words become inconsequential. "But actually, I wrote to you not to associate with any so-called brother if he should be an immoral person, or covetous, or an idolater, or a reviler, or a drunkard, or a swindler—not even *to eat* with such a one" (1 Corinthians 5:11, italics added). We saw earlier that at a minimum, this means the wayward brother cannot partake of the Lord's Supper, which necessitates either closed or semi closed communion.[156]

Simply stated, by definition, formal church discipline involves removing a person from the fellowship of a local church; therefore, there must be something that signifies one is "in" in contrast to one who is "out." Otherwise, one cannot be removed in a meaningful way. This is the definition of membership.

The Four Categories of Candidates for Discipline:

The first candidates are immoral members of the church, such as Paul wrote about in the church of Corinth.

It is actually reported that there is immorality among you, and immorality of such a kind as does not exist even among the Gentiles, that someone has his father's wife. And you have become arrogant, and have not mourned instead, in order that the one who had done this deed might be removed from your midst. For I, on my part, though absent in body but present in spirit, have already judged him who has so committed this, as though I were present. In the name of our Lord Jesus, when you are assembled, and I with you in spirit, with the power of our Lord Jesus, *I have decided* to deliver such a one to Satan for the destruction of his flesh, that his spirit may be saved in the day of the Lord Jesus. Your boasting is not good. Do you not know that a little leaven, leavens the whole lump *of dough?* Clean out the old leaven, that you may be a new lump, just as you are *in fact* unleavened. For Christ our Passover also has been sacrificed. Let us therefore celebrate the feast, not with old leaven, nor with the leaven of malice and wickedness, but with the unleavened bread of sincerity and truth.

I wrote you in my letter not to associate with immoral people; I *did* not at all *mean* with the immoral people of this world, or with the covetous and swindlers, or with idolaters; for then you would have to go out of the world. But actually, I wrote to you not to associate with any so-called brother if he should be an immoral person, or covetous, or an idolater, or a reviler, or a drunkard, or a swindler—not even to eat with such a one. For what have I to do with judging outsiders? Do you not judge those who are within *the church?* But those who are outside, God judges. REMOVE THE WICKED MAN FROM AMONG YOURSELVES (1 Corinthians 5:1–13).

Here we see several issues concerning discipline for an immoral church member.

The Rebellion in the Church—verse 1

"It is actually reported that there is immorality among you, and immorality of such a kind as does not exist even among the Gentiles, that someone has his father's wife" (verse 1). The word translated immorality is the Greek word *porneia* from which we get the word pornography. It involves "not only fornication or adultery but incest, sodomy, unlawful marriage, and sexual intercourse in general."[157]

319

The apostolic counsel that met in Jerusalem required Gentile believers to avoid four things, one of which is *porneia* (Acts 15:20), which is translated *fornication*. The sin in the Corinthian church was blatant, unrepented of, and ongoing. When someone lives unrepentantly and persistently in immorality, it is a clear call for church discipline. The particular case of immorality was incest, but immorality would also include things like those listed by Paul when he said, "Or do you not know that the unrighteous shall not inherit the kingdom of God? Do not be deceived; neither *fornicators*, nor idolaters, nor adulterers, nor effeminate, nor homosexuals, nor thieves, nor the covetous, nor drunkards, nor revilers, nor swindlers, shall inherit the kingdom of God" (1 Corinthians 6:9–10, italics added). *Fornicator* is the translation of the word *porneia* although in some contexts this word is translated fornication, the meaning is clearly more comprehensive. Thus, it is better to understand it as meaning extramarital relations of any kind, and other violations of God's moral laws, such as have been mentioned, and things like "hands that shed innocent blood" (Proverbs 6:17).

The particular sin being addressed in this passage is that of a son living with his stepmother. The present tense of the verbs, *reported* and *has*, indicates that this is a continuing relationship as opposed to a one-time sin. Since the Greek word for *adultery* is not used, it seems that the father and stepmother were divorced, or perhaps he was deceased. Finally, the woman apparently was not a believer since discipline for her is not mentioned.

This sin was explicitly prohibited by God in the Old Testament (Leviticus 18:7–8, 29; Deuteronomy 22:30). They were allowing sin in the church, which even the world viewed as wrong. Concerning such relationships, "Cicero (*pro Cluent* 5, 6) states 'it was an incredible crime and practically unheard of.' Such a marriage was strictly forbidden according to Leviticus 18:8 and Deuteronomy 22:30 and carried with it a curse" (Deuteronomy 27:20).[158]

However, some rabbis allowed for exceptions to this prohibition of Scripture. "Rabbinic law in the main seems to have allowed such a marriage when a proselyte married his stepmother, since his becoming a proselyte broke all bonds of relationship."[159] "It is possible that some who were now in the Corinthian church, may have come from the synagogue there and could have known of this allowance. Part of an inscription indicating the presence of such a synagogue has been found."[160] "Though as a Pharisee, (Philippians 3:5), Paul knew the system of Jewish law with its varying interpretations, and he applies the OT law and the teaching on marriage quite strictly."[161] The church was to exemplify Christ to the pagans, but they were living more corrupt lives than the pagans.

The Reprimand of the Church—verse 2

"And you have become arrogant, and have not mourned instead, in order that the one who had done this deed might be removed from your midst" (verse 2). Once the sin is exposed, the rest of the instruction and rebuke is not directed at the sinning brother, but toward the local church. They are responsible to deal with this sin within their fellowship just as Paul did, even though he was not physically present (verse 5). Paul exposed the sin of the "so-called brother" (verse 11), but he severely reprimanded the church for their sin of arrogance.

The Corinthians prided themselves on their tolerance of sin, and that is precisely what Paul condemns them for because it demonstrates a love of self rather than a love for Christ and each other. They should have mourned (refer back to chapter 7 for a full discussion of the attitude of arrogance and mourning).

Their attitude of arrogance shocked Paul more than the sin itself. They should have been in spiritual mourning, yet they were prideful and well satisfied with not doing anything in what surely was characterized as "the spirit of Christian liberty." It sounds much like the church today, which tolerates adultery, fornication, abortion, homosexuality, and every other immorality of choice under the banner of *grace*. For much of the contemporary church, the only real *sin* is denouncing something that is going on in the fellowship as sin.

The Response of Paul—verses 3–5

"For I, on my part, though absent in body but present in spirit, have already judged him who has so committed this, as though I were present. In the name of our Lord Jesus, when you are assembled, and I with you in spirit, with the power of our Lord Jesus, *I have decided* to deliver such a one to Satan for the destruction of his flesh, that his spirit may be saved in the day of the Lord Jesus" (verses 3–5). Paul is not an eyewitness to the event, but knows only by viva voce, which is sufficient for him.

Based on that, Paul invokes the name of the Lord Jesus Christ as his authority, and as an apostle, he acts on that authority by deciding "to deliver such a one to Satan" (verse 5). The premise is if he lives like a lost person, even though he claims to be Christian, he is to remain outside of the church. The "destruction of the flesh" (verse 5) refers to placing the individual in a sphere of greater susceptibility to Satan's fiery darts. Apparently, there is a protection afforded to believers in fellowship with a local church that is removed when they are not—even if their lives are not what they ought to be.

Paul's goal is to provide the sinning brother an opportunity to repent, which is what church discipline does, and what tolerance alone does not do. Since Paul did not call on the "so-called" (verse 11) brother to divorce, the implication is that either they were not married, or even if they were married, when he repented, he would be allowed to come into the church without having to divorce since that would violate the scriptural teaching of the indissolubleness of marriage (Genesis 2:24). The destruction of the flesh includes Satan's attacks, all the way up to, and including, physical death. God will go to great measures to protect his church (Acts 5:1–11; 1 Corinthians 11:27–30). This serves as a reminder to the church that physical death is to be feared less than the loss of holiness. Spiritual safety should always take precedence over physical safety.

The Reason for Church Discipline—verses 6–8

"Your boasting is not good. Do you not know that a little leaven leavens the whole lump *of dough*? Clean out the old leaven, that you may be a new lump, just as you are *in fact* unleavened. For Christ our Passover also has been sacrificed. Let us therefore celebrate the feast, not with old leaven, nor with the leaven of malice and wickedness, but with the unleavened bread of sincerity and truth." (verses 6–8). Leaven in the Scripture signifies influence, both good (Matthew 13:33) and evil (Matthew 16:6). The predominant usage is that of evil as it is here.

Leaven or yeast is that which is used to make dough rise. In ancient times, people would pinch off a small amount of bread dough and save it for the next time they were going to bake. This small amount of bread contained enough leaven to make the new bread rise. A very small amount of leaven will permeate the entire loaf and make it all rise; thus, the analogy that a little leaven permeates the whole lump. When the Jews left Egypt, they could not bring leavened bread with them. This was because they did not have time to let it rise; leaven represented the old life of slavery to Egypt, and unleavened bread represented their new life in the Promised Land that God had given them (Exodus 12:39). Consequently every Passover, all leaven had to be removed and only unleavened bread could be eaten to remind them of the deliverance of God from the old life to the new life in the promised land (Ex. 13:3,7).

Apparently, they boasted of things such as tolerance, being accepting, grace, numerical growth, etc. Paul condemns such attitudes because they not only violate Scripture, but also promote accepting the idea that one sin will not wound the body of believers . . . that everything is ok, because it is just one sin. This is a tragic place for a church to come to since sin is like a malignancy. It is its nature to spread. It will permeate every aspect of the body, ultimately resulting in minimal productivity and/or death . . . a spiritual death like that of the church of Sardis, that "you have a name that you are alive, but you are dead" (Revelation 3:1).

Those in Sardis probably thought they could excel in other areas and compensate for the failure to maintain purity. Tragically, in spite of clear and copious Scriptures to the contrary, this same fallacy continues to thrive today. As we all have heard, they must be doing something right, just look at how they have grown. However, the phenomenological should never be allowed to trump the theological. The Bible asserts that sin permeates everything; thus, the bigger the church that does not pursue purity, the bigger the malignancy and the greater the damage to the body of Christ and testimony of the One we are called to follow, Who is known as "The Holy One" (Acts 2:27). There is no escaping the fact that to allow sin to go unchecked in believers' lives or in the life of a local church is pure and simple disobedience, regardless what rationalization

324

is used. We are to live in a state of perpetual unleavenness since "Christ our Passover has been sacrificed" (verse 7) once and for all. We have been separated from the world that is perishing and spiraling toward a day of judgment from God.

The word for clean (verse 7) is *Ekkathairo* which is an intensified form and means "to cleanse," "to purge," "to separate" . . . "removing all abominations . . . setting aside what is shameful."[162] *Ekkathairo* means to clean thoroughly. The intensified form of this verb reminds us how serious God is about cleansing all leaven—sin. Every believer who sins (1 John 1:8,10) can either be cleansed by confession and repentance (1 John 1:9) or church discipline.

However, the command for the church to rid herself of all leaven obviously does not mean everyone who sins must go, for then there would be no church. It means that those who persist in their sin, unconfessed and unrepented of sin, must be removed because as sin cannot be compartmentalized in individuals' lives, neither can it be in the church. Living in the light of the infinite price that was paid on Calvary results in a passion to pursue purity and obedience—while minimizing it, forgetting about it, or not having experienced it, brings a low tolerance for the pursuance of purity.

The Responsibility of the Church—verses 9–13

The sphere of responsibility for applying church discipline rests with the local church. Apparently, Paul had already written the Corinthians concerning appropriate associations with immoral people.

"I wrote you in my letter not to associate with immoral people; I *did* not at all *mean* with the immoral people of this world, or with the covetous and swindlers, or with idolaters; for then you would have to go out of the world. But actually, I wrote to you not to associate with any so-called brother if he should be an immoral person, or covetous, or an idolater, or a reviler, or a drunkard, or a swindler—not even to eat with such a one. For what have I to do with judging outsiders? Do you not judge those who are within *the church*? But those who are outside, God judges. REMOVE THE WICKED MAN FROM AMONG YOURSELVES" (VERSES 9–13).[163]

He makes it clear that the suitable sphere for church discipline pertains only to those within the church who are "brothers" or "so-called brothers." Christians must associate with immoral people in order to evangelize.

The chasm between how a Christian is to deal with the woman at the well and a Pharisee or an Alexander (1 Timothy 1:20) is vast. Once someone is in the body of Christ by claiming to be a follower of Jesus Christ, the responsibility of both individual and the community is radically transformed. The person within the church is to demonstrate that they posses a new life in Christ. In contrast, the person outside of the church is to be dealt with like someone who is blind and dead.

The word *immoral* in these verses is the same word found in verse 1. Verse 11 makes it clear that Paul is not limiting church discipline to only incest, but is including things like immorality, covetousness, idolatry, reviling, drunkenness, and swindling. All of these qualities would fall under the category of immorality, but they are not exhaustive of the term. "Not to eat with such a one" (verse 11) has to do with fellowship at social gatherings and the Lord's Supper. Eating with this person has to apply to social gatherings since, if he is excluded from the fellowship, he would necessarily be excluded from the Lord's Supper; thus, the command would be superfluous. Regardless of whether he is a friend, family member, wealthy, poor, long-time or new member, leader or non-leader, influential or non-influential, he is to be removed if he acts and lives like an unbeliever.

Some maintain that we should not start, or even consider, practicing formal church discipline by removing people from the church roll who do not come to church. For example, Tommy South contends, "Outside the context of fellowship, discipline can only be destructive. . . . The situation is actually much worse than that! Apart from fellowship, discipline is not only meaningless, it is abusive."[164] This interpretation is based on the fact that, "'withdrawal of fellowship' could have little meaning or effect if there were no fellowship to withdraw."[165] He emphasizes that church discipline should be "the most that we can do to maintain fellowship with a brother or sister who has been overtaken by sin."[166] While this is a point well taken, to make it the determining criteria for the enactment of discipline is biblically unwarranted.

The problem with South's view is threefold. First, it seems to limit the purpose of discipline to how it affects the disciplined, which the Scripture never does. While there is a purpose intended for the disciplined, and that is to call them to repentance, there are also the purposes of purifying and protecting the church.

Second, it makes experiencing fellowship the acid test of whether you discipline someone or not, which the Scripture never does. Scripture makes unconfessedness and unrepentedness of sin the deciding factor; members should not be removed from the roll without a genuine attempt to fellowship with them and to restore them to fellowship with Christ and His church. Whether they choose to accept that offer is not the determinant of whether discipline is to be enacted.

My third reason to disagree with South is that while the best place to start practicing church discipline may vary from church to church because of the particular disciplinary needs, generally speaking, it seems quite appropriate to begin by concerning ourselves with those who make no effort to come to church or follow Christ, and who live lives that degrade the testimony of Christ and the church. Further, this at least gives a starting place for endowing church membership with New Testament significance. If you begin elsewhere, someone will inevitably raise the question of why nothing is done about those who make no attempt to live for Christ. At a minimum, a good question deserves a good answer. At least we should consider what to do with those that no one even knows who they are, much less *where* they are.

Thus, immorality is to be disciplined and the immoral person is to be removed from the life of the fellowship. Anything less is disobedience.

Paul tells us the events that happened to Israel are recorded in Scripture for our instruction and as an example for us (1 Corinthians 10:6,11). One lucid example of failing to deal with sin is Eli's failure with his sons (1 Samuel 2:12–3:13). Eli's sons had been taking the best of the offerings and leaving the rest for God. They had also been having sexual relations with several different women. When Eli heard of it, he talked to them about it and asked, why are you doing this? He then told them how the Lord would not be pleased. Rather than rebuking them for their willful sinfulness, he slapped them on the wrist. Consequently, God said, I am going to judge the house of Eli (1 Samuel 3:13). The tragedy of not dealing with sin is that God must intervene with divine discipline, which is always more severe.

The second genre of candidates for church discipline are the doctrinal deviates. Teaching false doctrine cannot be tolerated in the church. When someone is found to be teaching false doctrine, they must be dealt with and dealt with decisively. That is what Paul practiced and instructed the young pastor Timothy to do. "This command I entrust to you, Timothy, my son, in accordance with the prophecies previously made concerning you, that by them you may *fight the good fight*, keeping faith and a good conscience, which some have rejected and suffered shipwreck in regard to their faith. Among these are Hymenaeus and Alexander, whom I have *delivered over to Satan, so that they may be taught not to blaspheme*" (1 Timothy 1:18–20, italics added).

Timothy is told to fight the good fight of pure doctrine and live the life that Alexander and Hymenaeus had rejected. Theological aberrancy and immorality go together. You can hold to pure doctrine and be immoral, but you cannot hold to aberrant doctrine and remain morally pure. Immorality may be hidden, but it is there, and more than likely will emerge at some point. Often false doctrine arises not from intellectual differences but from immorality, and thus becomes a *justification* for the sin. Paul handed Alexander and Hymenaeus over to Satan, just like he did with the man involved in immorality in 1 Corinthians 5:5.

As we saw in 1 Corinthians 5:1–11, there is a sphere of protection afforded believers within the fellowship of the church which is not available outside of the church because "the whole world is under the control of the evil one" (1 John 5:19); but the church belongs to the Lord Jesus Christ and is to be a haven for His people. This is not to imply that Jesus is not sovereign over everything and everywhere, but to note the contrast that Scripture makes between the two domains. The phrase "delivered over to Satan" (1 Timothy 1:20) appears to refer to excommunication just as it did in the church of Corinth.

False doctrine destroys the conscience and faith of individuals. Therefore it must be exposed and removed lest it shipwreck the faith of others. Church leaders cannot prohibit someone from making a shambles of their faith, but they must prevent apostates from destroying the faith of others. Paul told Timothy, "Pay close attention to yourself and to your teaching; persevere in these things; for as you do this you will insure salvation both for yourself and for those who hear you" (1 Timothy 4:16). Pure life and doctrine are of immense importance because nothing less than salvation is at stake.

Anyone who brings false doctrine into the church is to be rebuked and then rejected if he continues. Paul instructed Titus, "Reject a factious man after a first and second warning, knowing that such a man is perverted and is sinning, being self-condemned" (Titus 3:10–11). This is the same idea expressed in Matthew 18:15–20. The wayward brother, in this case doctrinally wayward, is to be rebuked, but if he will not listen, he is to be turned out. False doctrine destroys faith, and it disunifies the body because it is false and comes from depraved minds out for their own gain (1 Timothy 6:3–5). Thus, it must be dealt with decisively.

If Christianity is about anything, it is about truth. God is called the "God of truth" (Isaiah 65:16), the Holy Spirit is called the "Spirit of truth" (John 16:13), and Jesus said of Himself "I am . . . the truth" (John 14:6). Christians are to love in truth, walk in truth and speak the truth (3 John 1:1, 4 and Ephesians 4:25). False doctrine is against everything that Christianity is and stands for. It is not to be tolerated in the church. False doctrine leads to dishonoring God, immorality, disunity, and corrupting the message of salvation.

In stark contrast to the Scripture, it is common today to hear disunity blamed on an emphasis of teaching doctrine. This comes from an errant understanding of what unity really is. Biblical unity is not everyone agreeing on some issue or even many issues, getting along, or being friends. Even the heathen can do that. That unity is purely human because it has its genesis and definition from man. Biblical unity is birthed by the Holy Spirit, grounded in the Scripture, and manifested in a desire to follow the teachings of Christ.

As long as Satan is able to work, there will always be false disciples and wolves that creep into the church that are desirous of corrupting true doctrine and unity; seeking unity with them requires selling out the faith. Simply put, unity is not defined by whether everyone gets along, but by whether everyone desires and seeks to follow the clear teachings of Christ. Those who undermine the clear teachings of God are to be removed. To agree with or allow the teaching of those who contradict the clear teaching of Scripture is to be in disagreement with the Lord Jesus Christ. This precludes the possibility of unity since unity definitionally means following Christ in spirit and letter (Philippians 2:1–11).

A caveat is in order here. Dealing with heresy is not equivalent to disciplining everyone who says something that is unorthodox or that the leadership disagrees with. If the church is carrying out the Great Commission, there will always be those in the local church whose beliefs are not orthodox because that is the nature of babes in Christ. They may say things that make you cringe at times, but they simply are repeating what they have learned during a life of following self—actually all of us do this since we all are learning.

Minor disagreements over obscure passages are not grounds for discipline. Rather, it is the willful rejection of the obvious truths of Scripture and/or seeking to corrupt the faith of others; however, the obvious and undeniable truth of Scripture does not have to be obvious and undeniable to the heretic. If that were the requirement of defining it, that would simply result in the non-existence of heresy or orthodoxy. The obvious and undeniable truth of Scripture is that which the leaders know and that which is available to anyone with an open heart.

331

If the leadership finds out that a teacher in the church is teaching heresy, that teacher must be approached and shown the error of his way. If he receives it, he can continue teaching provided that he has adequate correctness in other areas. If that same person is resistant to the pastor or elders of the church, he should be approached again, and if he still resists, he is to be removed. If his error is quite grave and jeopardizes the spiritual life of those whom he teaches, he may even have to be removed after the first encounter while someone works with him; or, he may have to be removed if he is resistant to follow the leadership of the church, which is another sign that his theology is wrong and probably his heart also.

The church need not fall into the error of failing to see the link between deficient or sinful behavior and false doctrine, even if someone espouses a belief in the Word of God as the Word of God. That alone does not mean that he truly believes it. Their lives are the best test for their true beliefs (James 2:17).

The third candidate for church discipline is the person who sows discord. This person can inflict untold devastation upon a church, and just one person can sow the seeds for a church split. Admittedly, it does take others to join in order to successfully complete his spiritual coup d'état; nevertheless, the unsettling reality remains that it only takes one to sow the seeds of discord. Paul says of the sower of discord, "Now I urge you, brethren, keep your eye on those who cause dissensions and hindrances contrary to the teaching which you learned, and turn away from them. For such men are slaves, not of our Lord Christ but of their own appetites; and by their smooth and flattering speech they deceive the hearts of the unsuspecting" (Romans 16:17–18). He instructs the believers in Rome to "turn away from them" (verse 17). If they are outside of the church do not fellowship with them, listen to their instruction, or allow yourself to be influenced in any way. If they are in the church, which these clearly were, the only way to avoid them is to remove them.

While Paul does not associate them with any particular false teaching, they are clearly espousing just that; you cannot have real disunity apart from a distortion of Scripture in letter, spirit, or truth. It may include rank heresy, or it may be someone who is unwilling to follow the leadership in the church and sows discord among the brethren; through their distortions and conniving they create dissention. Of course, all of this is done under the guise of loving Jesus and His church. If you are waiting for dissenters to wear a big sign that says, "I sow discord" then you will continue to wait as they unleash their spiritual "smart bombs" upon the fellowship.

For example, Mr. Discord may not think the pastor gives enough time and effort to what he thinks is important, or does not pay him enough attention; consequently, Mr. Discord will eventually have had enough and will initiate plans to remove or destroy the pastor regardless of certain harm to the church. He will say that he loves the pastor, but . . . ! All the while he is stalking the pastor and violating Scriptures on humility and following the leadership, to name a few (Philippians 2:1–11; Hebrews 13:17). God includes the sower of discord in the list of seven things that He says He hates, "There are six things which the LORD hates, yes, seven . . . one who spreads strife among brothers" (Proverbs 6:16, 19). The sower of discord embraces and promotes some kind of false teaching which is the genesis of the problem that ultimately will involve many. He gossips, which is euphemistically called sharing, and is a self-appointed leader; he will superciliously challenge the leadership and authority of God's appointed leader, the pastor.

Jude's description of apostates fits well with what Paul says in Romans about the "sowers of discord." He calls them "hidden reefs in your love feasts when they feast with you without fear, caring for themselves; clouds without water, carried along by winds . . ." (Jude verse 12) Notice, they are "hidden reefs"; you don't really know they are there until it is too late. *Hidden* reminds us again of their clandestine operations. Paul warned the Ephesian elders, "Be on guard for yourselves and for all the flock, among which the Holy Spirit has made you overseers, to shepherd the church of God which He purchased with His own blood. I know that after my departure savage wolves will come in among you, not sparing the flock; and from among your own selves men will arise, speaking perverse things, to draw away the disciples after them. 'Therefore be on the alert . . .'"(Acts 20:28–30). Jude warns, "For certain persons have crept in *unnoticed,*" (Jude verse 4, italics added). A significant part of these people's insidiousness is their ability to conceal what they really are.

Believing that one's own church does not have one or more of such people because they remain unknown is indeed Pollyanna. The words "caring for themselves" is a translation of the word *poimaino,* which is translated other places as shepherd or pastor. In other words, these people pastor themselves. They are not under the authority of God's leadership, and thus they are not under God, even though they parade themselves to be super spiritual. They are "clouds without water" (Jude verse 12) which pictures their deceptive nature and cunning escapades. They may appear to be supportive of the pastor, loving the church, godly, and humble, but they are pure deception. They shepherd themselves, which becomes glaringly and painfully evident when things do not go their way.

Commentators note the strangeness of Paul's warning at this place in chapter 16 of Romans. For example, one commentator says, "This warning concerning schismatics raises questions that cannot be answered with certainty. How can we account for its position between greetings from Paul to members of the Roman church and greetings from those who are with him?"[167] However, another way to look at it is that right in the middle of a greeting of love is the most appropriate place for such a caveat.

The word translated *urge* is the Greek word *parakaleo*, which means exhort, come along side, urge, beseech, desire, implore, or beg. It often has the idea of strong emotion or concern as seen in the word beg. Because of Paul's love for them, he interjects an emotional forewarning and begs them to keep their eyes open and to avoid these self-appointed shepherds. It is much like when a parent leaves their child with someone for a while and tells the child I love you; and immediately warns them to stay away from strangers. The parent, as well as Paul, is motivated by love, and consequently there is great pathos in his words. Paul then says, "keep your eye on them" (Romans 16:17), which is a translation of the word *skopew*, meaning, "to continue to regard closely—'to watch, to notice carefully.'"[168] Paul is begging them to be continually alert for those who cause divisions by what they say and do.

The Greek word for divisions is *dichostasia*. "In some languages the equivalent of 'causing division' is literally 'to cause two groups in place of one group,' but more frequently the equivalent is expressed in terms of attitudes, for example, 'to cause people to be angry at one another' or 'to cause people not to like one another' or 'to cause people to think of one another as enemies.'"[169] These people arduously and cunningly toil to divide the church that the Holy Spirit designed to be one. They first divide attitudinally and ultimately they split the church into identifiable groups. These divisions have a disastrous effect upon the body of Christ, the work of the Holy Spirit, and the testimony of the church, and have a damning impact on the lost that need to see the power and peace of God before they answer the call to accept the cross.

This same word, *dichostasia,* translated *dissension*, is listed as one of the deeds of the flesh (Galatians 5:20). Remember, unity is given by the Holy Spirit, maintained by the people of God, and demonstrated by following Jesus Christ according to His Word, and it is not causing disunity to emphasize doctrine and follow Scripture even though some turn against you. Biblical unity is only found in truth. When disunity is attributed to or seems to arise because of obedience to Scripture, it is deception. In reality, the disunity that was already in the hearts of those who do not want to follow Scripture is manifested. Naturally, they will bellow that the ones who seek to discipline a divisive person are causing the division. That is because they either do not know the Scripture or are not under its authority.

Again, unity does not mean that everyone is merely in agreement; that popular interpretation potentiates the entire church being held captive to the least spiritual people and principles. Sadly, that is a widespread understanding of unity. Biblical unity is everyone in agreement to follow Jesus' explicit and undeniable teaching. Those who do are unified. Those who choose not to follow these, regardless of what they say, are the ones who are divisive because they are not following Jesus; although they are quite accomplished in duping people into believing they are spiritual.

Hindrances is the Greek word *skandalon,* translated variously offense, stumbling block, and offends. It connotes the idea of trap, entrap, or ensnare; it refers to "the movable stick or trigger of a trap, a trap stick . . . any impediment placed in the way and causing one to stumble or fall . . . a rock which is a cause of stumbling."[170]

Paul had warned the Christians at Rome "not to put an obstacle or a stumbling block in a brother's way" (Romans 14:13). Sowers of discord trip people up spiritually and cause them to fall into sin by laying traps for them. These *disunifiers* will use friendship, family, lying, deception, slander, and anything else to get what they crave. They will split a church to save face or to get their way, and then call it the work of God. Many wonder how they could do such a thing. Paul gives the answer here if we will accept it, "for such men are slaves, not of our Lord Christ but of their own appetites" (Romans 16:18). Regardless how they seek to portray themselves, when they go against Scripture, they cause divisions and ensnare people into their *selfist* webs, they are slaves of themselves. They do not really care about the church or the Lord Jesus Christ because if they did, they would subjugate themselves to His Word. They will cause enormous harm to get their way although they claim the contrary.

How do you identify the person who inflicts this magnitude of evil upon the church of the Lord Jesus Christ? One would be inclined to think that this type of person must be easy to identify. He must be boisterous, ill-mannered, gruff, obnoxiously overbearing, foul-mouthed, and a hideous monstrosity of gargantuan proportions. If that were the case, we ought to stop him before he ever comes into the church. Oh, if it were only so easy, but Paul makes it clear this is not to be, "and by their smooth and flattering speech they deceive the hearts of the unsuspecting" (Romans 16:18). He flatters, speaks eloquently, or smoothly until his unsuspecting prey thinks he is the greatest. Jude says, "They speak . . . flattering people for the sake of gaining an advantage" (Jude verse 16). In other words they do not come as ministers of darkness but as "angel(s) of light" (2 Corinthians 11:14). Because of their disguise and cunningness, they slip in undetected, serve as spiritual loyalists, and gain allegiance from the unsuspecting. Add to this the church's confusion between a biblical characteristic like humility and a psychological characteristic like passive personalities, and the problem is exacerbated considerably.

When all of the Scriptures are combined, the profile of a dissenter may include the following qualities: well-mannered and polite, well-liked, maybe shy, intelligent, a hard worker in the church, a good friend, respected in the community, an excellent co-worker, etc. In addition to his winsome personality, he may be outwardly complementary of the pastor. However, make no mistake about it, he is a slave to himself. This is what makes him so damningly deceiving.

I once listened to a profiler of serial killers explain their characteristics. He described them as mild mannered, good neighbors, intelligent, loners, and liked by both neighbors and co-workers; this stands as a perennial reminder that they come as angels of light, but they are really emissaries of darkness. The *sower of discord* in your church is probably very involved, well liked, and may support the pastor for a while. His true nature is exposed when he becomes dissatisfied. By the way, this is an equal opportunity verse because the word "men" in verse 18, is better translated "ones"—sorry ladies, you are included. It is a solemn thought but a needed one, that the most mild-mannered man or woman in your church could be the spiritual equivalent of the Boston strangler.

I have heard of many who fit this profile and have seen it first-hand. The person seems quite spiritual in front of everyone. They may fool everyone for a while, but the unsuspecting, immature, and the pretenders are the most vulnerable to their "flattering speech" (Romans 16:8). Often, pastors speak of the meanest person in the church, the one causing more trouble than anyone, as being perceived by most as spiritual and a very nice person. What is unknown to many is that behind the scenes, they will act astonishingly ungodly, but when the need arises, they will pretend to be a humble and faithful servant of God; however, they are in reality a servant of their own "appetites" (Romans 16:18).

Everyone who is spiritual and knows the Word of God should be willing to sacrifice themselves for the good of the church. They should be willing to be silent when they have been hurt or wronged, rather than harm the church. They should follow the God-appointed leaders unless the leaders lead them to go directly against the explicit teaching of Scripture. If they cannot follow the leadership, they may very well have a spiritual problem that must be dealt with, and if it is not, they will take their venom to another unsuspecting church. This person is far different from a person who just does not agree with the direction of the church and thus opts, with no fan fare, to look for a church home where he can be supportive and serve.

I remember a man who was very much as Paul and Jude described. He was mild mannered, polite, very active in the church and could at times be heard praying for me. However, he and his wife worked in the most cunning, self-absorbed, and Machiavellian manner that I have seen in twenty-three years of pastoring. Little by little over several years, they gained significant credibility in the church. Then, when they did not get their way, they began to make their move, which defied any definition of spirituality, and the intricacies of their diabolical quest were so intertwined, seditious, and cunning that I simply am unable to do them justice on paper. However, many pastors will be able to figure out the essentials of the scenario by only changing a few names since they too have seen similar occurrences.

This couple deceived people that I would have staked my life that it would have been impossible for them to be lured into their web. In the presence of five pastors, the man repeatedly stated one story that he would relate to the church, but then he would stand before the church and unashamedly say the very opposite, even though he knew the pastors would be united in affirming his duplicity. He never spoke in a business meeting unless he was called on, but of course, he did not have to since he had deceived many others into carrying his banner. I must regretfully confess that I totally underestimated his ability to con and deceive, and overestimated the spirituality and maturity of many whom he deceived, and this much to the peril of the church. This is a haunting admission or reality that often emerges in my thoughts.

The full attack of this diabolical duo began clearly unfolding when my associate pastor was recovering from life-threatening cancer surgery and receiving chemotherapy. I had just come home from having emergency open-heart surgery at the age of forty-three. The coup d'état started within three days of my return home from the hospital. To put it mildly, I was in no shape to handle anything beyond walking to the kitchen table, much less something of this magnitude. It helps to remember that these people have no real compassion or love for the Lord, because they are slaves to their own appetite. If being compassionate or seeming to be holy feeds their appetite, then they will do it; but if not, their fangs begin to protrude farther than their diaphanous fleece can disguise. As he and his wife resisted every word of counsel from the pastors, biblical admonition, and opportunity to act spiritually; the deception spread to other deacons (he was a deacon), and the deacons began to act like they were the pastors of the church. This eventuated in their becoming the primary perpetuators of these passions from the pit.

I remember on one occasion the chairman of the deacons, in a meeting with the five pastors and the co-chairman of deacons said that he had been going back over some things in Scripture that I had taught them. He said he realized that the problem we were having was because the deacons were doing what pastors are supposed to do and not acting like deacons who are supposed to help and support the pastors. I asked him if he would tell that to the rest of the deacons, and he said he would. He did so in our next deacon's meeting, and it was met with deafening silence.

By this time the die was cast, sin was embraced, and deception had not only engulfed the deacons, but they had become co-conspirators—although thankfully not all of them were so easily bewitched. Without the complicity of the deacons, Satan could not have done his work. They never claimed any biblical support for what they did, and all five pastors remained unanimous every step of the way and repeatedly and consistently confronted the situation with the Scripture, but all to no avail because the Scripture was not the deacons' ultimate authority.

For the first time, I realized that there are just some things you cannot work through. Some people are simply unwilling; especially if they have sin in their lives, their pride has been hurt because they did not get recognized for something, or they have had an unspoken vendetta against you. I watched people begin to socialize together who had not done so in the decade I had been there. Meetings were held ostensibly to pray, but their actions betrayed their claim. It reminded me of the Pharisees and Sadducees, between whom there was no love lost, coming together because their abhorrence for Jesus was greater than their antipathy for each other. Sin, deception, and pride are formidable forces. Behind all of this laid the sin of a man and a woman who were willing to sacrifice the work of the Lord for themselves. I have never witnessed such demonism and pray that I shall never have to again. But I know that it is always "crouching at the door" (Genesis 4:7). I am not as naïve as I once was. No matter how well things seem to be going, Satan is *really* at work. The alternative is a spiritually lethal Pollyannaism.

Our church had experienced growth, spiritually and numerically, for ten consecutive years. Then, at a weak moment for the pastor and associate, and an opportune time for Satan and his emissaries of discord, he launched a formidable assault. Lest you think my words are extraordinarily harsh against these emissaries of the pit, a review of passages such as Matthew 23, Galatians, and 1 John reveal the Lord's view of these who deceive and damn. Actually, there are no words harsh enough to describe the nefariousness of these evil dogs of Satan (Philippians 3:2) and the spiritual damage and carnage they leave in their wake. They create a spiritual holocaust with both temporal and eternal damage. Unsuspecting baby Christians are drawn in by their alluring flattery and illusory veil of humility, and the lost are repulsed by what they perceive as the actions of Christians.

While I believe there are things churches can do, without compromising Scripture, to decrease the chance of these malevolent campaigns happening, there are no guarantees. The reality is if God is moving in your church, hell is strategizing to destroy you. Remember, Satan was in the perfect Garden of Eden, and rest assured, he is in our churches. He may not be there personally, but he is there in spirit through demons and people who are "following after their own lust" (Jude verse 16) and who wittingly or unwittingly become his primary instrument. In the garden he took on the form of a serpent. In our churches he takes on the form of people that you know and serve. Make no mistake about it, he or an emissary of his is there to steal, kill, and destroy; for that is his purpose in being. He works deceptively, cunningly laying the groundwork for the coup, and then like a matador in the faena he moves in for the kill. Thus, God warns, "Be of sober *spirit,* be on the alert. Your adversary, the devil, prowls about like a roaring lion, seeking someone to devour" (1 Peter 5:8).

It is a sobering thought to remember that Jesus did everything perfectly, and Satan was more visible around Jesus than anyone else. That ought to give us some insight into where Satan will spend most of his time. It will not be around those who have so humanized the church by the traditions of man or obsessions de jour, but with those who walk closest to our Lord Jesus Christ. If Scripture teaches anything about spiritual warfare, it is this; the more faithful you are to God and the more God uses you, the more Satan seeks to destroy your relationship with God, the work of God through you, and you.

I am well aware that I may go through this type of spiritual warfare again, and I may once again suffer profound losses, but this I believe: Jesus is worth it. Regardless of the cost, He is worthy. If He never poured out His blessings, He is worthy. His church deserves shepherds who will not allow His flock to be commandeered by self-shepherding wolves who seek to conceal their disingenuous bleats with their synthetic fleece. This mêlée is often the result of a lack of discipline, or unwise and undiscerning choices by the leaders. The latter is the case here, which allows them the opportunity to gain a loyal following for their day of overt revolt against the Word of God and the shepherds of the church. By this time, discipline becomes a battle for the soul of the church. It is a costly battle indeed, but an essential battle. For the shepherds to choose the path of avoidance is to become one of them. That should never be. I look back and wonder how I could have been so naïve. However, even now I know that someone can cause an eruption in the church if they so choose. That is the nature of human existence and the local church. I realize I do not know all of the devices of Satan, for to think otherwise would be the height of incredulity.

I am well aware that many of our fellow shepherds have walked through similar trials, and some are surely there now even as we ponder this all too frequent calamity. I pray that you will be faithful to the Word of God and our Lord Jesus Christ. I may walk through future similar fiery trials, but I know that I will never walk through it so naïvely again. I have now seen and lived through the pernicious, baleful, and insidious wickedness kindled by the fires of hell, and I now know that the flames have names.

The fourth recipient of church discipline is the disorderly disciple. Paul says of this one, "Now we command you, brethren, in the name of our Lord Jesus Christ, that you *keep aloof from* every brother who leads an unruly life and not according to the tradition which you received from us . . . For even when we were with you, we used to give you this order: if anyone will not work, neither let him eat. For we hear that some among you are leading an undisciplined life, doing no work at all, but acting like busybodies. Now such persons we command and exhort in the Lord Jesus Christ to work in quiet fashion and eat their own bread. But as for you, brethren, do not grow weary of doing good. And if anyone does not obey our instruction in this letter, take special note of that man and *do not associate with him, so that he may be put to shame.* And *yet* do not regard him as an enemy, but admonish him as a brother" (2 Thessalonians 3:6, 10–15, italics added).

Commentators are divided over whether this passage teaches church discipline including formal church discipline or just a form of social ostracizing. The *Expositor's Bible Commentary* and the *Bible Knowledge Commentary* interpret it as being less than formal church discipline. For example, *Expositor's* says, "Anyone refusing to comply with the work ethic set out in this letter was not to be associated with, so that he might be ashamed of his behavior. *He was not to be*

344

expelled from the church like the sinning brother referred to in 1 Corinthians 5. In Corinth the offense was so flagrant as to bring disrepute on the whole church. In Thessalonica, however, the lapse was not yet so aggravated as to bring the reproach of the pagans on the church. Here, the erring brother was allowed to continue in the meetings, but probably was denied participation in such things as the love feast and the Lord's Supper. Certainly he was not to be given food, because this would make the community appear to condone his offense. *Me synamignysthai* ("do not associate") implies "let there be no intimate association [with him]."[171] "To sum up, the recalcitrant idler was not to be treated as an enemy cut off from all contacts, but was allowed to continue in a brotherly status. So lines of communication were kept open for continued warnings about his behavior."[172]

Others like Calvin, Barnes, and Martin see it as referring to formal church discipline.[173] For example, Barnes teaches disfellowshipping but in direct contrast to the practice of the Roman Catholic Church. "This is the true notion of Christian discipline. It is not primarily that of cutting a man off, or denouncing him, or excommunicating him; it is that of withdrawing from him. We cease to have fellowship with him. We do not regard him any longer as a Christian brother. We separate from him. . . . How different is this from excommunication, as it has been commonly understood! How different from the anathemas fulminated by the papacy, and the delivering of the heretic over to the civil power!"[174]

He sees it as a local church action that withdraws the precious fellowship of fellow believers and the privilege of being a part of one of Christ's local churches, resulting in the removal of the recalcitrant from church life. Again Barnes says, "We simply cease to recognize him as a Christian brother, when he shows that he is no longer worthy to be regarded as such. A 'disorderly walk' denotes conduct that is in any way contrary to the rules of Christ. The proper idea of the word used here, upon him that he shall be shunned; that is, withdraw all Christian fellowship from him. . . . And have no company with him— The Greek word here means to mix up together; then to mingle together with; to have contact with. The idea is that they were not to mingle with him as a Christian brother, or as one of their own number. They were not to show that they regarded him as a worthy member of the church, or as having a claim to its privileges. The extent of their discipline was, that they were to withdraw from him."[175]

All things considered, it seems best and most natural to take the 2 Thessalonians passage to mean church discipline, which includes formal church discipline if the sinning brother does not heed godly instruction. Three things in the context seem to support this interpretation.

First, the phrases "keep aloof from" (verse 6) and "do not associate with him" (verse 14), are best understood as formal discipline. The first phrase is from the Greek word *stello,* which means to avoid or stay away from. It is hard to see how the full impact of that can be experienced while allowing the sinning brother to remain in the fellowship while not allowing him to participate in certain things. Although one can be excluded from certain privileges such as leadership as a form of discipline, that is not what is being talked about here because it puts the burden on the believers to avoid him, and the only way that can be even minimally done is to remove him from the fellowship.

Further, the verb *stello* is in the present tense, signifying continuous action of avoiding. Interestingly, this verb is in the middle voice, which signifies that the subject (the believers in the church) receives the action of the verb or the benefit from the action. In other words, God says to avoid these brothers who will not obey the Scripture so that the believers will benefit. This again underscores the reality that church discipline is not only redemptive but also protective. Thus, the church is protected from the permeating influence of sin.

The latter phrase, "do not associate with him" (verse 14) is a translation of *sunanamignusthai*. It means "to associate with one another, normally involving spatial proximity and/or joint activity, and usually implying some kind of reciprocal relation or involvement . . . to be in the company of, to be involved with, association."[176] This verb like the former one is also in the present tense and middle voice, thus signifying a continuous action and the subject receiving the benefit from the action.

Another evidence that this includes formal church discipline is the fact that *sunanamignusthai* is the exact same word and form that is used of church discipline in 1 Corinthians 5:9–11, which is clearly referring to formal church discipline. Thus, again it seems most natural to see this as formal church discipline. It is also difficult to see how a church could accomplish the full meaning of these words without removing the disorderly person from the fellowship. Michael Martin says, "Paul was instructing the members of the church to refuse to associate with fellow believers who persisted in living in a way contrary to 'the teaching' . . . they had received from Paul and his coworkers . . . several years later Paul would instruct the Corinthian believers also to withdraw fellowship from persons who claimed to follow Christ yet persisted in (and defended as a valid Christian lifestyle) some unchristian behavior . . . by ostracizing such persons the church as a body was able to express its disapproval in a manner that the offender could not dismiss lightly."[177]

Second, the direct intention of the discipline was "so that he may be put to shame" (verse 14). A true believer will feel shame when the entire local body confronts him with his sin and the wrongness of his actions. He also will feel ashamed because His Lord has forbidden him to have a part in the life of His church, which has to bring enormous shame upon any child of God. He is no longer allowed to be a part of the only thing His Lord promised to build. As long as someone is allowed to remain a part of the fellowship, they will be able to rationalize their behavior. Martin says, "the meddler would claim to help, the gossip would purport to share needed information, and the lazy always would consider 'supervision' their preferred form of participation. Such persons raise to an art form the ability to justify unchristian behavior and disguise obstructionism behind a mask of cooperation."[178]

The third reason for understanding the passage to include formal church discipline is the full consideration of what they were actually guilty. The word, *unruly* (verse 6) is translated in the NIV as *idle*. The reason for the difference is the former takes into consideration the fuller meaning of the Greek word *ataktos,* its corollaries, and other problems found in the context, while the latter focuses on the clear problem of being idle (verses 8,10–12). However, it is best not to limit this to people who do not work—idle—because that results in an unnecessary narrowness of the meaning and application of the word, making the passage have no relevance beyond dealing with people who refuse to work. There are several reasons to reject understanding the problem addressed here as merely being idle.

First, the meaning of the word, *unruly* encompasses more than that. It is defined as, "disorderly, out of ranks (often so of soldiers), irregular, inordinate, immoderate pleasures, deviating from the prescribed order or rule."[179] This seems to fit the context better, and that is why the New American Standard chose to translate the word *unruly*.

348

Second, the context seems to necessitate understanding it as *unruly* or *undisciplined* while recognizing that the most prominent fault is *idleness*. "In the verses we find that the *atakoi* were brothers (verse 15) who were living contrary to apostolic teaching (verses 6,10), contrary to the apostolic example of hard work and self-support (verses 7–9), and disrupting the church as *busybodies* (verse 12)."[180] Thus, their *atakoi* were clearly more than not working although that was a prominent part. Whether one views the problem as idleness or unruliness, it must not be forgotten that the root problem is the same here as in the other passages concerning church discipline: that is, refusing to obey the instructions of the Word of God from the Lord Jesus Christ, and heed the *reproof* of the church. Similarly, when Cain brought an offering, which the Lord rejected, it was not merely the offering that was the problem but the heart of the offerer, which the context makes clear (Genesis 4:1–15). The sin of idleness was the fruit of a wayward heart, similar to Cain's offering.

Therefore whether someone is disciplined because of immorality, heresy, sowing discord, or not working, the underlying problem is a recalcitrant spirit because formal church discipline is only enacted in the absence of repentance. As previously demonstrated, the call for discipline is not necessarily based on the kind of sin, but rather the response of the sinner to the admonition (Matthew 18:15–17); hence, the problem beneath the sin is always the attitude concerning the sin. A professed believer who lives a life that is contrary to the teachings of Scripture diminishes the holiness of the church, the testimony of the church, and his own spiritual progress; therefore, he must be handled according to Scripture. In this situation, the problem is in part idleness, but it could be someone who does not provide for his family, is involved in shady business dealings, or other such *unruly* behavior.

Paul also includes two well-needed caveats. The first one admonishes the brethren not to "grow weary of doing good" (verse 13). Once people have been *taken* advantage of by others, they can grow cold toward helping needy people. The fear or distaste of being taken again can transform their warm compassion into cold economics and management. Of course, this is all done under the guise of being a good steward of *the Lord's money.* Paul's warning is not to allow the slothful or shysters to extinguish the compassion of our Lord through His church. Paul may also have had in mind the potential discouragement that comes after discipling someone only to see him squander his work away. This can tempt Christians to believe that their work was in vain or that they failed, and this results in a loss of passion for discipleship. Surely this caveat would apply to other concerns embodied in Paul's admonition not to "grow weary of doing good" (verse 13). The main idea is not to let those who will not follow Christ keep you from following Him.

The other caution is "And *yet* do not regard him as an enemy, but admonish him as a brother" (verse 15). Those who see this passage as excluding formal discipline base some of their understanding on this verse. They posit that you cannot admonish someone if you disfellowship him. There are two obvious answers to this supposed dilemma. The admonishment could have gone on prior to the disfellowshipping and his failure to heed the counsel. This surely happened, but it does not seem to exhaust the warning. The more plausible answer is that it is always appropriate to go to a lost person to seek to win him to Christ, which is what the one under discipline may very well be, and it is equally appropriate to approach brothers or sisters in order to admonish them to repent and follow Christ. Admonishing a *brother* along the way is a valuable part of church discipline.

CHAPTER 10

Navigating the "Mind" Fields of Church Discipline: Facing the Factual, Theological, and Practical Realities of Church Discipline

So, you want to practice church discipline, but you do not know where to start. Nor do you want it to end with something similar to a spiritual neutron bomb. Therefore, the paramount question is, where are you supposed to start? Is Matthew 18, 1 Corinthians, or some other passage on discipline the place to start? Well, not exactly.

There are some things that need to be considered and practiced before and concomitantly with formal church discipline. Formal church discipline must be a part of comprehensive church discipline. Church discipline, understood rightly, encompasses prayer, evangelism, teaching, preaching, fellowship, and the entire life of the church. Therefore, this chapter will explore some factual, theological, and practical realities of church discipline. Seeking to practice church discipline without understanding the things in this chapter may result in enormous and unnecessary harm to the body of Christ. Conversely, if these things are grasped, the pastor and the church are postured to move through the full scope of church discipline successfully.

Coming Vis-à-Vis with Six Factual Realities

The first reality is that the church where you presently serve is probably not practicing church discipline and most likely has never practiced formal discipline. This reality produces a strong temptation to succumb to the idea that just because it is not being done, or has not been done, it need not be done. However, this is contrary to the whole spiritual experience. If we follow this line of reasoning, we will never implement the new things that God is showing us.

Because of the past neglect of church discipline, regardless where you start, you will appear excessive to some. This is, at best, because of the unfamiliarity with church discipline in most churches, and at worst, the pervasive carnality in our churches. Nevertheless, you must start somewhere lest you be unfaithful to our Lord Jesus Christ. Remember, if the reasoning reigns that it cannot be done because it has not been done previously or some would not like it, the church will never do anything other than wither away and die.

The second reality is that temple cleansing is arduous work. It is not enjoyable, fun, or exciting, nor is it the path to popularity. It will not earn the accolades of man nor invitations to speak on the subject. Of course, receiving the accolades of man and invitations to speak are not commanded by Jesus, but church discipline is. This fact is often forgotten—a kind of intentional senility. I am quite sure that Jesus did not experience exuberance or a rise in popularity from cleansing the temple. It was demanding and sacrificial work, and to most it probably seemed unwise and unnecessarily antagonistic. He could have spoken on missions or had a prophecy conference—each of these is wonderful and well needed; almost anything would have been better for His ministry than cleansing the temple, but nothing would substi-

352

tute for temple cleansing. Jesus knew that regardless of personal cost, He had to do the will of the Father—what is righteous. In like manner, we must judge our success by faithfulness to the Word of God and nothing else.

The third reality is that it takes supreme boldness, faith, truth, and love for God and His church to face the challenge of church discipline. Neither prayer, nor evangelism, nor Bible study, nor anything else can serve as a surrogate for following what God says concerning church discipline. To seek to replace the more difficult commands of Christ with the less demanding is, in reality, hypocrisy. If you ask your daughter to clean her room, and later you find her praying about the untidiness of her room or repairing her doll house while her room is still unclean, it will be seen, and rightly so, as disobedience. She did not need to do something different nor pray about what you told her to do. She merely needed to do it. Anything short of that is disobedience and is dishonoring to you. This same principle is applicable to the children of God.

The fourth reality is recognizing that the prevailing mentality in most churches is that of mediocrity and/or viewing numerical growth as the infallible guarantee of God's blessing. The corollary to this way of thinking is that discipline is something to be avoided since it requires spiritual excellence, and it does not connote images of numerical growth. This makes the implementation of discipline difficult but not insurmountable. It also serves as a reminder of the necessity for implementing the full scope of discipline.

Fifth, every church has its Sadducees and Pharisees. The Sadducees were the more liberal of the two groups; consequently, they did not accept the entire Bible as true. Their modern-day counterparts may not always be so bold as to deny outright the veracity of Scripture and the biblical mandate for church discipline, but they are more than willing to be equally selective in what parts of the Scripture they obey. Of course, true to Sadduceeism, they will cloak this infidelity under the guise of spirituality.

The Pharisees were halakist—people who either contributed to or followed the Halakah. The Halakah is the legal teaching of the Talmud and was considered authoritative for religious life. The laws and the discussions of the laws are extensive. These ultimately became more important in their practice than the law of God (Mark 7:8; Matthew 15:1–20). Like their predecessors, modern-day Pharisees are overly concerned with following their own ideas about how things should be done. They will turn their head, rationalize, ignore, or violate the law of God but never go against their own personal Halakah.

The sixth reality is that most short-term pastorates and worldly business meetings are directly related to the lack of church discipline. The lack of church discipline will assuredly and consistently produce these two results. The all too frequent display of carnality during church discipline is not the effect of church discipline but rather a consequence of the absence of church discipline.

Coming Vis-à-Vis with Five Theological Considerations

First, the biblical order of discipline is laid out by Peter, under the inspiration of the Holy Spirit, where he says, "*It is time for judgment to begin with the household of God; and if it begins with us first,* what *will be* the outcome for those who do not obey the gospel of God?" (1 Peter 4:17, underline added). The first thing God judges is not the lost and the wicked but the church.

The judgment of the church is not judgment in the sense of judging our sins, because they have been laid on Jesus, but the judgment is discipline that results in our purity. Peter says,

354

"In this you greatly rejoice, even though now for a little while, if necessary, you have been distressed by various trials, that the proof of your faith, *being* more precious than gold which is perishable, even though tested by fire, may be found to result in praise and glory and honor at the revelation of Jesus Christ" (1 Peter 1:6–7).

God allows persecutions and difficulties to come upon His people as disciplinary actions to purify the family of God, which is also the precise point of church discipline. The vicissitudes of life are part of God's disciplinary plan and so is church discipline. These are all temporal disciplines. The writer of Hebrews says, "It is for discipline that you endure; God deals with you as with sons" (Hebrews 12:7).

It is most interesting that Peter transitions from the appropriateness of God's disciplining His church prior to judging the world, directly into the responsibility of the elders (1 Peter 5:1 ff.). It implies if discipline is going to be implemented it, must be understood and modeled by the elders. This was also the pattern in Ezekiel 9. In Ezekiel's vision, God called His city guards and instructed them not to hurt the faithful, but concerning the unfaithful He said, "But to the others He said in my hearing, 'Go through the city after him and strike; do not let your eye have pity, and do not spare. Utterly slay old men, young men, maidens, little children, and women, but do not touch any man on whom is the mark; and you shall start from My sanctuary.' So *they started with the elders who were before the temple*. And He said to them, 'Defile the temple and fill the courts with the slain. Go out!'" (Ezekiel 9:5–7, italics added). God was going to bring judgment against all of Israel, the unsaved and the saved, but He began at the temple with the elders and then the people since that is the way the corruption flowed, from the temple to the people.

Therefore, there seems to be a general biblical pattern, which indicates that discipline is to begin with the elders first. From this, I would deduce that deacons would be considered next since they are set apart servants in the local church, then lay leaders, and then the church. Granted, something could arise in the congregation that warrants discipline first, but as a matter of practice, you cannot overlook the problems with the elders or deacons and begin in the church. For one reason, it is not the general biblical and logical pattern; and another is, the church will rebel against the hypocrisy of such practice. If the elders seek to implement discipline within the body when they are unwilling to practice it among themselves, they will experience a well-deserved mutiny because as pastors we are to teach by our doctrine and our lives (1 Timothy 4:16).

Second, accept that you will do what Jesus says even if it is hard and unpopular. This is the first battle of the mind, and it is present throughout the entire process of church discipline. I fear that too often, when someone says that they sense the Lord telling them to stop midway, a task that earlier they said He clearly told them to do, it is most often an unwillingness to stay the course because of the difficulties being encountered. The old saying, "Do not doubt in the dark what God has clearly shown you in the light," is a good rule of thumb for walking through difficult battles. Meaning, what you clearly understood Jesus to tell you to do before the spiritual warfare began is probably still true.

It is not unusual for doubts to creep in during the heat of battle. Therefore, to be successful during spiritual warfare, it is crucial that you determine the will of the Lord beyond doubt (to the best that you can) before embarking on the mission. If it is commanded in the Scripture, you can be sure it is His will, regardless how things look. One warning I would offer is, if the details are not spelled out in Scripture, God can change the direction because He is leading you. All formulas are limited. You cannot put God in a box, no matter how popular the formula is. However, we should not use this as an escape hatch from following God in the difficult times. At some point, even a Western Christian must "take up his cross" (Luke 9:23).

Third, church discipline is biblically intertwined with all of church life, and without it, the church simply cannot fulfill the purpose for which she was designed. This has been corroborated in the previous nine chapters. If we fail to follow the Lord in this area, there will be hypocrisy in our preaching. Politicians are often criticized for saying and doing what the people want them to say and do while avoiding the difficult things because of the personal cost it exacts. Their hypocrisy is repugnant, but if found in the *man of God*, it is repulsive indeed. Exhorting the flock to take up their cross and follow Jesus will be hollow words unless it begins with the pastor.

Fourth, prayer is strategically important. I recognize that prayer is important in every area of the Christian life, and many books have been written on this very subject. However, my emphasis here has to do with prayer as related to church discipline. It is strategically important for accomplishing church discipline in a God honoring way and potentially seeing the wayward come to Christ. Regardless how many books you read, or how experienced at church discipline you are, each time is somewhat different and only prayer can prepare you for the "mind" fields that lay before you. Because of the nature of church discipline, it is crucial to pray for yourself and others who are involved.

Fifth, expository preaching is a prerequisite for maturing the church on the Word of God, because consistent topical preaching leaves the church spiritually anemic. This is because topical preaching is built upon three false premises.

The first false premise is that the preacher will always objectively preach the whole counsel of God and will not be sidetracked by his own pet topics or idée fixe; in other words, the topical preacher would claim to preach the whole counsel of God. The reality is, all of us have certain things that we gravitate to; and we often gravitate to the things we like or what others will like and concomitantly will cause them to like us. Therefore, we consciously or unconsciously avoid passages that appear to be less exciting, less conducive to preaching, or may prove difficult to explain or follow. By topical preaching, the preacher limits his depth and breadth of knowledge of the Scripture because his study will be topical; thus, his decisions about what to preach on and what to say about them will be necessarily limited.

The second false premise is that the felt needs of the people are the real needs of the people. There is no doubt that at times people can express needs that they feel are important, which necessitate being met, and the pastor can surely preach on these subjects. In addition, the pastor should know his flock well enough to be able to sense some things that need to be addressed. Having said this, it is undeniable that only God can know the real needs of an individual and the flock. Only God can know what it will take to equip his children. That is why He gave the Scripture and not just certain topics. Only the Word of God can reveal the *true* needs of people, which lie deep in their souls (Hebrews 4:12).

I have often thought how presumptuous it is for a mere human to believe that he can know the spiritual needs of the church. Frankly, I have come to realize that I do not know. I may know what some are going through or facing, but they may merely be the more vocal ones or the ones that I talk to more regularly. Topical preaching exposes people to the Scrip-

tures you know while exposition exposes people to the whole
counsel of God.

The third false premise is that what man has to say is more
important than what God has to say. Too often, thematic
preaching, which takes a biblical theme and expounds upon
it, is confused with contemporary topical preaching, which
relies more on current events, psychology, stories, trends, and
the emphasis of the preacher or his oratorical abilities. Topical preaching will inevitably have an undue focus on man
whereas expository preaching causes the preacher and the
church to listen to what God says, much of which would otherwise be overlooked. Expository preaching gives a diet that
nurtures biblically mature thinking. It exposes all of the nuances of discipline that might otherwise be missed when only
the more obvious are dealt with. Biblical expository preaching has authority because it is not what the preacher says or
planned to say, it is what God has said. It also allows the
preacher to address controversial subjects with more courage
and credibility because the preacher does so as he preaches
through books. The timing is of the Lord and not him, and
everyone knows it.

Following are the three essential aspects of expository
preaching.

1. *Observation:* This answers the question, what does the
   passage say? This is the linguistic analysis of the passage. Technically, this is referred to as *exegesis*. It is
   studying the grammar and syntax. The emphasis of
   observation is, what does the passage *say*, because that
   determines the parameters of the message—what it
   means. This is foundational.
   Paul Enns comments on the importance of thoroughly
   studying grammar in order to know what the passage

says. "Biblical theology has a direct relationship to exegesis ('to explain; to interpret'), inasmuch as biblical
theology is the result of exegesis. Exegesis lies at the
foundation of biblical theology. Exegesis calls for an
analysis of the biblical text according to the literal-gram-
matical-historical methodology.

    a. "The passage under consideration should be
studied according to the normal meaning of language. How is the word or statement normally
understood?

    b. "The passage should be studied according to the
rules of grammar; exegesis demands an examination of the nouns, verbs, prepositions, etc., for
a proper understanding of the passage.

    c. "The passage should be studied in its historical
context. What were the political, social, and particularly the cultural circumstances surrounding it? Biblical theology does not end with exegesis, but it must begin there. The theologian
must be hermeneutically exacting in analyzing
the text to properly understand what Matthew,
Paul, or John wrote."[181]

2. *Interpretation:* This answers the question, what does
the passage mean by what it says? In interpretation,
the passage is compared to other relevant passages in
the Scripture. Commentaries, dictionaries, and other
tools are used to determine precisely what God meant
by what He said. Interpretation is primarily concerned
with the authorial intent of the verse or passage. Authorial intent means what did the author—God—mean

by what He said, and how did the initial recipients understand His words.

3. *Application:* This answers the question, what does it mean to me or to the people who will receive the message. If this aspect of exposition is ignored, much of the Scripture's meaning to your audience will be lost. This is particularly true for those who do not think inferentially. If application is done first, the Word of God is distorted and held captive to the whims of man. What does it mean to me is an appropriate question, but it is not the first question to be asked. Application moves the message from the original recipients to the present recipients.

Exposition ties these three—observation, interpretation, and application—together in a deliverable, understandable, and meaningful way. Without these three, biblical exposition cannot be done, maturing of the church will be hindered, and church discipline will almost inevitably remain hidden away in the non-mentionables of Scripture.

Richard L. Mayhue lists the following benefits of expository preaching:

1. Expositional preaching best achieves the biblical intent of preaching; delivering God's message.
2. Expositional preaching promotes Scripturally authoritative preaching.
3. Expositional preaching magnifies God's Word.
4. Expositional preaching provides a storehouse of preaching material.
5. Expositional preaching develops the pastor as a man of God's Word.

6. Expositional preaching ensures the highest level of Bible knowledge for the flock.
7. Expositional preaching leads to thinking and living biblically.
8. Expositional preaching encourages both depth and comprehensiveness.
9. Expositional preaching forces the treatment of hard-to-interpret texts.
10. Expositional preaching allows for handling broad theological themes.
11. Expositional preaching keeps preachers away from ruts and hobbyhorses.
12. Expositional preaching prevents the insertion of human ideas.
13. Expositional preaching guards against misinterpretation of the biblical text.
14. Expositional preaching imitates the preaching of Christ and the apostles.
15. Expositional preaching brings out the best in the expositor.[182]

Coming Vis-à-Vis with Some Practical Realities

First, the church must be led to practice all the other disciplines of the faith like reverence for God, Bible study, worship, prayer, etc. De-emphasizing discipline in several areas while seeking to implement it in another will produce confusion and unnecessary disruption.

Second, the pastor needs to have served at the church for a while. While this is not always possible, it is the best. The problems that have been going on in the church for years are *not* a new pastor's responsibility to solve in his first year or two. Take your time and make sure your approach to church discipline is comprehensive and thought through. If church discipline is your first act, it may very well be your last act. As the saying goes, "There is a way that seemeth right unto a young preacher, but the end thereof is to be put out."

Third, make sure that you really love the flock and do not merely see them as a steppingstone to bigger and better things. The pastor's heart needs to be committed to loving and serving that flock for the rest of his life. If it is not, leave church discipline to someone who can love the flock as the great Shepherd does. Churches do not exist to help pastors further their *careers*, but rather pastors exist to help churches honor Jesus. The church is to be a place of nurturing, love, discipleship, and preparation for God's people to go into the entire world to make disciples. If the pastor is not deeply devoted to God and His flock, he will most likely never implement discipline because it may mar his reputation. If he does implement it without sufficient love, more than likely he will neither do it the right way nor complete the task. Discipline is difficult enough, but to fail to do it in the right way is catastrophic.

Fourth, the level of commitment needs to be raised in all areas of the church, including what is expected of pastors, staff, deacons, teachers, leaders, secretaries, custodians, and any others who participate in the life of the church. Then, church discipline becomes a part of an overall strategy and works to elevate the measure of what it means to follow Christ. This is not an artificial elevating of the standard, but unless your church is trying to do everything that the Bible says, there is room for improvement. If you are doing everything you should, including church discipline, then you need not read this book or any other for that matter. One of the areas that must be held up as the highest criterion is the studying and teaching of the Word of God. The people must see that the Word of God is that which the shepherds give their lives to in order to know and serve God more faithfully because, ultimately, the church's willingness to follow in the exercise of church discipline is based on her respect for God and His Word.

Fifth, I would advise that you teach thoroughly on church discipline before it is implemented. This is crucial. This needs to be done before you are facing a discipline case if at all possible. This will produce a more conducive atmosphere for the church to receive the biblical mandate for exercising church discipline. Most churches have no concept of what church discipline is other than something that ought to be avoided. It is the dinosaur of the church, and like the dinosaur, we are better off with stories about them and not the real thing. The church must be taught both the necessity of church discipline and the beauty of it. If the teaching is shallow, the support for church discipline will be shallow, but if it is thorough, in most cases it will produce a more godly response to church discipline.

Sixth, church bylaws need to reflect the commitment to practice church discipline. Changing the bylaws may not be one of the first things that you are able to do—unless you are indeed a miracle worker—but it is important to review and update your bylaws to reflect the commitment to church discipline. This is more of a legal necessity than a theological issue.

Your bylaws do not have to go into great detail about the practice of discipline, but they do need to state that the church practices it according to the New Testament—see appendix II for a sample. If you have bylaws, they need to be current with the practice of the church since calling people to obey one part while ignoring other parts is a bad practice and a high protein diet for a lawsuit.

Some churches have both a constitution and bylaws, but as Barry C. McCarty writes, "The practice of having a separate constitution and bylaws is becoming less common"[183] I would recommend eliminating the constitution and including the necessaries in the bylaws. This simplifies administration of the necessaries, and the safeguard, which keeps someone from changing them without due process, is still intact.

In addition, I would change, as much as possible, the bylaws into standing rules or guidelines. This facilitates maintaining current rules of procedure and greatly increases protection from potential lawsuits. Bylaws can be kept current without changing any of them to standing rules or guidelines, but the cumbersomeness of doing so may prove to be poor stewardship of time. Regrettably, we must consider the potential of the church being sued. I do not think man's laws can trump the law of God, but if we can keep the law of man without violating the law of God, we should. *Church Discipline and the Courts* by Buzzard and Brandon is a good book on the legalities related to the church and church discipline.

Seventh, confidentiality is of the utmost importance. Not only do people being disciplined deserve this, but it is also essential to make sure that the disciplinary process is not thwarted. When you choose another counselor, even if at the second level of public disclosure or at the first encounter if the primary level of privacy has already been lost, the commitment of this person to maintain confidentiality should be given significant consideration. Any particular case of discipline may take from six months to a year to resolve, and during that time, confidentiality is of the utmost importance. Further, if the one being disciplined repents at any time during the process, those who are privy to the facts are love bound to keep what they know to themselves. The more mature and committed the church is generally, and the ones involved in the discipline are particularly, the more probable confidentiality is.

Eighth is the need to forgive. The church must realize that regardless what the wayward has done or how many times he has done it, if he repents, the church must genuinely forgive the transgression. It cannot be held against him. However, forgiveness is not to be understood as synonymous with being qualified for particular responsibilities as is done so often and was addressed previously. Disallowing the repentant from serving in certain areas of responsibility is not tantamount to holding a grudge, but rather it is to protect the repentant and the church.

If someone has repented of stealing, and the church forgives him, he does not need to be made treasurer in order to demonstrate that the church has really forgiven him. To make him treasurer too early is to unnecessarily expose him to temptation, which he may not be able to resist. It is also unwise to require the church to trust someone who has given no evidence of trustworthiness. Fellowship requires forgiveness, but leadership requires trust. Forgiveness is given at the time of repentance, and trust is given in response to a sufficient demonstration of trustworthiness. Leadership is bestowed upon those who demonstrate sufficient ability, spiritual giftedness, commitment, and trustworthiness.

Ninth, let the discipline case arise naturally, and take the most obvious case first if at all possible. Do not go looking for someone to discipline, and do not begin with a questionable case. When you go into a church that has not practiced discipline, there will probably be several things that need to be dealt with, but it is a grave error to seek to correct all of the wrongs from the last fifty years in a year or two. Something that cannot be denied or avoided is the place to start. Do not force the issue. Keep your eyes on building the church up in the faith, raising the standards, and calling the church to follow Jesus in everything. Then, when the situation arises that warrants attention, do what must be done. Prayerfully, sufficient time will have lapsed before the need arises. Although there may be some difficult members who merit discipline because of their carnality and recalcitrant spirit, you can work around them until a later time. The ones that cannot be avoided—heretics, the one who sows discord, and those living in flagrant immorality—are the ones to concern yourself with.

Tenth, realize that it is normal for a case of formal church discipline to take six months or more from the time of awareness of the problem until the time of formal discipline. There is no need to rush. Take time between each encounter with the wayward brother or sister to pray for them to repent—and for your own heart, spirit, and wisdom—and pray diligently. During the whole process, seek counsel from others involved or others whom you know have practiced church discipline—without violating confidentiality.

Eleventh is courage. Get some people who are as convicted as you are about discipline, who pray, are respected by the church, and whom you believe will weather the storm and be there in the end. This is of monumental importance. If the ones who support you at first turn against what you are doing before the process is completed, it may very well undermine everything. Satan could seek to involve someone whom he will pull out halfway through in order to counter your attempt to follow Jesus. This is warfare. It is a war for holiness and against sin. We have heaven on our side, but hell is in front of us. It is war, and it is hellish war.

Appendix III contains a true story of a church that practiced discipline, and as a result, a couple's love and marriage were saved. The church disciplining loved, prayed, and forgave. This is what God desires; may we desire it as well.

Appendix 1—Resolution on Church Discipline by LeRoy Wagner

The following circumstances prompted Pastor LeRoy Wagner to offer the resolution that involved church disciplining.

During the time that Bill Clinton was president, some leaders and pastors spoke publicly on the need of his home church, Immanuel Baptist Church in Little Rock, Arkansas, to exercise church discipline on him. This prompted some to react by denouncing these leaders for challenging Immanuel to exercise discipline on one of her members because, they argued, that violated local church autonomy. LeRoy's resolution demonstrates the tragic marginalizing of church discipline and the fallacy and danger of such thinking, which seeks to silence any criticism of a local church by those outside the church.

LeRoy Wagner described the event as follows:

"On November 3, 1998 at the 145th session of the Arkansas Baptist Convention, I submitted a resolution to the Resolutions Committee. I was informed later in the day that the committee had rejected the resolution on the grounds that the language was divisive and inflammatory. They wanted to keep their resolutions on a 'high plane.'

I submitted the same resolution during an open business session on November 4. This convention was at Ouachita and the "deck was stacked." After an opportunity to speak for my resolution, the committee chair, Mike Seabaugh, attacked the resolution with fervor, *scoffing at the idea of church discipline having any connection with the Great Commission* (italics added). The fervor of the chairman was unlike anything I have ever heard in 22 years of attending conventions. The resolution was soundly defeated with no one rising to speak for it."

Voted: Resolution from LeRoy Wagner—Cherished Baptist Doctrines

> President Kirksey recognized LeRoy Wagner, messenger from Pearcy Baptist Church, Pearcy, who presented a resolution from the floor on Cherished Baptist Doctrines, and moved for adoption. Motion seconded. Following a report from Mike Seabaugh on the decision of the Resolutions Committee on this particular resolution, the resolution failed.

The Cherished Baptist Doctrines resolution reads as follows:

> WHEREAS, we cherish the autonomy of the local church; we also cherish the God-given mandate for lay persons and leaders alike to "speak the truth in love" (Ephesians 4:15); and
>
> WHEREAS, local church autonomy, in reality, can only be violated when it is externally controlled to act or think contrary to its self-governance, not merely by a person expressing their opinion, and

WHEREAS, the New Testament clearly and unequivocally commands the church to practice church discipline (Matthew 16:15–19; I Corinthians 5); and

WHEREAS, the authority for church discipline resides totally within the local church: this in no way precludes those outside the church from addressing scriptural matters in a prophetic voice; and

WHEREAS, church discipline is not less important than the Great Commission, since both are given by our Lord Jesus; and

WHEREAS, we publicly challenge, chronicle, exhort, and bemoan churches and denominations who fail to fulfill the Great Commission mandate without violating their autonomy.

Therefore, be it RESOLVED, that we cherish both the principle of local church autonomy and the command to speak the truth in love.

Be it further RESOLVED, that it is no more possible for a person to undermine local church autonomy by speaking their opinions than it is to undermine an individual's priesthood by calling on them to repent of sin.

Be it further RESOLVED, that seeking to silence or censure individuals from speaking their God-given convictions is not only unmerited but implicitly validates the emerging gales and dangerous notion that we should never speak about an individual's sin; thus while seeking to protect autonomy, we legitimize the claims of those who seek to thwart the proclamation of the gospel.

Be it further RESOLVED, that we recognize the church and nation is in desperate need of clear biblical insight, strong moral leadership, and scriptural exhortation, knowing that it is impossible to be under the direction

of God's Holy Spirit if we are not submitting to God's
Holy Word.

Be it further RESOLVED, that we will never place political
correctness above biblical correctness.

Be it finally RESOLVED, that we, the messengers in the Arkansas Baptist State Convention, meeting at Quachita
Baptist University. Arkadelphia, November 3–4, 1998
gladly and humbly submit to the authority and verdict
of Scripture by recognizing the validity and compatibility of the biblical principles of local church autonomy,
the command to exercise church discipline and the right
and responsibility to "speak the truth in love."

The officers for 1998 were presented: Greg Kirksey, Benton,
president; Bill Bowen, Mena, first vice-president; Tim Reddin,
Hot Springs Village, second vice-president. The one hundred
forty-fifth session of the 150th year of the Arkansas Baptist
State Convention was adjourned with prayer by President Greg
Kirksey. There were 1168 messengers registered for the 1998
convention.

Appendix 2-Bylaws on Church Discipline

$\mathcal{B}$laws adopted by Lakeside Baptist Church, 1990

Section 6—Corrective Discipline

(a) *Basic Purpose and Types.* It shall be the basic purpose of the church to emphasize to its members that every reasonable measure will be taken to assist any troubled member. The pastor, other members of the church staff and deacons are available for counsel and guidance. Redemption rather than punishment should be the guideline which governs the attitude of one member toward another.

Corrective discipline is necessary because of conduct or doctrine contrary to Biblical standards. Matthew 18:15–19 is a general procedure for church discipline unless prohibited by danger, distance, or some other prohibitive obstacle. Corrective discipline is always intended for the glory of God, the welfare and purity of the local church and the restoration and spiritual growth of the offender.

(i) *Suspension.* There are occasions when a member's slackness in the performance of duty, disorderliness, and/or departure from the traditions and instructions of the Word of God require church discipline but of a less severe nature than excommunication (II Thessalonians 3:6, 11, 14–15). Therefore, if a member's disorderliness requires discipline, the church may suspend the offender from church membership at a duly called congregational meeting. The congregation has the right and responsibility to suspend such a one by three-fourth majority of the members present and voting. The discipline consists of temporary suspension of rights to participate in the Lord's Supper, to serve publicly in the church, to vote in congregational meetings, and to participate in the general life of the church. The offender is not to be treated as an enemy but admonished as a brother.

(ii) *Excommunication.* It is right and in harmony with the scriptures for the congregation to exclude from fellowship any member who persistently holds false and/or heretical doctrines, is unwilling to settle differences in a scriptural manner, openly and persistently lives inconsistently with his Christian profession, lives in violation of Biblical morals or the law or persistently disturbs the peace and unity of the church. This discipline occurs when suspension fails to secure the offender's repentance or may be enacted without prior corrective steps. After hearing the charges against the accused, the congregation

has the right and responsibility to excommuni-
cate an offending member by three-fourths majority of the members present and voting. The
church is required subsequently to deal with excommunicated individuals according to Matthew
18:17 and I Corinthians 5:13.

(b) *Reasons Revealed.* It is not an infringement upon a
member's rights when they are being disciplined to have
the reasons, if so deemed by the leadership, revealed
to the church and other churches in which that person
might seek membership or a church which might have
an interest in the particular incident. Every precau-
tion would be taken to not harm the person's reputation any more than absolutely necessary.

(c) *Restoration.* The church must restore to fellowship in
full forgiveness those persons who show satisfactory
evidence of repentance (II Corinthians 2:6–8). Persons shall be restored at a duly called congregational
meeting upon recommendation of the deacons and
pastor and three-fourths majority of the members
present and voting.

Appendix 3-
A Story of Temptation, Tragedy, and Triumph: A True Story of How a Church's Willingness to Practice Church Discipline Resulted in Restoration and Rejoicing

The following is a story of temptation, tragedy, and triumph, which took place in the lives of two of my dear friends, Jason and Melissa.

I have known each of them since they were children. They both grew up in a church where I pastored for thirteen years. I have watched them walk through this difficult and heart wrenching time in a way that honored our Savior and His kingdom.

At my request, Jason and Melissa have consented to share their story. The church they were members of practiced church discipline, which played a significant role in their lives being reunited and made new by the Holy Spirit.

Their prayer in sharing their story is that it will encourage churches to embrace the New Testament practice of church discipline, and that their story will give hope to others whose lives are devastated by sin.

Jason and Melissa:

> We were the *ideal* Christian couple if there ever was one. We sought to honor God even in our dating life. We had abstained sexually, saving ourselves only for each other. We had spent much time in prayer with and for one another, so that when our wedding day came, we were confident that God had created us for each other.

Jason:

> I was already serving as a youth director in a small church just outside of Hot Springs, Arkansas when Melissa and I were married. Just a few months into our marriage, God made it very clear to us that our lives were to be fully surrendered to His ministry. We were obedient to that calling, and during the next six years of service, I became licensed, and then ordained as a minister of the gospel. I never felt more in the center of God's will than when we were serving and ministering in that little church. My eyes were focused on Christ, and I was daily searching His word to know Him more. God was blessing my efforts and my humble attitude of service.
>
> We saw God do some amazing things with that little youth group. A youth group that consisted of maybe six or seven students when we first arrived exploded into a group of more than forty. God was opening doors of ministry to us constantly. I was being asked to speak at camps, revivals, and mission trips. In this time of

growth and exciting new opportunities, my focus began to shift. I started to have a pride in what I had accomplished, or at least what I thought I had accomplished. I knew all the right things to say; all of the
churchy words ran from lips as if it were second nature. I knew who to give the credit to in public, but my
heart was swelling with pride and arrogance.

My time of Bible study had dwindled greatly, even to the
point of not studying the Word when I was teaching or
preaching it. I had enough head knowledge to get by and
just relied on my own talents and skills, or so I thought.
After all, it was all about me right? My eyes were no
longer fixed on Christ and on knowing God more but on
me and my aspirations. As my relationship with God
suffered, my relationship with Melissa began to suffer as
well. While I put on a mask of holiness, Melissa could
see and feel me drawing away from her.

Melissa:

Some situations arose in our church as we were ending
our fifth year of ministry in 2000, and through a series of
circumstances and events, Jason became very hurt. Over
the next few months, I watched him slip into some other
personality; he became someone I had never known. He
had chosen unforgiveness and bitterness, and although
our marriage had nothing to do with the hurt he experienced at church, it was our marriage that began to suffer.
It would be just a few months later into 2001 that the
outcome of this bitterness would spring up.

Jason:

All of these things led to a tragic decision in February 2001. I became involved in an adulterous relationship with a college girl from our church. My pride and bitterness drove me to a decision to be unfaithful to my wife during a two and a half month affair with this girl. I drug my Savior's call and my wife's love through a cesspool of sin, showing no respect for either of them.

I will never forget the May afternoon when my pastor called me into his study to confront my sin. Our church was led by a ministry team that was comprised of six men, a mixture of paid staff and lay pastors. Each man was there to support his pastor as he confronted me with what I had done. I was numb with fear and disgust. My first instinct was to deny as much as I could and try to save as much face as possible. After nearly three hours of hearing my pastor wrap each of his words with Scripture, God's word broke me and I confessed to my sin. What happened over the next few months changed my life forever.

The next day was Sunday, and I stood before my church and confessed my sin of adultery. This began my process of being disciplined by the church. My first step was to confess all I had done and ask the church to forgive how I had sinned against my Lord, my wife, and my church. I also resigned from my staff position. I was only beginning to see the consequences of my sin. In a matter of weeks, I went from a full-time staff member of a growing church to a gas station attendant. Over the next few months, I was involved in two different types of separations. One was from my wife, and the other was from my church family. During this time of separation, however, I was never separated from my pastor. He was vitally involved in the discipline process. It would have been much easier, I am sure, for my pastor and my church to have dismissed me quietly and to never hear from me again. The only problem is, that is not how Scripture commands the church to deal with sin inside the body. It was during this time of discipline that God was able to completely break me of all my pride. I was at the end of me, and I was able to see all of the filth and evil things I was capable of when I put my desires over His. During this same time God was doing a work in Melissa's heart as well.

Melissa:

There is no way to adequately describe the intense pain and emotions that were raging within me. I had vowed that nothing in my life would ever resemble any of the paths and mistakes my parents had made, and now here we were, about to enter a time of separation because of an affair within the church. How much more could my marriage resemble the lost world? I knew in my head I had to forgive both parties, but in the beginning there was no room in my heart for forgiveness.

I had to cling to the Lord, for He alone is my rock. I had to draw from His grace daily, for He alone is my source of hope. The more I trusted and asked the Lord to meet with me and reveal truth, the more He began to peel the layers of sin and selfishness from my own life. God began to open my eyes to my own arrogance, and He broke me. It wasn't just about Jason, but about areas in my life that needed refining, and I would venture to say that every other marriage walking this road requires that both husband and wife be taken through a refining process. I had to ask for forgiveness and give my broken marriage to Him, the ultimate healer.

Jason:

This time of discipline in my life was used by God, not only to humble me and draw me near to Melissa, but also to give our church an opportunity to choose God's way. Everyone in the church was not supportive of the practice of discipline. Our pastor and leadership team were questioned about the actions they were taking. With each question and challenge that arose, our pastor stood firm on the word and was obedient to walk the church through this time of crisis.

In hindsight, I understand why many are uncomfortable with the practice of church discipline. If you are involved in a church that is practicing discipline, this process forces you to see your own sin and your own unworthiness to be called a child of the King. For some, this is too much, and they would rather not deal with such thoughts. During this time, members of our church, and those visiting as well, were able to see firsthand a church that is obedient to every command in God's word. This drove some away, but it drew in many more. Many of those that God brought to our church during this time are now playing vital roles in the life and ministry of our body.

As my relationship with the Lord was restored, and He began drawing me nearer and nearer to Him, He was also healing my marriage. God used a precious couple from Little Rock to counsel us through a very tumultuous time. Their godly wisdom and example are still an inspiration to us today. This time of counseling was crucial in the healing and restoration of our marriage. Melissa, more out of love for her Savior than her husband, forgave me and allowed me back into her heart and our home. The Lord was continuing to heal and do a restorative work in each of our lives.

Melissa:

My prayer all along had been that Jason would be a new creation and the same would be true for our marriage. The Lord was answering that prayer before my very eyes. In the seven months we were separated, God continually gave me Scriptures like 2 Corinthians 5:17. The Greek word for *new* used in this passage is *kainos*, which means never before. God doesn't make it better, but literally something new. What a source of encouragement these Scriptures were and are. I began to see that our situation could actually be used to bring God glory.

There is a passage in Mark 2 that I remember reading during this time. It is the story of the paralytic man whose friends had faith enough that if they could just get the paralytic to Jesus, he would be healed. What made an impression on me was verse 12. "And he got up and immediately picked up the pallet and went out in the sight of everyone, so that they were all amazed saying, "We have never seen anything like this." In the margin of my Bible I penned the words "Be true in my life." I trusted and believed that God could do such a work in our marriage that people would glorify God and say, "We have never seen anything like this." This has become a prayer of ours as we seek to give God all the glory He deserves. In December of 2001, Jason and I renewed our vows in the same church where just a few months earlier he had resigned.

Jason:

After some time of visiting other churches in search of a new church home, Melissa and I became frustrated. We knew that our old church was home, but we saw no way we could ever go back. Our pastor asked us to consider coming back, to consider coming back home. I saw no way that it would be humanly possible for a staff member who was forced to resign because of immorality could ever come back and be a part of that body again. In one aspect I was right; there is no way this could be humanly possible. Fortunately, our God loves to do the impossible. Melissa and I came back to our home church and were loved like I never thought possible. Words cannot describe the feelings I had when person after person came to me, forgave me, and loved me again. I knew then we were at a special place with special people. I understand now that this is what God intended the outcome of discipline to be. He does not discipline us to drive us away, but to draw us back to Him.

Melissa and I are still a part of that church today. We are currently teaching a young couples Sunday school class. It amazes me every Sunday that my God loved me enough to choose to forgive and allow me to serve Him. I understand there are still consequences to my sin, but I understand even more that I am an example of how holy and gracious our Lord is. We still do not know all of God's plan for our lives, but we are anxiously awaiting the next door He will open. I am so thankful for a pastor and a church that loved me enough to do things God's way, so that I could experience a new life in Him. God's word is true yesterday, today, and tomorrow and I know He can, will, and has made all things new.

Index

A

Anabaptist 107

B

baptism 97, 106, 107
believe 10, 19, 23, 24, 33, 62, 63, 64, 72, 73, 75, 79, 89, 101,
     109, 125, 134, 140, 148, 152, 159, 162, 165, 166, 170, 176, 183, 195, 200, 202,
     203, 205, 213, 218, 231, 235, 236, 239, 263, 266, 268, 271, 290, 291,
     312, 313, 314, 315, 342, 343, 350, 358, 367

C

Calvin 105, 345
Catholic 345
church growth 173
confidentiality 292, 365, 367
convict 220, 264
corporal punishment 28, 29
correct 30, 57, 58, 59, 114, 147, 161, 162, 165, 166,
     180, 194, 200, 235, 288, 366
corrected 295
correcting 57
correction 25, 57, 59, 60, 74, 83, 106
correctional 58, 63
corrective 57, 58, 59, 89, 374
correctives 42

correctly 32, 109, 295
correctness 332, 372

D

determinant 63, 327
determinants 63, 65, 82, 86, 192, 211
determinate 73, 312
determinates 78
determinative 98
determine 18, 71, 119, 177, 183, 189, 197,
221, 232, 273, 312, 317, 356, 360
determined 19, 63, 64, 65, 66, 71, 72, 78, 81, 86, 137, 162, 177,
182, 192, 236, 252, 283, 294
determiner 221
determines 26, 35, 63, 201, 312, 359
determining 109, 146, 311, 327
determinism 62, 65, 66, 67, 77, 82, 192, 193, 317
determinist 73
deterministic 19, 79, 81, 82
discord 103, 332, 333, 334, 337, 338, 342, 349, 367
disorderly 344, 346, 347, 349
disunity 225, 226, 227, 228, 229, 330, 333, 336
divine 26, 28, 35, 38, 39, 43, 44, 45, 46, 51, 97, 121, 140, 206,
207, 213, 214, 215, 246, 305, 328
doctrine 49, 62, 106, 107, 109, 139, 141, 149, 191, 193, 217,
218, 281, 304, 328, 329, 330, 331, 332, 336, 356, 373

E

evangelism 33, 42, 45, 78, 90, 96, 132, 147, 148, 153, 158, 169,
194, 195, 197, 201, 204, 232, 238, 281, 283, 351, 353
exposition 79, 146, 152, 155, 174, 226, 361, 361

F

faith 5, 32, 34, 39, 46, 49, 69, 73, 76, 84, 94, 99, 106, 107, 124,
150, 158, 159, 160, 164, 186, 193, 230, 257, 259, 260, 263, 267,
279, 287, 308, 329, 330, 331, 353, 355, 362, 366, 383
fear
39, 45, 59, 71, 142, 158, 159, 160, 190, 199, 207, 209, 223, 225,
234, 237, 250, 307, 317, 334, 350, 356, 380
forgive
75, 140, 142, 215, 256, 258, 259, 260, 262, 263, 267, 268, 269, 270,
286, 296, 304, 366, 380, 381, 385

forgiveness 20, 24, 33, 60, 80, 86, 97, 123, 139, 140, 141, 215,
256, 257, 258, 259, 260, 263, 264, 267, 268, 269, 270,
272, 276, 289, 304, 307, 309, 366, 375, 381, 382
free 19, 62, 65, 66, 67, 68, 71, 75, 77, 78, 81, 82, 84, 85, 134,
136, 145, 165, 192, 202, 222, 236, 257, 261, 262, 263, 264, 266
freedom 19, 34, 47, 61, 67, 68, 70, 71, 72, 73, 74, 84,
85, 121, 134, 165, 222, 234
freely 67, 71, 72, 84

G

glorification 129, 139, 208
glorified 207
glorifies 208
glorify 98, 204, 205, 206, 208, 384
glorifying 206
glorious 15, 20, 76, 136, 207
gloriously 24, 76
glory 37, 41, 50, 51, 74, 130, 152, 167, 205, 206, 207, 208, 229,
308, 355, 373, 383, 384
gospel
15, 17, 18, 19, 20, 33, 34, 38, 42, 43, 45, 69, 71, 77, 78, 79, 80, 81,
82, 85, 86, 90, 91, 94, 105, 112, 113, 126, 134, 158, 179, 188, 192, 194, 195, 196,
197, 199, 200, 201, 203, 204, 209, 215, 253, 267, 309, 316, 354, 371, 378
govern 49
governing 39
government 35, 39, 40, 41, 44, 46, 51, 53, 129, 130
governmental 26, 28, 39, 45, 214
governments 39
governs 373
Great Commission 17, 42, 79, 88, 89, 91, 92, 93, 94, 95, 96, 98,
105, 166, 168, 194, 217, 331, 370, 371
grief 242, 243, 244, 245, 246, 251, 252, 268, 283
growth
18, 24, 36, 37, 42, 74, 99, 153, 165, 166, 167, 168, 169, 170,
171, 172, 173, 174, 183, 230, 231, 324, 342, 353, 373, 378
guns 31, 64, 234, 235

H

heresy 80, 91, 100, 103, 148, 199, 231, 331, 332, 333, 349
holiness 5, 57, 74, 75, 89, 107, 109, 111, 112, 121, 122, 123,
125, 126, 127, 128, 129, 130, 131, 132, 133, 137, 138, 139, 142,
143, 168, 170, 171, 188, 195, 196, 197, 211, 212, 217, 222, 223,

225, 230, 231, 232, 233, 237, 252, 266, 271, 272, 275, 279, 280, 281, 282, 283, 303, 323, 350, 367, 379
Holy Spirit
36, 44, 45, 69, 91, 96, 125, 147, 186, 189, 191, 199, 213, 223, 224, 227, 244, 262, 263, 264, 265, 266, 267, 330, 331, 334, 335, 336, 354, 372, 377
humility
18, 134, 136, 137, 160, 226, 237, 244, 246, 247, 248, 250, 251, 252, 268, 284, 333, 338, 342
hypocrisy
10, 91, 104, 113, 114, 120, 132, 179, 196, 197, 198, 201, 204, 210, 224, 244, 281, 282, 287, 288, 290, 312, 313, 314, 317, 353, 356, 357

I

image of God 20, 31, 34, 35, 56, 61, 65, 66, 69, 70, 73, 74, 76, 77, 78, 79, 84, 85, 86, 115, 191, 192, 207, 235, 261, 262, 263, 266, 283
imago dei 139, 194, 262, 264
immoral 18, 42, 71, 116, 135, 286, 301, 302, 318, 319, 325, 326, 328, 329
indeterminate 63
inerrancy 99, 114, 115, 218

J

judge 19, 83, 113, 114, 115, 116, 118, 119, 134, 137, 209, 213, 224, 250, 284, 319, 326, 328, 353
justice 52, 62, 65, 74, 77, 83, 96, 208, 265, 339

L

law 40, 55, 64, 66, 95, 117, 118, 120, 121, 135, 165, 202, 206, 209, 214, 215, 248, 249, 257, 280, 287, 293, 314, 321, 354, 365, 374
love 5, 9, 11, 15, 16, 30, 32, 42, 43, 45, 52, 53, 55, 56, 57, 60, 71, 74, 75, 76, 79, 80, 89, 96, 97, 99, 102, 104, 108, 109, 130, 133, 134, 135, 136, 137, 138, 139, 140, 142, 159, 162, 167, 168, 186, 198, 200, 203, 206, 208, 211, 213, 215, 216, 217, 218, 219, 220, 222, 228, 230, 237, 241, 243, 245, 249, 251, 252, 253, 254, 255, 259, 260, 266, 267, 268, 269, 277, 280, 281, 282, 284, 289, 290, 294, 312, 322, 330, 334, 335, 340, 341, 345, 353, 363, 365, 367, 370, 371, 372, 380, 382, 383

M

membership 11, 12, 13, 18, 106, 109, 110, 185, 186, 201, 281, 293, 301, 317, 318, 328, 374, 375

modernity 77, 111, 125, 128
mourn 242, 244

P

parental 23, 26, 27, 29, 30, 31, 32, 33, 34, 40, 43, 44, 46, 56,
57, 97, 163, 214, 311
parenting 29, 33, 82
parents
27, 29, 30, 31, 32, 33, 34, 41, 56, 59, 154, 168, 188, 262, 381
post modernity 169
pray 22, 44, 89, 90, 97, 147, 161, 177, 187, 211, 251, 288,
302, 304, 305, 307, 308, 341, 344, 353, 357, 367
predetermine 66
protect 40, 45, 58, 59, 70, 162, 164, 187, 189, 190, 245, 260,
283, 311, 323, 366, 371
protected 41, 63, 74, 170, 190, 191, 284, 347
protecting 45, 74, 187, 190, 191, 327
protection 73, 74, 83, 190, 281, 322, 329, 365
protective 58, 73, 74, 83, 89, 295, 347
protector 295
protects 74
psychology 31, 80, 81, 82, 83, 85, 99, 152, 192, 359

R

redemption 24, 45, 50, 55, 56, 59, 83, 127, 172, 202, 257, 294
redemptive 45, 51, 52, 55, 56, 57, 58, 59, 74, 89, 347
relativism 49, 91, 127, 165, 204
repent 20, 25, 109, 138, 141, 162, 170, 179, 187, 197, 199,
214, 215, 216, 217, 220, 245, 251, 260, 265, 266, 295, 296,
299, 300, 302, 305, 315, 323, 351, 367, 371
repentance 19, 51, 97, 134, 163, 214, 220, 229, 249, 257, 258,
259, 260, 263, 264, 265, 267, 268, 270, 274, 283, 285, 287, 289,
293, 295, 297, 298, 299, 303, 315, 325, 327, 349, 366, 374, 375
response 22, 26, 81, 94, 102, 118, 162, 189, 200, 201, 205, 244,
245, 249, 251, 256, 259, 269, 279, 296, 312, 349, 364, 366
responsibilities 61, 189, 190, 243, 366
responsibility 10, 33, 36, 38, 39, 40, 44, 61, 62, 67, 71, 77, 86,
136, 141, 163, 166, 175, 177, 186, 190, 191, 193, 194, 225, 230,
234, 236, 244, 248, 276, 280, 286, 289, 297, 299, 302, 325,
326, 355, 362, 366, 372, 374, 375
responsible 18, 27, 33, 34, 62, 63, 64, 65, 67, 68, 69, 70, 71,
73, 75, 84, 191, 193, 200, 236, 261, 262, 283, 284, 301, 321
responsibly 63
responsive 153

S

save 72, 94, 137, 262, 279, 282, 323, 337, 380
self-determined 66, 70, 72, 73, 192
self-discipline 26, 34, 35, 36, 39, 40, 44, 214
self-governance 262, 372
self-governed 135
self-protection 26
sin 19, 20, 25, 26, 33, 45, 47, 52, 55, 66, 67, 68, 69, 74, 75, 76,
    78, 80, 83, 84, 97, 100, 102, 105, 106, 109, 111, 117, 118, 119,
    120, 127, 128, 129, 134, 138, 139, 142, 143, 144, 158, 159,161,
    162, 179, 187, 188, 189, 194, 196, 198, 201, 203, 208, 209, 211, 212,
    215, 216, 217, 221, 222, 223, 224, 226, 227, 232, 238, 242, 243, 244, 245, 246,
    248, 249, 250, 251, 253, 254, 255, 256, 257, 260, 261, 262, 263, 264, 265, 266,
    267, 268, 271, 275, 276, 280, 281, 282, 283, 284, 286, 287, 288, 289,
    290, 292, 295, 296, 300, 302, 303, 304, 307, 308, 309, 312, 317,
    320, 321, 324, 325, 327, 328, 329, 337, 341, 347, 348, 349, 367, 371, 377, 380,
    381, 382, 385
society 25, 30, 31, 33, 40, 41, 46, 52, 58, 59, 60, 61, 64, 65, 66,
    73, 76, 77, 79, 80, 111, 158, 162, 163, 165, 166, 191, 192, 205, 234, 236
spiritual discipline 36, 37, 38, 41, 91, 164, 229, 237, 238

T

teaching 9, 10, 18, 26, 38, 41, 69, 87, 91, 93, 94, 95, 96,
    98, 103, 104, 107, 109, 111, 112, 113, 116, 118, 126,
    127, 132, 136, 144, 145, 148, 150, 151, 171, 181, 187,
    191, 193, 194, 202, 215, 217, 218, 226, 228, 236, 237,
    241, 251, 253, 254, 269, 281, 284, 286, 291, 301, 305,
    321, 323, 328, 330, 331, 332, 333, 336, 339, 347, 349,
    351, 354, 363, 364, 379, 384
theology 9, 42, 140, 149, 151, 152, 174, 179, 198, 308, 332, 360

U

unity
    18, 49, 77, 88, 89, 100, 129, 167, 223, 224, 225, 226, 227, 298,
    330, 331, 336, 374
unredemptive 137

W

witness 46, 69, 70, 107, 116, 152, 168, 179, 197, 233, 244, 294
worship 42, 55, 73, 90, 103, 104, 110, 130, 141, 145, 146, 147,
    148, 149, 150, 151, 152, 153, 154, 155, 159, 217, 237, 273,
    274, 275, 276, 305, 316, 317, 362

Notes

[1] By society, I do not mean to refer only to society in the sense of a city, state, or country, but rather to any group of individuals living as members of, or associated together as, a religious, cultural, political, or other purposed community. This can be groups as varied as a nation such as Israel, a church body, or family.

[2] Lynn R. Buzzard and Thomas S. Brandon, Jr., *Church Discipline and the Courts* (Wheaton: Tyndale House Publishers, 1987), 65.

[3] D. M. Jackson, *The New Schaff-Herzog Encyclopedia of Religion*, (Grand Rapids: Baker Book House, 1950), III:8.

[4] Johannes P. Louw and Eugene A. Nida, *Greek-English Lexicon of the New Testament based on Semantic Domains,* electronic edition of the 2nd edition, (New York: United Bible Societies, 1989), s.v. "paideia."

[5] Deborah Ausburn, "Child Abuse Investigations," *Action*, (August 1988).

[6] "America and God: Abolishing Corporal Punishment in the School and the Home," *Family Life*, (August 1990), 1.

[7] Ibid.

[8] Gene Edward Veith, "Hating our Children," *World*, (12 June 1999), 23–24.

[9] Punishment and discipline are often distinguished because of some grammatical dissimilarities. However, I am using these two terms interchangeably throughout this book based on their similarities. They both acknowledge right and wrong, and both are brought to bear in order to correct the behavior or consequences of the behavior. Additionally, both are based on the nature of God, which will be demonstrated in chapter 2.

[10] The popular undermining of the value of corporal discipline can be seen in studies like the one on "The Growth Of Conscience," where physi-

cal punishment was deemed to have a negative impact in Charles G. Morris' *Psychology an Introduction*, (New York: Appleton-Century-Crofts, 1973) 106; or William Glasser's view as seen in his "Reality Therapy" in *Perspectives on Counseling Theories,* ed. Louis E. Shilling, (Englewood Cliffs, New Jersey: Prentice-Hall Inc., 1984) 113 and 116.

[11] Donald S. Whitney, *Spiritual Disciplines for the Christian Life* (Colorado Springs: Navpress, 1991) 15.

[12] James Strong, *The Exhaustive Concordance of the Bible: Showing Every Word of the Test of the Common English Version of the Canonical Books, and Every Occurrence of Each Word in Regular Order,* electronic edition (Ontario: Woodside Bible Fellowship, 1996), s.v. "gumnazo."

[13] Synergistic is not used in its strictly theological sense of discussing the nature of salvation being synergistic vs. monergistic as is debated between Calvinism and Arminianism. It is used only to emphasize the interaction of the human and the divine. The dictionary defines synergistic as the "interaction of elements that when combined produce a total effect that is greater than the sum of the individual elements, contributions, etc." *Random House Webster's Unabridged Dictionary*, 1996 electronic edition.

[14] J.I. Packer, *Concise Theology: A Guide to Historic Christian Beliefs*, (Wheaton, Ill.: Tyndale House Publishers, Inc., 1993), Matthew 18:15–17, s.v. "discipline."

[15] Ibid.

[16] Francis A. Schaeffer, *Trilogy: God Who Is There,* (Wheaton: Crossway Books, 1990), 197.

[17] Paul Lee Tan, ThD., *Encyclopedia of 7700 Illustrations: [A Treasury of Illustrations, Anecdotes, Facts and Quotations]* (Garland, Tx: Bible Communications, 1979), s.v. "googol."

[18] Robert E. Clark, Joanne Brubaker, and Roy B. Zuck, *Childhood Education in the Church*, (Chicago: Moody Press, 1975), 303.

[19] In order to quote and interact with different writers and views, I at times use the term "free will." However, unless I am quoting or referring to another's writing, or referring to Adam and Eve and/or Lucifer before they chose to sin, I use terms or phrases such as: "free choice," "free moral agent," "freedom," "responsible," "responsible for his actions" and/or "not responsible for his actions" rather than free will.

The Bible is clear that man was created in the image of God (Genesis 1:26–27) as a free moral agent, capable of real free choice of whether to obey or disobey God. However, the Bible is equally clear that Adam used his free choice to sin, fell, and he and his offspring became sinners not only by choice but also by nature (Romans 5:12–14, Ephesians 2:1–3, 4:17–19).

Consequently, man, since the fall of Adam, does not have true free will or free choice in the same way that Adam did. However, the Bible does hold man accountable for his decisions and societies are to hold members of the society responsible for their choices (Matthew 18:15–20; Romans 13:1–7).

Therefore, man's will is in bondage (Romans 3:10–11). Man is incapable on his own to perform any spiritual righteousness, whether this means meriting the favor of God or coming to God on his own. Without the work of the Holy Spirit, man will never come to saving faith in Christ. The Holy Spirit must convict (John 16:8) before anyone will be in a position to either receive or reject the gospel.

Having said that, it is important to remember that even after Adam sinned, and became spiritually dead and separated from God (Genesis 2:17), he responded to God's summon (Genesis 3:9–10). This is because the fall did not destroy or eradicate the *image of God* in man (Genesis 9:6; James 3:9); therefore, man, even lost man, can, with certain limitations, choose to do civil righteousness or good. In addition, the Bible repeatedly puts choice before man with the clear indication that he can choose and will receive based on his choice (Deuteronomy 30:19; Isaiah 7:16).

It is obvious that every man is not as evil as he could be. It is also obvious that we condemn certain actions and praise certain actions on the undeniable basis that man can choose to commit certain acts or not to commit certain acts. For example, speeding tickets are given out because a person could have chosen not to speed and hopefully the ticket will remind him to do so in the future.

My point in all of these discussions is to emphasize that fallen man still retains the image of God because while the fall corrupted the image, it did not destroy it. Consequently, apart from works of spiritual righteousness, man can and does make choices. These choices are uncoerced, although they may be influenced (Romans 2:4; Ephesians 2:1–3), which means that man could have chosen to do otherwise. Therefore, man is free enough in his choices to be accountable for his actions and the consequences of his choices. The devaluing of this premise, regardless if that devaluing is the result of natural or spiritual determinism, devalues man as created in the image of God and thereby dishonors God. This results in devaluing discipline, which ultimately emasculates the gospel.

20 Sue Titus Reid, *Crime and Criminology*, (New York: CBS College Publishing, 1985), 72.

21 Ibid., 73.

22 Ibid., 74.

23 Ibid., 76.

24 *Newsweek*, 20 September 1982, p. 30, as quoted by Reid in *Crime and Criminology*, 125.

25 Reid, *Criminology*, 76.

[26] Chuck Colson, *How Now Shall We Live*, (Wheaton: Tyndale House Publishers, 1999), 181.

[27] Norman Geisler, *Chosen But Free*, (Minneapolis: Bethany House Publishers, 1999), 175.

[28] By self-determined, I mean to indicate that the person's choice is generally, within limits, what determines his actions. Therefore, he is responsible for his actions. This is not to imply that there are not influences, whether natural (family, background, etc.) or spiritual (Romans 2:4: Ephesians 2:1–3). Nor is it to imply that God cannot override man's self-determination. In addition, this in no way suggests that man can choose spiritual good without God's initiation and grace. "Only the grace of God can bring man into his holy fellowship and enable man to fulfill the creative purpose of God." *The Baptist Faith and Message*, a statement adopted by The Southern Baptist Convention June 14, 2000 (Nashville: LifeWay Christian Resources). Article III Man.

[29] Russell Chandler, *Understanding the New Age*, (Dallas: Word Publishing, 1988), 274.

[30] Robert Gordis, "The Book of Job" *Thesis Theological Cassettes* (audiotape) 15, no. 7 (December, 1984).

[31] *The Baptist Faith and Message*, Article III Man.

[32] Peter Kreeft and Ronald K. Tacelli, in *Handbook of Christian Apologetics*, (Downer's Grove, Ill.: InterVarsity Press, 1994), chapter 6, s.v. "freewill."

[33] Schaeffer, *Trilogy*, 266–267.

[34] Kreeft, *Apologetics*, 18.

[35] E.B. Batson, article on John Bunyan in *Who's Who in Christian History*, eds. J.D. Douglas, Philip W. Comfort, and Donald Mitchell, (Wheaton: Tyndale House Publishers, Inc., 1992).

[36] Paul Meier, Frank Minirth, and Frank Wichern believe that Christian psychiatrist Johann Christian August Heinroth should be considered the father of psychiatry. They say, "Since his discoveries preceded Freud's by a hundred years, Heinroth could be considered the father of psychiatry, as well as the father of Christian psychiatry." He may be the father in the sense of being the first, but in influence and definition of psychiatry, Freud is unchallenged. *Introduction to Psychology and Counseling: Christian Perspectives and Applications* (Grand Rapids: Baker Book House, 1982), 21.

[37] Louis E. Shilling, *Perspectives on Counseling Theories*, (New Jersey: Prentice Hall, Inc., 1984), 21.

[38] Ibid., 31.

[39] Ronald. L. Koteskey, *General Psychology for Christian Counselors*, (Nashville: Abingdon Press, 1983), 19.

[40] Schilling, *Perspectives*, 31.

[41] Ibid., 113.

[42] Ibid., 116.

[43] Appendix I—Resolution made by LeRoy Wagner at the Arkansas Baptist State Convention.

[44] Frank E Gaebelin and J.D. Douglas, eds. "Matthew, Mark, Luke" Vol. 8 of *The Expositors Bible Commentary*, (Grand Rapids: Zondervan Publishing House, 1984), 595.

[45] Strong, *Exhaustive Concordance*, s.v. "tarco."

[46] Louw and Nida, *Greek-English Lexicon*, s.v. "tarco."

[47] *Theological Dictionary of the New Testament Theology*, Vol. 4, 390–461.

[48] Dietrich Bonhoeffer, *The Cost of Discipleship*, (New York: Simon & Schuster, 1959), 44–45.

[49] Buzzard and Brandon, *Church Discipline*, third page of book.

[50] Buzzard and Brandon, *Church Discipline*, 46.

[51] Marlin Jeschke, *Discipling the Brother*, (Scottsdale, Penn.: Herald Press, 1972), 32.

[52] George Davis, "Whatever Happened to Church Discipline," *Criswell Theological Review*, Spring 1987, 346.

[53] William R. Estep, *The Anabaptist Story*, (Grand Rapids: William B. Eerdmans Publishing Co., 1975), 186.

[54] J.A. Oosterbaan, "The Theology of Menno Simons," *The Mennonite Quarterly Review*, no. XXXV, (July 1961), 191–192.

[55] Estep, *Anabaptist*, 186.

[56] Ibid., 182–183.

[57] Ibid., 188.

[58] Estep, Anabaptist, 189.

[59] Ibid.

[60] Winthrop S. Hudson, *Religion in America*, (New York: Charles Scribner's Sons, 1981), 129–130.

[61] Strong, *Exhaustive Concordance*, s.v. "holy."

[62] D.R.W. Wood & I. Howard Marshall, *New Bible Dictionary*, third edition (Leicester, England; Downer's Grove, Ill.: InterVarsity Press, 1996), 5.T, s.v. "holy."

[63] Gerhard Kittel, Gerhard Friedrich, and Geoffrey William Bromiley, eds., *Theological Dictionary of the New Testament*, Abridged in One Volume, (Grand Rapids, Mich.: William B. Eerdmans Publishing Co., 1985), s.v. "holy."

[64] *Random House Dictionary*, s.v. "integrity."

[65] *The New Bible Dictionary*, s.v. "holiness."

[66] *The Academic American Encyclopedia*, 1998 edition Grolier Multimedia Encyclopedia, s.v. "narcissism."

[67] Ibid.

[68] John F. MacArthur, *The MacArthur New Testament Commentary*, (Chicago: Moody Press, 1983), Matthew 16:24–27.

[69] Buzzard and Brandon, *Church Discipline*, 23.

[70] John MacArthur, Jr., *The Love of God*, (Dallas: Word Publishing, 1996), 36.

[71] Martyn D. Lloyd -Jones, *The Love of God*, (Wheaton, Ill.: Crossway Publishing, 1994), 52.

[72] Some argue that she was not sincere for various reasons. However, she was sincere enough to accept Jesus exposing her sin and rejecting her worship, and she embraced the truth when she heard it from Him and became a great witness.

[73] David Wells, *No Place for Truth: Whatever Happened to Evangelical Theology*, (Grand Rapids, Mich.: William B. Eerdmans Publishing Co., 1993), 281–282.

[74] Al Fasol, *With a Bible in Their Hands*, (Nashville: Broadman & Holman Publishers, 1994), 2.

[75] Ibid., 3.

[76] Ibid.

[77] Ibid.

[78] Martyn Lloyd-Jones, *The Sacred Anointing*, (Wheaton, Ill.: Crossway Books, 1994), 84.

[79] Ibid., 85.

[80] Jones, *Sacred Anointing*, 65.

[81] Donald S. Whitney, *Spiritual Disciplines Within The Church*, (Chicago: Moody Press, 1996), 68.

[82] Martin Luther, quoted in John Blanchard's *Gathered Gold,* (Welwyn, England: Evangelical Press, 1984), 238.

[83] J. I. Packer, *The Preacher and Preaching: Reviving the Art in the Twentieth Century*, (Phillipsburg, New Jersey: Presbyterian and Reformed, 1986), 20.

[84] Doug Murren, *The Baby Boomerang,* (Ventura, Calif.: Regal, 1990), 217–218.

[85] John F. MacArthur, *Ashamed of the Gospel*, (Wheaton: Crossway Books, 1993), 121.

[86] "Division over music styles displeases God, Mohler says," Laura Rector, quoted in *Baptist Press*, 22 October 1999.

[87] Davis, *Church Discipline*, 349.

[88] Williston Walker, *A History of the Christian Church*, (New York: Scribner's Sons, 1959), 208–209. (This story is relayed in part).

[89] Davis, *Church Discipline*, 347.

[90] Ibid.

[91] Os Guinness & John Seel, *No God But God*, (Chicago: Moody Press, 1992), 155.

[92] Paul C. Vitz, *Psychology as Religion: The Cult of Self-Worship*, (Grand Rapids, Mich.: William B. Eerdmans Publishing Co, 1977), 20.

[93] Needless to say, Chesterton uses the word gay in the sense of happy or joyful

[94] G.K. Chesterton quoted in Guinness & Seel *No God But God*, 138.

[95] Os Guinness, *Fit Bodies Fat Minds; Why Evangelicals Don't Think and What To Do About It*, (Grand Rapids, Mich.: Baker Books, 1994), 139.

[96] Buzzard and Brandon, *Church Discipline*, 77.

[97] Ibid., 75–76.

[98] Ibid., 74–75.

[99] John MacArthur, Jr., *Rediscovering Pastoral Ministry*, (Dallas: Word Publishing, 1995), 336.

[100] Davis, *Church Discipline*, 355.

[101] This term is explained fully in chapter 2.

[102] Guinness, *Fit Bodies*, 38.

[103] R. C. Sproul, *The Holiness of God*, (Wheaton, Ill.: Tyndale House Publishers, Inc, 1998), 57.

[104] Will Durant, *The Story of Philosophy*, (Garden City, NY: Garden City Publishing Co., Inc., 1943), 127.

[105] Ibid.

[106] Ibid., 184.

[107] Sproul, *Holiness*, 57.

[108] Faithism is an inordinate emphasis on the material results of faith like found in the faith movement or quasi faith movements

[109] The New Bible Dictionary, 415.

[110] Kittel and Friedrich, *Theological Dictionary*, 179.

[111] Ibid.

[112] Ibid.

[113] Ibid.

[114] Ibid.

[115] Kittel, Friedrich, and Bromiley, *Theological Dictionary*, 180.

[116] Davis, *Church Discipline*, 359.

[117] Albert Barnes, *Notes on the New Testament*, (Grand Rapids, Mich., Baker Book House, 1983), First Edition, Revelation 2:5, Revelation commentary 65.

[118] John F. Walvoord, Roy B. Zuck & Dallas Theological Seminary, *The Bible Knowledge Commentary: An Exposition of the Scriptures*, (Wheaton, Ill., Victor Books, 1985), Revelation 2:5.

[119] Jay E. Adams, *Handbook of Church Discipline*, (Grand Rapids, Mich.: Zondervan Publishing Co., 1986), 21.

[120] Ibid., 22.

[121] Ibid., 24.

[122] Ibid., 25–26.

[123] Whitney, *Christian Life*, 166.

[124] Kittel and Friedrich, *Theological Dictionary*, s.v. "pentheo."

[125] Louw and Nida, *Greek-English Lexicon*, s.v. "fusiovo."

[126] Barnes, *Notes*, I Corinthians 10:12.

[127] MacArthur, *MacArthur Commentary*, Galatians 6:2–5, 180.

[128] Vitz, *Psychology*, 132–134.

[129] Kittel and Friedrich, *Theological Dictionary*, s.v. "convict."

[130] Strong, *Exhaustive Condordance*, s.v. "convict."

[131] Expositors Commentary, Volume 9, John 16:8, 157.

[132] Adams, *Church Discipline*, 53.

[133] Ibid., 93

[134] Tommy South, *That We May Share His Holiness*, (Abilene, Tex., Bible Guides, 1997), 17.

[135] Ibid., 16.

[136] Richard Lovelace, *Dynamics of Spiritual Life* (Downers Grove, Ill.: InterVarsity Press, 1979), 83–84.

[137] MacArthur, *MacArthur Commentary*, Matthew 7:1.

[138] Kurt Aland et al., eds., *The Greek New Testament*, 26th Edition, (West Germany: United Bible Societies, 1975), Greek text, page xiii.

[139] James S. Spiegel, *Hypocrisy: Moral Fraud and Other Vices*, (Grand Rapids, Mich., Baker Books, 1999), 10.

[140] Strong, *Exhaustive Concordance*, s.v. "sin."

[141] Kittel and Friedrich, *Theological Dictionary*, s.v. "reprove."

[142] MacArthur, *MacArthur Commentary*, Matthew 18:18–20.

[143] The Expositors Bible Commentary, Volume 8, Matthew 18:19, 403.

[144] Craig S. Keener, *IVP Bible Background Commentary: New Testament*, 2nd Edition, (Downers Grove, Ill.; InterVarsity Press) Matthew 18:15–20.

[145] Adam Clarke, *Adam Clarke's Commentary on the New Testament*, 1st Edition, (Cedar Rapids, Iowa: Parsons Technology, Inc.), Matthew 18:20.

[146] Ibid.

[147] Bonhoeffer, *Discipleship*, 22.

[148] Life Together, (New York: Harper & Row, 1954), 112–113.

[149] Louw and Nida, *Greek-English Lexicon*, s.v. "hypocrisy."

[150] Spiegel, *Hypocrisy*, 43.

[151] Ibid., 33.

[152] Ibid., 33–34.

[153] Piers Benn, "What is Wrong with Hypocrisy?" *International Journal of Moral and Social Studies*, (1993), 223–225.

[154] Spiegel, *Hypocrisy*, 39.

[155] Ibid., 80.

[156] Semi closed communion is sometimes known as transient communion, which is basically the closed communion position with exceptions. These exceptions do not normally allow for things like someone in the area who chooses not to belong to a church or someone who does not live the Christian life to partake of the supper. The exceptions are intended to allow for the rare times when the church partakes of communion and a brother or sister, who is dedicated to God, is visiting the church when

communion is shared. This could be someone like a guest speaker, or a members' family visiting for the holidays. Thus, the local church aspect is maintained while allowing for the expression of the universal body of Christ.

[157] Kittel and Friedrich, *Theological Dictionary*, s.v. "porneia."

[158] *Expositors Bible Commentary*, Volume 10, 1 Corinthians 5:1, 217.

[159] Strack-Billerbeck, *Kommentar zum N.T. aus Talmud und Midrasch*, Munich, Beck, 1922–1961, 3:343–358.

[160] J. Finegan, *Light From the Ancient Past*, (Princeton, New Jersey: Princeton University Press, 1959), 361–362 (as quoted in *Expositors Bible Commentary* p 336).

[161] *Expositors Bible Commentary*, Volume 10, 1 Corinthians 5:1, 217.

[162] Kittel and Friedrich, *Theological Dictionary*, s.v. "ekkathairo."

[163] Verse 9 "That not all of an apostle's writings have been preserved presents no problem regarding the completeness of the canon. The church has all of the inspired writing God intended his people to have." *Expositors Bible Commentary*, Volume 10, 219.

[164] South, *Holiness*, 31.

[165] Ibid., 30.

[166] Ibid., 31.

[167] *The Expositors Bible Commentary*, Volume 10, Romans 16:17, 166.

[168] *Skopew* is the word we get our English word "scope" from, and it is in the present tense signifying continuous action.

[169] Louw and Nida, *Greek-English Lexicon*, s.v. "dichostasia."

[170] Strong, *Exhaustive Concordance*, s.v. "skandalon."

[171] As quoted in *Expositors Bible Commentary*, 336.

[172] *Expositors Bible Commentary*, Volume 11, 336.

[173] John Calvin *Calvin's Commentaries* (Grand Rapids, Mich.: Baker Book House, 1979), Barnes, *Barnes Notes*, and D. Michael Martin, *New American Commentary*, Vol. 33, (Nashville: Broadman & Holman Publishers, 1995) 2 Thessalonians 3:6.

[174] Barnes, *Barnes Notes*, Volume 12, 2 Thessalonians 3:6, 99.

[175] Ibid.

[176] Louw and Nida, *Greek-English Lexicon*, s.v. "sunanamignusthai."

[177] Martin, *New American Commentary*, Vol. 33, 273.

[178] Ibid., 283

[179] Strong, *Exhaustive Concordance*, s.v. "unruly."

[180] Martin, *New American Commentary*, 274.

[181] Paul P. Enns, "Biblical Theology Relative to Exegetical Studies," *The Moody Handbook of Theology* (Chicago: Moody Press, 1989), 21.

[182] Richard L. Mayhue, *Rediscovering Expository Preaching*, chapter 1 in *Rediscovering Expository Preaching* by John MacArthur, Jr. and the Master's Seminary Faculty, (Dallas: Word Publishing, 1992), 20.

[183] C. Barry McCarty, *A Parliamentary Guide for Church Leaders*, (Nashville: Broadman Press, 1987), 29.

To order additional copies of

UNDERMINING
the
GOSPEL

Have your credit card ready and call:

1-877-421-READ (7323)

or please visit our web site at
www.pleasantword.com

Also available at:
www.amazon.com
and
www.barnesandnoble.com

Printed in the United States
19858LVS00003B/40-96